A Wall in Palestine

A WALL IN PALESTINE

RENÉ BACKMANN

Translation by A. Kaiser

Picador

New York

A WALL IN PALESTINE. Copyright © 2006 by René Backmann. English translation copyright © 2010 by A. Kaiser. All rights reserved. Printed in the United States of America. For information, address Picador, 175 Fifth Avenue, New York, N.Y. 10010.

www.picadorusa.com

Picador® is a U.S. registered trademark and is used by St. Martin's Press under license form Pan Books Limited.
For information on Picador Reading Group Guides, please contact Picador.
E-mail: readinggroupguides@picadorusa.com

Maps by Mehdi Benyezzar

Designed by Kelly S. Too

Library of Congress Cataloging-in-Publication Data

Backmann, René.
    [Mur en Palestine. English]
    A wall in Palestine / René Backmann ; translation by A. Kaiser. — 1st Picador ed.
        p. cm.
    Includes bibliographical references and index.
    ISBN 978-0-312-42781-8
    1. Israeli West Bank Barrier.   2. Arab-Israeli conflict—1993–   I. Title.
    DS119.65.B33 2010
    956.9405'4—dc22   2009041548

This book was originally published in France by Librairie Arthème Fayard, 2006, and was republished in an expanded and updated edition in 2009 by Editions Gallimard, collection Folio-Actuel.

First U.S. Edition: February 2010

10   9   8   7   6   5   4   3   2   1

Contents

Prologue   1

CHAPTER 1 : Even the Color of the Light   7

CHAPTER 2 : We're Here. They're There.   23

CHAPTER 3 : The Eve of Pesach   35

CHAPTER 4 : The Dayan Campaign   51

CHAPTER 5 : How Many Olive Trees?   61

CHAPTER 6 : The Kibbutz Monteneros   75

CHAPTER 7 : The Great Lie   87

CHAPTER 8 : Qalqiliya in the Net   101

CHAPTER 9 : The Siege of Sheikh Sa'ad   117

CHAPTER 10 : Spartheid   129

CHAPTER 11 : The E-1 File   141

CHAPTER 12 : The Good Side of the Barrier   153

CHAPTER 13 : Settling   167

CHAPTER 14 : Two Roads for Two Peoples   177

CHAPTER 15 : Force Is the Problem   189

CHAPTER 16 : A New Border   201

Chronology   213

Notes   235

Bibliography   247

Acknowledgments   251

Index   253

A WALL IN PALESTINE

The barrier at Abu Dis, East Jerusalem, on the Palestinian side. *Courtesy of Nick Marcroft*

PROLOGUE

"You have family in Israel?"

For nearly twenty-five years I've heard this question each time I've shown my passport to security at Ben-Gurion Airport, in Tel Aviv. For nearly twenty-five years I've answered, "No, I don't have any family in Israel."

"But your name . . ."

"My name comes from eastern France."

"You have friends in Israel?"

Yes, I have friends in Israel. I also have friends in that "country to come,"[1] Palestine. Through a quarter of a century, one has time to make a lot of friends—and some enemies—in this corner of the Middle East where people have so much trouble living together.

Thanks to these friends, and perhaps those enemies, I gradually learned to decipher the codes, the countless codes that make daily life in Israel so complex and difficult to comprehend. And so I discovered, for example, that the cars with yellow license plates (Israeli) can drive anywhere—with the exception of some places strictly forbidden by the army (black plates) or the police (red plates). And that cars with white or green plates (Palestinian) are not authorized to enter Israel; nor can they travel in the West Bank, except in zones for which the drivers have obtained a permit.

I also came to understand that the use—or the refusal to use—certain words often revealed covert beliefs. Take, for example, the words "West Bank." To geographers, these words refer to a territory to the west of Jordan, occupied by Israel since June 1967. These politically "neutral" words, which appear in official international documents, are generally used by journalists, diplomats, and observers. Palestinians, too, commonly call this area the "West Bank," but some use the phrase "occupied territory," which reflects a more militant vocabulary common among Islamists. In everyday conversations with Israelis, the use of the words "West Bank"—rare—expresses a desire to stick with geography, even an implicit critique of the occupation. More disturbing, but perhaps more revealing, is the widespread habit of saying, "the territories." It's impossible to trace the disappearance of the adjective "occupied." Perhaps it caused discomfort to those who may themselves have lived under occupying regimes. Or perhaps they simply wish to save time—everyone knows the territories to which they are referring. Official Israeli documents refer to the land as Judea-Samaria—a distinctly unmysterious reference to the bible—as do many people within the settlements, and their supporters.

"Colonists" and "colony": two more words that are, to put it lightly, debated. They are never used by the people living in the colonies, or by those who support them. Israelis living in the West Bank say that they live in the "Jewish localities of Judea and Samaria." Those who live in the colonies on the outskirts of Jerusalem built to the east of the armistice line of 1967 (geographically, in the West Bank) say that they live in the "Jewish neighborhoods" of Jerusalem. In designating the "colonies," English-speaking Israelis who don't believe in the biblical justification of this enterprise use the word "settlements," a word that carries fewer negative connotations.

The phrase "Civil Administration" is another example of coded language, a form of semantic camouflage. At first glance, there's nothing remarkable or troubling in these two seemingly technocratic words. But what is the Civil Administration? It is the branch of the army in charge of relations with people living in the Occupied Territories. It is they who, for example, give out—and in most cases refuse to give out—travel permits to Palestinians. It is difficult to imagine an administration less civil than this uniformed military unit, whose mission consists of imposing the rules of the armed occupation on civilians.

And the wall? Is it, to begin with, a wall or a barrier? Both. Along most of its path, it's essentially a fifteen-foot electric fence and a security zone between 135 and 300 feet wide at varying points. Within the security zone are barbed wire, an anti-vehicle ditch, one or two intrusion-detection pathways, and at least one patrol route, all under constant surveillance by remote-control cameras and other detection systems. For about twenty-five miles, a concrete wall about sixteen inches thick and twenty-three to thirty feet high replaces the barrier. Whether it is called a barrier or a wall is determined officially by the army.

According to official Israeli documents and the military, it is a "security barrier." To the Palestinians, it's an "annexation wall." Israeli organizations who oppose its construction call it a "separation barrier." Several Palestinian organizations have christened it an "apartheid wall." In its advisory opinion of July 2004, the International Court of Justice of the United Nations decided to use the word "wall" for the whole of the wall/barrier. In the pages that follow, I will use the word "barrier" when I'm talking about a barrier and the word "wall" when I'm talking specifically about a wall.

Why dedicate a book to this enterprise? Because, like many of my friends, Israeli and Palestinian, I believed in peace when the Oslo Accords were signed in 1993, and then witnessed, along with them, the failure of the peace process. Because I still can't believe that what the entire world saw fall down yesterday in Berlin could be a solution tomorrow in Jerusalem. Yasser Arafat expressed this same sentiment in an interview in Gaza some days after the assassination of the Israeli prime minister. It seemed to me at the time that if the successors of Rabin and Arafat remained faithful to their commitments, all would not be lost, despite the death of one of the principal architects of the peace process.

On the other hand, I was not among those who placed their hopes in the Camp David negotiations of July 2000, or the Taba Summit in January 2001. Once the Second Intifada had exploded, it became unreasonable to remain optimistic. The increase in suicide attacks, Hamas's rise to power, the Israeli army reoccupation of the majority of the West Bank, and the spectacular development of settlements all conspired to create the worst conditions possible, once calm was restored, for the renewal of negotiations.

It was at the beginning of 1995, when Yitzhak Rabin was still in power, when I first heard that a "continuous obstacle" between the Israelis and Palestinians was under consideration. I didn't quite believe it. Of course, it was easy to see the trauma that pervasive suicide attacks had wrought on the Israeli population, but I had a hard time imagining that the Israeli government would respond to this challenge with such a project. A wall or a barrier of several hundreds of miles, designed to deter and trap terrorists: the idea seemed at once anachronistic and overblown. But the project was reviewed by the army, the government, and the Knesset, and was on the verge of becoming a construction site—one of the most important in Israeli history. I wanted to understand how and why, at the dawn of the twenty-first century, the leaders of a modern, sophisticated country would choose to resolve its biggest problem with such an archaic strategy. Later, when I saw the first sections of the wall, I wanted to understand why it frequently meandered into Palestinian territory. Why the length of this continuous obstacle was estimated at nearly 435 miles when the line that serves as the border between Israel and the West Bank is no longer than 202 miles. *A Wall in Palestine* is both the story and the result of this investigation.

Israel is a small country; the West Bank, an even smaller territory. In little more than an hour, you can drive from Tel Aviv to Jericho; in two hours, you can reach any town in the West Bank from Jerusalem. This allows one to travel easily between Israelis and Palestinians, and to contrast mere words with reality; to separate lies from propaganda, and the myths of militant discourse from fact. Thankfully, among both Israelis and Palestinians, there is no lack of competent journalists, serious intellectuals, or men and women of good faith, who are open to dialogue and disposed to hope, and who are willing to make that short but arduous journey across.

·Children crossing between the cement blocks that constitute the wall in Abu Dis. *Courtesy of MachsomWatch/Neta Efroni*

CHAPTER I

Even the Quality of the Light

One morning in early August of 2002, the residents of Chiyah, El-Azariyeh, and Ras al-Amud, the Palestinian villages that form the eastern boundary of Jerusalem, discovered that pieces of paper printed with a message in Hebrew had been tacked to the trees during the night. The message, bearing the stamp of the Israeli Defense Forces, was a military order informing residents that some of their land was going to be requisitioned by the army to erect a wall. It listed the plots of land that would be affected and specified that those who wished to file an objection had one week from the time that the notices had been posted to do so. In the time it took to translate the flyers into Arabic, access the land title registry, identify the requisitioned tracts of land and the path of the future wall, the week was over.

"Finding a lawyer to bring our case before an Israeli court and have it translated into Hebrew would have taken us at least another whole week. Assuming, that is, we managed to raise the money," says Terry Boullata, principal of an elementary school in Abu Dis and an impassioned activist for peace between Israelis and Palestinians. Four years later, she still hasn't come to terms with the brutal legal maneuvering of the Israeli army. Sitting on the flowered sofa in her living room, this energetic woman in her forties is agitated. While serving coffee, then cold drinks, she chain-smokes, glancing out the window at her concrete enemy every time she mentions it. "Why is it that for us, the soldiers are satisfied to nail military orders to trees, but they'll go door to door, house to house, to explain to the settlers that they're going to be evacuated from Gaza? What happens when the rain washes away the message or when the wind tears it loose?"

The residents never filed an objection in the manner required, so on August 14, the bulldozers, protected by a large detachment of soldiers, began demolition to clear the way for the wall and to open a roadway for construction vehicles. As a first step, concrete blocks in the shape of upside-down *T*s, each about two yards high, were haphazardly set down by cranes. There was enough room in between some sections for a child or a slim adult to slip through. But: "We could see that there was something temporary about that wall," remembers Terry Boullata. "It prevented cars from getting through, except at crossings controlled by the Israeli army. For people on foot, it was exasperating and humiliating, if not entirely insurmountable. But when the checkpoint was moved from Ras al-Amud to Abu Dis, along the planned route of the wall, it was clear that something else was in the works. In fact, it appeared that the Israelis intended to transform the municipal boundary of Jerusalem, which had been arbitrarily drawn after the annexation of the eastern part of the city in 1967, into a genuine border between Israel and the territories under control of the Palestinian Authority. For those of us here, that was a disaster."

A member of an old Jerusalem family, Terry had married Salah Ayyad, the son of a successful businessman from Abu Dis, toward the end of the First Intifada. Terry was Christian; Salah, Muslim. Both were members of the Democratic Front for the Liberation of Palestine (DFLP), and had spent time in Israeli prisons for having belonged to an outlawed political party. Neither one saw their religion as an issue. "We were married during the Gulf War, but we still had a party at the Cliff Hotel, which belonged to my husband's family, until it was confiscated by the Israeli army in 2003 in order to set up quarters for the Border Police," Terry recounts. "The municipal boundary of Greater Jerusalem, drawn by the Israelis after capturing the eastern part of the city in 1967, ran straight through the hotel. The bar was in Jerusalem, the restaurant in the West Bank. This was just one of the countless absurdities of the occupation, and it sometimes caused problems with the Israeli military bureaucracy. But it didn't get in the way of the hotel's daily functioning, nor did it hinder customers coming from the West Bank or from Jerusalem. They simply had to cross the army checkpoints, wait, and run the risk of being turned back. But the Palestinians of my generation have been used to doing that since birth."

By the time the 1993 Oslo Peace Accords had been signed, Terry had left the DFLP to join an organization working to reform the status of women in Palestinian society. She and her husband moved to the second floor of a little white-stone apartment building within the municipal boundaries of East Jerusalem, about twenty yards from the Cliff Hotel. The building had been built in 1958 by Salah's family.

"I was filled with hope," Terry admits today, now regretting her naïveté. "I really believed we were finally going to have our State and live as neighbors with the Israelis. I was so full of enthusiasm that I decided in 1999 to open a kindergarten and elementary school in Abu Dis, to contribute to the education of the new generations of Palestinians. 'New generation' was actually the name that I had chosen for it. I borrowed thirty thousand dollars, then twenty thousand, then ten thousand, and I started with fifty children. Five years later, I had two hundred children and twenty-two teachers. It was a heady time. The school was a five-minute walk from my home. All I had to do was cross the street near the mosque, walk the length of the Palestinian parliament building that was under construction, pass by Al-Quds University, and I was at work.

"Like many of my pupils and teachers who lived within Jerusalem city limits, I continued to take the same route to the school, despite the wall that appeared in 2002. There were openings in this wall where Border Police soldiers let children and people they recognized pass, when they didn't have orders to the contrary. Their tolerance worked well for us, but I will never forget how humiliating it was to crawl through those holes, and especially to see old women in traditional embroidered dress or grandfathers in keffiyehs struggle to pass through while these young people looked on. And in spite of it seeming temporary, this wall was, for the first time, a concrete separation between East

Jerusalem and the West Bank, and an additional physical obstacle to what was already heavy regulation."

Indeed, since March 1993, six months before the signing of the Oslo Accords on the White House lawn, the Israeli army had put into place a system of cordons and controls in the West Bank and Gaza Strip designed to regulate—in fact, reduce—Palestinian movement within the Occupied Territories and at crossings into Israel. Any travel was laden with a multitude of checkpoints and military roadblocks. Entry into Jerusalem was forbidden, except to those who had authorization from the Civil Administration—that is, the army. This authorization was difficult to obtain, and the smallest incident could nullify it. With the onset of the Second Intifada in September 2000, the military and police tightened security; ditches were dug, clay roadblocks were put up, and cement blocks were laid across the roads, paths, and alleyways that had previously allowed people to avoid checkpoints.

For those who lived in the neighborhoods or Palestinian villages on the outskirts of East Jerusalem, such as Ras al-Amud and Abu Dis, these measures were a nightmare. They had been casually breaking the rules of the occupation for years and now faced a clampdown. The Israeli authorities forbade Palestinians, whether they had an orange or a green identity card, to remain in Jerusalem between 7:00 p.m. and 5:00 a.m. under penalty of prison and a fine. And Palestinians living in East Jerusalem holding blue "permanent resident" cards were now forbidden to live outside of the city for more than seven years. Those who exceed this time limit and are caught by the police lose their right to residency and visiting privileges, authorization to work in Israel, the benefits of social security and the Israeli school system, their yellow license plates (like the Israelis') for their cars, and the freedom to travel in Israel or to use the Tel Aviv airport. At the same time, the cost of living in Jerusalem, the exorbitant price of housing and its scarcity on the Palestinian side, has forced many beneficiaries of the "permanent resident" status to live in the villages or neighborhoods on the outskirts of the city, while keeping a fictitious address in Jerusalem.

In those parts of East Jerusalem where, until the erection of the wall, nothing (except occasionally the checkpoints) marked a border, where no one knew exactly where Ras al-Amud ended and Abu Dis began—and borders were established communally—the circumstances of day-to-day life determined the geographic boundaries. It was like a big village stretching along the road to Jericho where everyone knew his neighbor and where families and clans had lived for generations. At the beginning of 2005, close to 55,000 Palestinians from East Jerusalem—out of 215,000—lived, in reality, outside of the city limits, and 75 percent of the residents of Az Zayyem, a town of about 3,000 people to the north of El-Azariyeh, held identity cards from East Jerusalem. In other words, putting up a wall here, between Abu Dis and Ras al-Amud, would tear families apart and sever the human, social, and economic ties established over the course of decades.

Which is exactly what happened. One morning in January 2004, the neighborhood found itself under siege, living in a "closed military zone." Bulldozers and cranes, hired from the private sector and escorted by Israeli soldiers, took over the area. No vehicles, not even school buses, were authorized to enter or leave. The site was guarded day and night by a private armed militia, which, according to the residents, was made up of Druze and Bedouin. In place of the short temporary barrier, a cement wall almost thirty feet high, made up of slabs of concrete about four feet wide and sixteen inches thick, had suddenly been raised between neighbors. There was no longer any possibility of slipping through a gap between two cement slabs to go to work, or of climbing on a stepladder to pass a tray of *knafeh* or a basket of Jericho strawberries over to friends. In the blink of an eye, the other side of the road had disappeared, along with the neighbors, the storekeepers, the horizon, the rising sun—erased overnight by the wall.

For a few months, one passageway under the watch of the Border Police remained half-open. It was essentially a gap between a section of the wall and a fenced enclosure around a Christian monastery. Like everyone else, Terry Boullata crawled on all fours through the fencing to make the shuttle between Ras al-Amud and Abu Dis, until that hole also was closed up. Now she has to drive to her school. She heads toward the center of Jerusalem through the tunnel under Mount Scopus, follows the road of the Ma'ale Adumim settlement, turns toward the entrance to Abu Dis, and winds through traffic jams for a total of about nine miles, with at least one checkpoint—in other words, she must drive thirty to forty minutes in order to reach a point some nine hundred feet from where she started, on the other side of the wall.

"The problem today is deciding whether or not I should keep my school open. The majority of my students and teachers living in East Jerusalem can no longer come, for lack of transportation. I still owe the bank twenty-five thousand dollars. How am I going to pay them back if I lose a good part of my students? In a single year, seventy-seven out of two hundred have left. I had thirty-four students in sixth grade before the wall. Now I have six. And I have to pay my teachers, who are working even if they have only a handful of students. How will I manage?"

The worst part for Terry is that the wall has divided her own family. Her husband, Salah, who has an orange ID card from the West Bank, is not authorized to live in Jerusalem. In order to travel between Abu Dis, where he works, and Ras al-Amud, he is forced to play a game of hide-and-seek with the police and the Israeli army. Like most Palestinians, he used to cross the invisible line between the West Bank and East Jerusalem by sneaking through gardens and alleyways, in order to stay out of sight from the Israeli patrols—risky before the construction of the wall, but now impossible, since there is only one heavily guarded point of passage. "Well before the construction of the first wall," Terry says, "we had asked the Israeli authorities three times for a permanent resident permit for family reunification reasons. It was refused three times for 'security reasons,' because Salah, like me, was imprisoned during the First Intifada. My husband ended up obtaining a permit that allows him to stay in Jerusalem from five a.m. to seven p.m., but for professional reasons only. His company sells stones for construction, and they have some big Israeli clients.

"If he sleeps here, in our apartment, he's breaking the law. All it takes is for the Border Police to enter in the middle of the night, which they have no problem doing, and he will be arrested, imprisoned for at least three months, and fined. As for me, I would have harbored a West Bank resident who does not have the right to be in Jerusalem past seven p.m.—even if he is my husband—so I risk prison and a fine, too. I will also be punished if I give Salah a ride in my car." Regulations forbid anyone holding a blue ID card from East Jerusalem to transport a Palestinian from the West Bank in his or her vehicle, even if they are husband and wife. The police could confiscate her car and revoke her license, and she could face six months in prison and a thousand-dollar fine.

There was one solution for Terry and her children: they could surrender their ID cards for East Jerusalem and go live in Abu Dis.

"Out of the question," Terry says. "That would be falling into the Israelis' trap. They make our daily lives more and more difficult so that we will leave. My daughters, who are thirteen and eighteen years old, go to school in Beit Hanina, on the north side of Jerusalem. They would have to change schools, and I don't want to add more trauma to their lives. And I also want to continue using the Tel Aviv airport for trips abroad. Even if every time I use it I run into endless problems with security because of my former political activities, it's still quicker and less expensive than passing over the Allenby Bridge at the Jordanian border and using the Amman airport. So we chose to live on different sides of the wall: me here, on the East Jerusalem side, and Salah in the family home in Abu Dis. Our daughters, Zeina and Jasmine, spend three nights with me and three nights with their father. That's the life the wall has condemned us to!"

ROLLING UP HIS RUG, ON WHICH HE HAS JUST FINISHED MIDDAY PRAYER, Hassan Ikermawi glances desperately around his small souk, which smells of cumin, saffron, and freshly roasted coffee. "Before, at this time of day," he says, "customers were practically on top of each other." Besides the two kids counting their shekels in front of the candy rack, there's no one here at the Al-Hilal grocery store that Ikermawi runs, to his chagrin, on this embankment on the far eastern boundary of Jerusalem. Nor are there any customers in front of the freezers of ice-cream bars that sit outside under an awning protecting them from the burning sun of the Holy Land.

At a gas station next door, the same despair is felt by Youssef al-Khatib. An unemployed engineer now working as an attendant at the station, he dozes off in his rundown office, a newspaper on his lap, while his young employee watches a soccer match on an old television. "No one has come by for more than an hour," says the Ronaldinho fan, in his worn soccer jersey and grease-smudged overalls. "I was able to watch the whole first period and go buy myself a Pepsi at halftime without one customer stopping by."

"This station has belonged to my family since 1955," says Munir al-Khatib, Youssef's brother. "Before the wall, we had a good business going. Really good. Now we have a hard time making ends meet. We have lost four fifths of our revenue."

Across the way, on the other side of what was Jericho Road, it's worse: most of the stores have been closed down for months. Iron doors are locked down over the windows and covered with posters and graffiti.

"I think I'll have to do the same thing," says Hassan Ikermawi. "Today I don't even earn enough to cover the twelve hundred dollar rent and the eight hundred and fifty shekels I owe in taxes on the store. How can I support my wife and children? My father-in-law has a business in Jerusalem. I'm going to work for him. At fifty years old, I have lost three fourths of my customers and some of my best suppliers. Every day I had fresh fruits and vegetables from Jericho and the Jordan Valley—much better quality and much less expensive than the produce you find in Jerusalem. Even the Israelis from the Ma'ale Adumim[1] settlement came here to do their shopping. For a business like mine, it was the perfect location. Before."

Anyone who may have come to visit here "before" knows that Hassan Ikermawi, a short, bearded man with oval-shaped glasses and a defeated look in his eyes, isn't making any of this up. Here, in front of the store, the Jerusalem–Jericho Road, with its stream of cars, trucks, buses, and taxis, intersects with another, narrower road linking this Jerusalem neighborhood to Ramallah and Bethlehem. In the days before the wall, one had to wait as long as fifteen minutes to fill up at Youssef and Munir al-Khatib's pumps. While waiting, the customers in their cars and trucks would buy mineral water, sodas, fruit, or little bags of pistachios or grilled watermelon seeds from the Al-Hilal grocery store. Today, this once-busy intersection no longer exists. It's a dead end.

Hassan Ikermawi's "before" is not some idealized long-ago era rendered peaceful and prosperous by imagination and time. "Before" was yesterday. The same military occupation was in place, the same Israeli army checkpoints, the same harassment, inconvenience, and lassitude. But there was not yet the wall.

It stands only fifteen feet from Ikermawi's store. Gray, massive, more impenetrable than a tank, with cylindrical watchtowers fitted with security cameras and bulletproof windows—it is twice as high as the Berlin Wall. It crosses Jericho Road, slices in between apartment buildings in Chiyah, loops around and through various religious properties (Christian monasteries, pilgrim hostels, churches, schools, and retirement homes), and then climbs the hills to the south of the Cliff Hotel, bluntly slicing the landscape like a giant chain saw. It spans miles, and meanders through highly sensitive territory.

One might assume that Israelis live on one side of the barrier and Palestinians on the other, but this is not quite the case. Here, near Ikermawi's store, the wall actually separates Palestinians from Palestinians. Besides the soldiers, the only Israelis present in the vicinity are a few settlement families living in two old Palestinian homes, where now flies the blue-and-white Israeli flag. This "wild" settlement, called the Kidmat Zion, is not on the list of official settlements published by the Israeli Central Bureau of Statistics (CBS). Nevertheless, it is protected by the Border Police detachment that has set up shop in the former Cliff Hotel.

"My windows used to open onto the rising sun; they open now on this monster," says Elie Yacoub, a retiree from the tourism sector, who speaks French with a delicate, melodic cadence he learned in Catholic school. He lives two steps away from the wall of concrete. "It's so depressing that I can't stay at home anymore. Even deep in a book, I can't forget about it. It changed everything, even the quality of the light. In the morning, I leave the house as soon as I can and I go visit my friends who run a hotel near the Damascus Gate, in Jerusalem. I help out, I cover for the receptionist when she takes a break, I read the international press, and I chat with the foreign tourists. I tell them what we are going through. I send them off to discover the wall so they talk about it when they return home."

A little higher up on the hill, in the direction of the Mount of Olives, concealed behind a wall of rocks and a metal door equipped with an intercom, is the Community of the Daughters of Charity. Italian, Palestinian, and Lebanese nuns maintain a hostel for pilgrims and a boardinghouse for boys ages five to thirteen, who come from Christian villages in the West Bank. From the terrace of the boardinghouse you can see all the way to the Judea Desert. The view of the wall is entirely unobstructed. "Look: our garden once extended down into the valley," explains Sister Laudy Fares, pointing to the olive, lemon, fig, and palm trees and a beautiful vegetable garden. "It was the children's playground. In summer we organized picnics there. But since the wall, that's all done with. The Israelis didn't hesitate to take over a part of the valley, tear apart the gardens, and uproot trees to build it."

ABOUT A HUNDRED OR SO YARDS FROM THERE, ON A LITTLE ROAD THAT climbs farther up the hill from the Community of the Daughters of Charity, just at the foot of the wall, a vast shaded garden shelters the "Home of Our Lady of Suffering," a retirement home run by Christian nuns. "Out of our forty-five residents, Islamic and Christian," explains Sister Amal, one of the heads of the institution, "twenty are from East Jerusalem, and their families can visit them with no problem. For the twenty-five others, though, who are from the West Bank, everything has changed, because now the Palestinians from the West Bank must obtain a permit to enter Jerusalem. They can no longer leave their cars or get out of their taxis at the checkpoint and enter into East Jerusalem on foot along little pathways. There no longer *are* any little pathways, and at crossings, the checks are merciless. If you have a permit, you pass; if you don't, you turn around. Some of our residents whose papers are not completely in order have not had a visit from their family in months. Our personnel have the same problems. Only one of our staff lives in East Jerusalem; for him, nothing has changed. But the others come from Ramallah, Bethlehem, and Abu Dis. They have work permits, so they can come in legally, but they have to cross the wall in the morning and in the evening. In other words, they have to wait at several checkpoints. Some, like our chef, prefer to sleep here, even if they are not authorized to spend the night in Jerusalem, and so they are taking significant risks. Considering the fact that now it is impossible to get our supplies from the other side of the street, in Abu Dis, and we have to go to Jerusalem, where everything is almost twice as expensive, I wonder how we are even going to survive."

Near the Home of Our Lady of Suffering, Helmut Konitzer, a German volunteer at the facility, was allowed to live in the garden cabin. He arrived in the Holy Land some years ago to work with the Christian communities of Jerusalem. Indefatigable, curious, always on the move on his motorcycle, Helmut points out a troubling coincidence: the wall broke ground on the night of August 13, 2002, forty-one years to the day after the sealing of the first perpend of the Berlin Wall—a coincidence that no German could help noticing.

"COME, I HAVE BEEN WAITING FOR YOU, AND I HAVE ALL THE TIME IN THE world. You are welcome here."

At the other end of the line, the voice of Yahia Izhiman is warm, almost playful. He is giving me directions to his store.

"Drive to the Abu Dis taxi station, and there ask for the Izhiman store; it's my brother's. If you can't find it, ask anyone in the street. Everyone knows us."[2] Yahia Izhiman is not exaggerating about his family's local fame. His name is a brand in this region. It's impossible to go into a grocery store, café, or restaurant from Khan Younis to Jenin without seeing Izhiman tea, coffee, chocolate, sugar, or spices.

How is this old family business faring under today's present difficulties? The answer is on the other side of the wall, literally ten yards from where I am calling Izhiman, nearly three quarters of an hour's drive away. On the way there, I hit traffic jams in the center of East

Jerusalem, a checkpoint, plus an annoying mobile checkpoint[3] near the Ma'ale Adumim settlement, then traffic again, and total anarchy looking for a parking spot in the main street of Abu Dis. The Izhiman store, run by Soufian, the younger brother of Yahia, is in the center of town, on what was once the Jerusalem–Jericho Road. It is a bulk store where customers can buy a half dozen different types of freshly roasted coffee, pistachios, and spices from Asia and Latin America, all displayed in brown wooden containers at the back of the store.

Yahia Izhiman is there, pouring hot cups of coffee. A short man in his fifties with a lively look, he is clearly proud to belong to a large and respected old family of businessmen. "I have eight brothers, one who works at Arab Bank, here in Abu Dis, and three sisters, one living in Iraq. My grandfather started importing coffees and spices in the thirties. At that time, he used caravans of donkeys from Aden to Jerusalem, across Arabia. And it was my father who started to sell the products we imported under the brand name Izhiman. When he died, I took over the company. My brothers manage the stores in East Jerusalem, Azariyeh, and Ramallah. The company has continued to function, despite the checkpoints, the barriers, the permit system, and the import taxes taken by the Israelis, who have greatly disrupted our raw material supplies and deliveries to our clients. But now, with the wall, I'm no longer sure of anything. Let me show you why."

Five minutes' walk from the boutique, on a quiet little street, Yahia Izhiman pushes open the heavy door of a warehouse filled with the aroma of roasted coffee beans. "This is our roasting and packaging center," he explains as he slaloms among the piles of burlap sacks marked Colombia, Costa Rica, Brazil, India, to his office, where the only decoration is a black-and-white portrait of his father. More than half of the machines have been switched off, apparently for several days. "This is our problem," he says. "The Palestinian economy is bankrupt. People no longer work, so there's no more money. No orders are coming in. And with this wall, and the ban on working in Israel, things are going to go from bad to worse. Look around you: Before the wall, we had more than twenty employees. Now there are five. We often worked thirteen hours a day, even around the clock, to fill the biggest orders; we now work seven hours."

At the end of the main street in Abu Dis, where the wall cuts right through the road, Yahia Izhiman had a supermarket across from Hassan Ikermawi's Al-Hilal grocery store. At first he kept it open for a few hours a day, before permanently closing it and opening up a new one in Anata, another suburb of East Jerusalem. "Most of the customers were passersby, people from East Jerusalem especially frequented my store; it was less expensive than in town." In the neighborhood, all other businesses—the drugstore, bakery, furniture store, rotisserie, tailor—closed down a long time ago. All of the business along nearly five hundred feet of the wall, including the medical center and dentist's office, have closed. The heavy metal doors in front of each building are locked up and covered with several layers of posters and graffiti.

But Eitaf Labadi, the pharmacist, is still there: "For how much longer, I don't know," she says. "I did the math, and it's not very encouraging. My rent is nine hundred dollars. My daily revenue has dropped off since the construction of the wall, from eight hundred dollars a day to fifty or sixty. Many people have lost their jobs and have no savings left. And now, because of problems traveling from place to place, I can't get certain medications."

Eitaf is patient when faced with the requests of her embarrassed customers, who are ashamed to admit that they have no money. With her gray chignon and glasses, she looks like a kindly schoolteacher. Kindly but weary, on the cusp of retirement, over having to weather so much uncertainty and pain that she is powerless to change.

Among the pharmacy's customers is Abu Mohammad, a husky, mustachioed man in his forties who is angered whenever he hears talk of the wall. And with good reason. Formerly a construction worker, he lost his job because the barriers and checkpoints made him perpetually late for work. He is very proud to have bought a piece of land on the outskirts of Abu Dis, across from the Cliff Hotel, and to have built a small house there, with a veranda facing the hills. But "since I couldn't find regular work here," he explains as he walks the gravel path that runs around the Palestinian Parliament building, abandoned before completion, "I decided to raise sheep. I had about forty, and I brought them to the hills to graze every day. When the Israelis started to clear the area in front of my door, I complained that they were going to build their wall only fifteen feet from my house, on my land. They said that it was too late for protesting. Today, I have thirty feet of concrete outside of my windows, and I have to leave the light on all day on the veranda. The wall bars me from my pastures. I no longer have any means to feed my herd. I sold a part of it to make a little money, and slaughtered the others, one by one, to feed my family. May Allah punish the Israelis for what they do to us!"

"THE CITY IS GOING UNDER," REMARKS IMRAN EL-KHATIB, FORMER HEAD of a transport company, now a real estate agent since the sharp drop in tourism. With little work to do, he is seated at a table with two friends at one of the neighborhood's last falafel vendors, before plates of hummus, foul, labneh, and salad. Perhaps to save face, he has kept up his appearance as a successful businessman—short-sleeve shirt, tie, carefully combed hair, gold lighter—but his heart is no longer in it. "I have a piece of land in the center of the city; it was valued at almost eight million dollars before the construction of the wall. Today, it's worth two million. I can't find renters. The apartments that used to go for two thousand dollars a month now hardly rent for five hundred."

The only prosperous business in the neighborhood is the new household goods store owned by Sbitany and Sons, whose enormous red sign lights up this dismal cul-de-sac as soon as the sun goes down. "It's the wall that forced us to open this new store," explains one of the young salesmen, Mahmoud Arikat, dressed in the Sbitany uniform, a red cardigan and white shirt. "Since our clients in the West Bank can no longer travel to East Jerusalem, where our stores are located, we opened new ones on the other side of the wall. Of course, this means that our trucks need Israeli authorization to cross the checkpoints. For the time being, they have it. Our director, Mr. Mohsen Sbitany, negotiated with the Israelis himself."

Across from the brazen Sbitany store, Dr. Adnan Anafeh, along with his wife, Mona, runs a busy pediatric center. "Everyone is doing badly," he says. Now in his fifties, the doctor has lived here since his youth. "They are worried, anguished, tense. Each family here is more or less cut in two by the wall, and wonders what life will be like in the coming months. They don't hope for anything; they feel abandoned. The children in particular have reacted very badly to what they see as a sort of amputation of their natural space. And I'm not sure that people fully understand the risks of our situation here. We are now cut off from all emergency medical assistance. There is no maternity, cardiology, or surgical service, not even an MRI, in Abu Dis, or in the neighboring villages, where about seventy-five thousand people live. Before the wall, whenever we had a serious case, we called an ambulance, and fifteen minutes later at worst the patient was at Makassed or at Augusta Victoria, the two big Palestinian hospitals in East Jerusalem. Today, these two hospitals are on the other side of the wall. Inaccessible.

"At Augusta Victoria, seven employees out of ten reside in the West Bank and have to request a permit every three months from the Israeli army in order to enter East Jerusalem, a permit that is sometimes granted, sometimes not. The hospital has already lost thirty percent of its patients. The administration might cut sixty of its one hundred and sixty-five beds. Makassed has just gone from two hundred and fifty beds to one hundred and fifty.[4] In case of an emergency or complication, we have to get an ambulance to come from either Bethlehem or Ramallah and then take the patient to Ramallah Hospital. In other words, we have to contact the Israeli authorities, obtain the necessary authorizations for passing the checkpoints, and then transport the patient on the narrow, winding roads around Jerusalem. This can take anywhere between thirty-five minutes and three hours, especially at night. If we're dealing with a heart attack or internal hemorrhaging, this lost time can prove fatal. You think the Israelis thought of that?"

The wall under construction at night. *Courtesy of Gali Tibbon*

CHAPTER 2

WE'RE HERE. THEY'RE THERE.

Who invented the wall? Who came up with the idea for it? "Maybe it was me," Dany Tirza says half-jokingly as he weaves his car through Gilo morning traffic. Adjacent to the southern neighborhoods of Jerusalem, this truly "new" city of thirty-seven thousand people, which dominates the nearby Palestinian enclaves of Bethlehem and Beit Jala, is considered by the Israelis to be a natural extension of the Holy City. In fact, Gilo was built on the outskirts of "Greater Jerusalem," as it was redefined by Israel in 1967 after the Six-Day War, on approximately seven thousand acres of annexed Palestinian land. But Gilo is on the Palestinian side of the "Green Line," which, since 1949, separates the State of Israel from the present-day West Bank. Thus, it is a settlement, one of twelve built by Israel since 1967 at the periphery of Greater Jerusalem.[1]

Colonel Dany Tirza lives in Kfar Adumim, a settlement near the Jordan Valley. He is a strapping man with salt-and-pepper hair who wears the crocheted yarmulke of a settler. Forty-six years old, he has recently been relegated to the Reserves, but remains in charge of "strategic and spatial" planning at the Ministry of Defense. This grants him a plastic ID card authorizing passage at any crossing. He travels with an armed soldier in the backseat of his car for protection.

Tirza never goes anywhere without a thick folder of daily updated aerial maps. He is considered by the military forces to be one of their top experts on the West Bank. He has trekked its villages and pathways in all directions in his Jeep. Perhaps only Ariel Sharon possesses as much ground-level intelligence about the region. At the beginning of the Oslo peace process, Tirza was put in charge of the Rainbow Project, planning military withdrawals and redeployments in the West Bank, during the region's initial period of self government.² As such, he was also part of the Israeli delegation involved in negotiations with the Palestinians. It was during this time that Yasser Arafat, amused to see Tirza arrive at the meetings every day with a roll of maps under his arm, gave him the nom de guerre Abu Karita, or "the father of maps."

When the Sharon government decided in 2001 to launch a study on a barrier project between Israelis and Palestinians, Dany Tirza was naturally put in charge of it, and of sketching the barrier's path. Today he supervises the construction sites, works on modifications called for by the Supreme Court, and adds the finishing touches. He has even become a diplomat, traveling to the Vatican to negotiate the course of the wall on Catholic-owned lands. "Here's where it all might have begun," he says as he gets out of his car and steps onto a rocky promontory at the southern edge of Gilo, across from the village of Beit Jala, on the other side of the valley.³

"At the beginning of the Second Intifada, in October 2000, this area was under attack by snipers. They were taking potshots at people in the street from their apartment windows." The snipers were located in Beit Jala, which sits on a hill overlooking Gilo. "A policeman was killed nearby. At that time, we knew the liaison to the Palestinian police in Bethlehem very well. He was a part of the town's security force, he spoke Hebrew, and he had four thousand men with Kalashnikovs at his disposal. But when we asked him to stop the shooting, he said that it was impossible, because the snipers were young people from the refugee camps hiding in the Beit Jala mayor's house, and that he could not take them out by force. So we brought two tanks to a parking lot in Gilo and fired shells on the mayor's house from here." Indeed, the tanks had a remarkably clear shot of the building from this parking lot. "As you can see from here, the mayor's house has never been repaired. After this, we conducted military operations and engagements inside Beit Jala, but we could not stay forever and watch every house.

"Then the idea came to me that in order to prevent the snipers from targeting the people of Gilo, we could build a wall six feet high and some sixty feet long, with concrete upside-down *T*s, simply arranged side by side. The wall worked. The shooting stopped, and people were able to live normally again."

Five years later, the Gilo wall is still standing. Local artists have had fun covering it with a mural of the Palestinian hill that it hides, perhaps hoping to help it blend in with the surroundings.

"Back then, ensuring security in the neighborhood was a nightmare," Dany Tirza continues, as he glances over the arid hillsides overlooking the road from Bethlehem to Hebron. "Each morning, the thousands of Palestinians who work in Jerusalem come into town through the checkpoint near Rachel's Tomb, but they also take one of the many paths etched out in the hills. At one time, we deployed up to fourteen Border Police Jeeps here to try to filter who was coming in. But even with the best-laid plans and the best-trained soldiers, you couldn't intercept all the terrorists among the innocent workers. In 2003, a border patrol broke up a group of three young Palestinians from the Deheishe refugee camp, to the south of Bethlehem. They had been trained for suicide attacks, and were trying to get into Jerusalem from Beit Jala. Two of them apparently were turned back, but the third succeeded in reaching the bus station, which connects Gilo to Jerusalem's center. He got on the bus and set off his belt near a school. Twenty-three children were killed.[4]

"There are not a thousand ways to prevent this sort of thing. There is one: build a very effective, impenetrable barrier, and establish a rigorous policy at crossings."

As stated in multiple documents from the government and the Ministry of Defense, and by many Israeli politicians, the objectives of the "security barrier" were to prevent the infiltration of terrorists, forbid the entry of clandestine arms and explosives, and protect the lives of 6.7 million Israeli citizens. This preoccupation with security is not unfounded. Between September 28, 2000—the date of Ariel Sharon's controversial visit to the Temple Mount (to Muslims, the Noble Sanctuary), in Jerusalem, which triggered the Second Intifada—and

January 31, 2006, 992 Israelis, including 683 civilians, were killed in attacks or bombings. More than 40 fell during the first three months of conflict. The following year, total fatalities reached 188, then 420 in 2002, before they began to decline: 185 in 2003, 108 in 2004, and 50 in 2005. In the same period, Israeli army operations and attacks on settlements caused 3,399 deaths among Palestinians.[5]

THE IDEA OF BUILDING A WALL OR BARRIER AS PROTECTION AGAINST INvaders, immigrants, smugglers, or neighbors, or to separate sectors of the population, or, as in Berlin, to prevent people from fleeing an intolerable regime, is neither new nor original. Between 220 and 206 B.C., during the short-lived Qin Dynasty, the neighboring Chinese sovereign rulers already had a network of fortifications in place to protect them from one another, but also to contain attacks from nomadic tribes from the north. Other lines of defense were erected in the middle of the sixth century by the northern Qi Dynasty, then by the Sui. To the south of these fortresses, of which almost nothing remains, the Great Wall of China, extending close to four thousand miles long, was undertaken by Ming emperors beginning in 1368. Completed in 1620, it was intended to protect the Chinese from Manchu invasions. History shows that its strategic efficacy is debatable, as the Manchu Dynasty of the Qing conquered Peking in 1644.

Much less spectacular and ambitious was the seventy-five-mile wall built in 122 in the north of England by Emperor Hadrian, which served to delineate the northern boundary of the Roman Empire. Even though its garrison of more than ten thousand men resisted many attacks, it was abandoned by Hadrian's successor, and a good many of its stone blocks were reused elsewhere. Its central section was spared pillage and, named a World Heritage site in 1987, is now a major tourist destination in the region.

As for the Wall of the Farmers-General (fifteen miles long, with sixty toll barriers), which Claude-Nicolas Ledoux built around Paris in 1785 to enforce the taxation of merchandise flowing into the capital, it did not survive through the French Revolution or the "Grands

Boulevards" a century later. Today, all that remains are a few of the toll barriers that escaped revolutionary fury, and an anonymous alliterative ditty: "Le mur murant Paris rend Paris murmurant . . ." ("The wall walling Paris keeps Paris murmuring").

These experiments, along with their spotty results, have hardly discouraged modern leaders from seeking recourse in walls or barriers, whether to resolve political or territorial disputes, prevent hostile incursions, discourage illegal immigrants, or simply buy time while negotiating compromises with the people on the other side of the wall.

A dozen walls or barriers of this type exist today between China and Hong Kong (20 miles); China and Macao (1,000 feet); India and Pakistani Kashmir (340 miles); Morocco and the Spanish enclaves of Ceuta (6 miles) and Melilla (7 miles); Morocco and the western Sahara (1,550 miles); North Korea and South Korea (155 miles); the Republic of Cyprus and the northern region of the island, occupied by Turkey since July 1974 (205 miles). Others are under construction between Saudi Arabia and Yemen, Thailand and Malaysia, and Bangladesh and India, where the Indian government has undertaken the construction of a 2,500-mile-long barrier that will cost $565 million. The United States has already walled in several sections of its 2,000-mile-long border with Mexico. Today it is planning to construct a 690-mile-long wall along the most porous zones of this territory to deter the entry of illegal immigrants.

Danny Tirza, with his bulletproof partition in Gilo, was perhaps the first in Israel to fully actualize a protection wall and demonstrate its efficiency, but the desire for a line of physical separation between the two peoples had long been lurking in the minds of Israeli ideologues, military people, and politicians.

Twenty-five years before the creation of the State of Israel, Vladimir (Ze'ev) Jabotinsky, the ideological father of Likud, had first suggested the idea. In a famous article dated November 1923, the theoretician of Zionist revisionism, who dreamed of creating a Jewish State on the two banks of the Jordan, envisioned the erection of a "wall of iron" as protection from the "Arab insubordinates." "All autochthonic people," he wrote, "struggle against foreigners who settle on their land, and there always remains for them the hope, however faint, that they can avert the dangers associated with settlement. Such is how the Arabs of Palestine will feel, as long as the spark of hope remains that they can prevent the transfiguration of the Arab Palestine into Eretz Israel, that is, a Jewish Palestine. . . . That is why those who hold that an accord with the Arabs is a *sine qua non* of the Zionist political stance must say to themselves from today on that it is definitively out of the question, and that there is nothing else to do but to give up the Zionist project. Our emigration to Palestine must continue without consideration of the Arab position, in a way that our settling can develop there under the protection of a power that is not dependant on the local population, under the shelter of a wall of iron that this population can never break down. This must be our political stance regarding the Arab question."[6]

IN YISHUV, THE JEWISH COMMUNITY IN PALESTINE BEFORE THE CRE-ation of the State of Israel, the idea of separation, founded on the conviction that the Arabs would never accept the existence of the State of Israel between the Mediterranean and Jordan, was omnipresent. This idea continues to be an obsession among the settlement communities, and in Israeli political circles on both the Right and the Left today.

On July 26, 1967, less than two months after the Six-Day War, it was a Labor Party representative, Yigal Allon, who proposed to the government a "territorial compromise" to divide the West Bank between Israel and Jordan. At the time a former commander of Palmach, the assault forces of Haganah (which served, unofficially, as Yishuv's army), Allon was minister of labor under Prime Minister Levi Eshkol. His plan did not explicitly call for a wall or barrier among the Palestinian enclaves that had been handed over to Jordan, but rather a "strategic defense zone," controlled by Israel, about six miles wide between Jordan and the eastern foothills of the West Bank. It also proposed the creation of a string of settlements along the ridgeline, to delineate the new border and to serve as an early warning post. This plan, which implied the Israeli annexation of 33 percent of the West Bank, was never endorsed by the government or by the Labor Party (even if it remained for a long time the unofficial program of the party in terms of settlements).

Today, there are twenty settlements along the Jordan, and the spectacularly scenic Allon Road runs across the Judean Desert to the Jordan Valley, where it terminates near the Green Line, nine miles to the south of Beit She'an. Just under fifty miles long, and mostly off limits to Palestinians, Allon Road connects ten settlements, constructed between 1968 and 1979, with more than six thousand inhabitants. From the vantage point of these well-guarded hills overlooking the western side of the Jordan Valley, one can see as far as the Jericho Oasis and, when the weather is clear, to the ochre-colored summits of Djebel Amman, in Jordan.

Over the following decades, other separation and settlement plans gained momentum in Israeli political and military circles. None of these initial proposals would materialize into a real, concrete separation between Israelis and Palestinians, but many resulted in settlements and "bypass roads" reserved for Israelis. The proliferation of settlements with special-access entries would gradually enclose the Palestinians of the Occupied Territories in a series of pockets, separated from one another by military roadblocks and checkpoints, and transform their daily travel into a Kafkaesque obstacle course.

MORE THAN TWENTY YEARS BEFORE BECOMING PRIME MINISTER OF IS-rael, Ariel Sharon, at the time minister of agriculture of the "religious Likud" coalition government formed by Menachem Begin, had also conceived of a way for Jews to populate the West Bank. On September 29, 1977, his plan was submitted to the government and adopted that October. It opened the way for the construction over four years of nearly sixty settlements designed to ensure the security of Israel, and to satisfy the territorial and messianic demands of Gush Emunim (Bloc of the Faithful),[7] who were allies of Begin. Like Gush Emunim's founders, the Israeli prime minister felt that Judea-Samaria was the cradle of the Jewish people, and that it was Israel's right to settle there.

Did Sharon imagine, as far back as 1977, the construction of a security barrier around the settlements, and their, de facto, annexation to Israeli territory, ignoring the existence of the Green Line? One of his ardent supporters, Ron Nachman, mayor of the Ariel settlement, believes the answer is yes. In 2003, Nachman told a journalist from the mainstream daily newspaper *Yedioth Ahronoth* that his friend "Arik" had envisioned a barrier since the 1970s, and that at each one of his meetings with Sharon, from 1978 onward, he had seen in Sharon's hands the map showing the outline of a wall in the West Bank.[8]

It was not until the 1990s that the Israeli army constructed the first true barrier between Palestinians and Israelis, around the Gaza Strip. Thirty-seven miles long, it is composed of a nine-foot-high fence fitted with several kinds of intrusion-detecting devices and sensors, and has a patrol road running alongside it. It was heavily influenced by the barriers installed along the Lebanese, Syrian, and Jordanian borders. The Gaza barrier was designed not only to clearly demarcate the "Autonomous Areas" as drawn by the Oslo and Cairo accords, but also to prevent terrorism and armed infiltration from Gaza into Israel. After the withdrawal of its troops, the Israeli military feared that the police force of the Autonomous Palestinian Territories would constitute a threat to Israelis, particularly in Jericho and Gaza. The Israeli army symbolically gave the keys of Jericho back to the Palestinians on May 13, 1994. On May 18, it withdrew from most of the Gaza Strip, but not from the settlements there, which account for close to 20 percent of the territory. Yasser Arafat, coming from Egypt, arrived in Gaza the following July. It was not until August 2005 that the Israelis finally left the settlements.

In truth, this first barrier did not hold up long against Palestinian aggression after the explosion of the Second Intifada in September 2000.

"During my first tour of duty in Gaza as chief of the Southern Command[9] in December 2000," notes Major General Doron Almog, head of the Israeli division deployed in the Strip from 1994 to 1996, "I noticed that the Palestinians had dismantled most of the barrier. At the same time, the army received ten to thirty reports each day from army and police intelligence that terrorists were trying to infiltrate Israel to bring in explosives and organize suicide attacks. So my first decision was to build the barrier back up. This took six months, from December 2000 to June 2001. In tandem, we created a half-mile-deep buffer zone along the fencing[10] cleared of any obstacle. Sometimes the orchards made it possible for the terrorists to approach up to 150 feet from the barrier without being detected. So we got rid of all the trees so we could watch over the area better. We also built high-tech[11] observation towers which allowed soldiers to watch over a 3.72-mile section of the barrier while cameras recorded each incident. Finally, we created a new protocol for how soldiers manage Palestinians who approach the barrier. The result was that from 2000 to 2003, when I quit my post, out of more than 400 attempts to cross the barrier detected by the army, none succeeded."[12]

Another man whose opinion greatly influenced how the wall was constructed arrived at the same conclusion. His name is Avraham (Avi) Dichter, head of the southern sector of Shin Bet, the General Security Service of the State of Israel. At the beginning of the 1990s, he also noticed that the barrier around Gaza had succeeded in preventing suicide bombers from entering Israeli territory and that, even though the terrorist networks of Gaza were well armed with explosives and mine detectors, they had become much less effective in Jenin, Nablus, Ramallah, and Hebron. His opinion would bear even greater influence when, on May 14, 2000, he was appointed to the head of Shin Bet by the prime minister from the Labor Party, Ehud Barak.[13]

A devastating attack on a group of soldiers returning to base after a weekend of rest on January 22, 1995, would ultimately move the Labor Party prime minister at the time, Yitzhak Rabin, initiator and signer of the Oslo Accords, to commission the first study of a wall project between Israel and the Palestinians. The attack fell on Beit Lid Junction, about twenty miles northeast of Tel Aviv. Several dozen soldiers were gathered at the intersection of Highways 4 and 57, waiting for a ride back to their unit, when two suicide bombers almost simultaneously detonated. Islamic Jihad, one of the organizations hostile to the Oslo Accords, claimed responsibility for the attack, which killed twenty soldiers and one civilian. Sickened by Yasser Arafat's inability to control "his" extremists, Rabin appointed his minister of police, Moshe Shachal, to the head of a commission charged with studying the construction of a wall.

Shachal, who had participated in the conception of the barrier around Gaza, with the support of the army and the security services, went to work. Since the signing of the Oslo Accords, fifty acts of violent terrorism against Israeli civilians and military personnel had been recorded.[14] The number of victims had reached one hundred. "In fact," remembers General Uzi Dayan (Reserves), at the time head of the Department of Planning for the IDF General Staff, "the project was aimed at combating both petty and organized crime, and arms and car trafficking between Israel and the Autonomous Palestinian Territories. The leaders at the top of the political hierarchy still believed that a true peace agreement with the Palestinians was possible, and that once such an agreement was in place, things would be simpler, especially thanks to the collaboration between our forces and theirs. I can't say that I shared this opinion. Like other heads in the security service, I began to think that the Palestinians would never come to effectively fight their own terrorists and that a barrier would undoubtedly be an efficient tool of protection, barring anything better."

Mired in endless discussions, the "Shachal Project" did not survive past Yitzhak Rabin, who was assassinated on November 4, 1995, in Tel Aviv, by Yigal Amir, a young religious nationalist who accused Rabin of selling Israeli land to the Arabs.

A slightly modified version of the same project—estimated by Dany Tirza at 2 billion shekels, or $535 million—was briefly discussed under Binyamin Netanyahu, who was elected prime minister in May 1996, but abandoned under pressure by Defense Minister Yitzhak Mordechai. Of Iraqi origin, Mordechai arrived in Israel in 1949 at the age of five, and would go on to command a battalion of paratroopers at the Suez front during the October War of 1973. He thought that the barrier was dangerous because it might become a true border over time.

In the fall of 2000, Ariel Sharon, elected president of Likud a year earlier, visited the Temple Mount, which set off the Second Intifada. The Labor Party prime minister Ehud Barak, who was in a delicate political situation because his party had become the minority in the Knesset in July, announced that he, too, was in favor of a barrier. The plan that was submitted for his approval in November was founded on a core principle: "We are here, they are there." He foresaw a barrier that would filter the passage of vehicles and pedestrians along the Green Line, as well as around the big settlements—notably Ariel, Ma'ale Adumim, Gush Etzion, and those at the periphery of Jerusalem. The status of the isolated settlements was still up for discussion. It would, in effect, never be addressed under Barak: endless haggling over the constitution of a national unity government, or "national emergency," would postpone the question of the barrier for another year. That is, until Ariel Sharon was elected prime minister of Israel on February 6, 2001, with 62.39 percent of the vote.

A forest license, issued by the IDF, empowering the army to uproot and "move" 350 olive trees, near the West Bank town of Zufim. *Courtesy of B'Tselem*

CHAPTER 3

The Eve of Pesach

Who was against the "security wall"? With the exception of a few West Bank settlers terrified by the possibility of finding themselves isolated on the "wrong" side of the barrier, some Israeli human rights organizations pushing for a diplomatic alternative, and of course the Palestinians, apparently no one opposed it. In today's Israeli society, the idea of the wall enjoys overwhelming support. It is hard to find politicians or military personnel involved in its construction who would admit to the slightest doubt. Yet, the idea of building a "zone of separation" between Israelis and Palestinians didn't immediately take hold, even among those who claim to have brought the idea to life.

When Sharon became prime minister on March 7, 2001, he was more than a little wary of the plans he inherited from the Barak government. He feared that a wall built along the Green Line, which Barak's advisors had imagined, would become a real border, isolating the settlements in Palestinian territory. But he had been intrigued—and perhaps rattled—by a presentation he had seen by Professor Arnon Sofer, director of the Department of Geostrategic Studies and co-president of the National Security Studies Center at the University of Haifa. As a specialist on the "Arab Demographic Danger," "Sofer, the Arab Counter," as some of his colleagues called him, had argued for years for a true separation between Israelis and Palestinians, which, in his view, was necessary to preserve the Jewish character of the State of Israel. To support his argument, he had drawn an actual map of the separation, with 80 percent of the 220,000 settlers in the West Bank and all of the 180,000 settlers in East Jerusalem on the Israeli side of the "closure."[1]

The West Bank, he explained, should be divided into three parts, or, as he put it, three "sausages": the first sausage, to the north, from Jenin to Ramallah; the second, to the south, from Bethlehem to Hebron; and the third, smaller sausage, around Jericho. An electric fence would be built around these three Palestinian sausages, enclosing the majority of the territory's Arab population in a little less than half of the West Bank. The Jordan Valley would remain under control of the Israeli army, which, in case of an attack from the east, could cut off the Palestinians from the rest of the Arab world.

Sharon, at the time leader of the opposition party, had a long talk with the professor after his presentation. Sofer was therefore not surprised when, on the heels of Sharon's election to prime minister, one of his advisors invited him to come see the new PM, maps in hand.[2] According to one of his military advisors at the time, Sharon was considering the strategic advantages of a separation barrier, the route of such a barrier, and how to conduct the unilateral withdrawal of Israeli settlements from the West Bank. He consulted the maps, and met with the representatives of the settlements. He seemed to realize that before long he would have to make crucial strategic and political decisions.

In January 2001, he declared in his political policy plan that he was in favor of an intermediary long-term agreement with the Palestinians, and went as far as saying that the final phase of this plan would be the creation of a Palestinian State on 42 percent of the West Bank—compared to 94 percent proposed by the Israeli delegation in Taba. But at the beginning of March 2001, after the failed Israeli-Palestinian negotiations in January in Taba had sealed the end of the Barak government, and the Second Intifada had already killed 64 Israelis—including 36 civilians—and 343 Palestinians, the new PM seemed more concerned with ending the Palestinian uprising as quickly as possible than with the blueprints for a future separation wall. The Israeli desire for security had been a major focus of his campaign, and he responded to that desire for security by laying siege to the Occupied Territories and by directing the army to aggressively track and attack the terrorists, often with heavy collateral damage among the Palestinian population.

"When he called me, shortly after taking office, Sharon didn't show me any map," remembers Uzi Dayan, the general presiding at that time over the National Security Council.[3] "He simply asked me what I thought of the idea of a separation. So I went to work, first analyzing the security situation, how to deal with the terrorists, the mood among the population. In the span of six months, nearly eighty Israelis had perished in terrorist attacks. The majority were killed in Israeli territory. A bombing some days before had particularly affected people; the target was Dolphinarium, a night club in Tel Aviv, where more than twenty young people were killed and more than one hundred and twenty injured.[4]

"I had submitted my first plan in July. We needed to respond to the distress of the Israelis and put an end to the terrorism; we needed to study and plan for a security barrier. Sharon then appointed me to the head of a commission in charge of preparing the project. But the government wasn't completely behind it. At least five cabinet members, including the minister of foreign affairs, Shimon Peres, and the minister of national infrastructure, Avigdor Lieberman, had reservations. Lieberman thought that this plan would ruin his dreams of a 'Greater Israel.' Peres, who was convinced that an accord with Yasser Arafat was still possible, felt that the barrier went too far off the Green Line.

"Sharon, too, was against the idea. Since his days as a soldier he had always hated defensive strategies and he imagined the problems that the creation of a barrier would stir at the heart of the coalition, notably among the settlements. He also wanted to avoid being dragged into a discussion about 'disengaging' the settlements from the Territories. When I learned the substance of his objections, I asked him: 'Well, what will you do if there are more attacks? Give the usual answers, tell the Israelis that those who died were precious and that we will miss them? And what would you say to those who believed that the barrier could have saved them?' After consulting with the government, Sharon decided that the wall was not urgent, but he did ask me to continue working on measures to prevent the infiltration of Palestinian terrorists in Israel. And on July 18, the Security Cabinet approved what I had recommended."

In fact, the only decision that the Sharon government made, as documents published by the Israeli minister of defense show, was to order, on July 23, 2001, the creation of a "zone of separation" between Israel and the regions under control of the Palestinian Authority. In this zone, the Border Police (to the west) and the army (to the east) would be responsible, under the authority of a coordinating task force, to step up patrols and inspections for more effective interception, arrest, and interrogation of Palestinians attempting to enter Israel illegally. The deployment of soldiers and police in this area was reinforced. Measures that had been adopted in November 2000 to prevent Palestinian vehicles from entering Israel were tightened. But there was no further consideration of constructing a continuous obstacle,[5] that is to say, a wall or a barrier, except in three sectors: Um el-Fahm, Tulkarem, and Jerusalem—about fifty miles of territory considered to be "high-risk zones."

With thirty-six years of distinguished military service behind him, Uzi Dayan was disappointed by Sharon's "wait and see" approach (he and his colleagues in the military knew Sharon better as a rapid, even audacious decision-maker). Wearing blue jeans and a plaid shirt, his square-jawed face rarely lit with a smile, Dayan himself thinks like a military man, though he is now in the Reserves. He reasons that once the danger has been identified, the risks assessed, and the plan of attack drawn, there is nothing left to do but give the orders. This is no doubt why, at the age fifty-eight, with the support of a few friends and a squad of young militants, he decided to launch his own political movement, called Tafnit, or "Turnaround."

The movement, which chose a green-and-blue Star of David as its logo, until recently had not met with much success.[6] In the apartment that serves as Tafnit's headquarters, on the twenty-sixth floor of the Sheraton Tower on the edge of Tel Aviv, are stacks of boxes full of brochures describing, in Hebrew and English, the movement's mission. Their map of the "Line of Disengagement" proposes the annexation of a third of the West Bank, the construction of a barrier around the annexed territories containing the majority of the sizeable Israeli settlements, and abandoning thirty-two smaller settlements home to twenty-one thousand Israelis. This plan, in other words, closely resembles both the project presented to Ariel Sharon in July 2001 and the project under way today.

"Look," he says while tracing the barrier's route on a piece of paper. "What happened in Gaza should be enough to convince you that a barrier was the solution. In five years, not one group of terrorists was able to infiltrate Israel from the Gaza Strip. It was this fact that finally encouraged Sharon to concede. So why, then, did we wait so long to launch the construction of the barrier around the West Bank? Why, when attacks were multiplying, did we need to waste a year?" Despite the repeated requests of IDF chief of staff Shaul Mofaz and the director of Shin Bet, Avi Dichter, who tirelessly argued for a continuous obstacle between Israelis and Palestinians, it was not until April 2002, after a series of targeted operations, bombings, attacks, and counterattacks that killed 123 Israelis and 605 Palestinians in four months, that the Sharon government officially made the decision to construct a barrier or a wall in three regions of the West Bank.

"ON THE EVE OF PESACH," REMEMBERS BINYAMIN "FOUAD" BEN-ELIEZER, minister of defense at the time, "I had decided to bring my wife and children to Bethlehem, where one of my former units was stationed, so we could spend the evening with the soldiers.[7] You understand what Pesach means to the Jews: it's the celebration of the exodus of the Hebrews from Egypt, one of the most important days on our calendar. I had planned on spending the evening with these young men who couldn't be with their families. But we weren't in Bethlehem more than an hour when a telephone call warned me that a suicide bomber had detonated explosives in the reception room of the Park Hotel in Netanya, where two hundred and fifty people had gathered to celebrate Pesach. It was carnage, thirty dead and one hundred and forty injured.

At that moment, I said to myself, 'This must stop.' I don't care what people might say about me. I have to build this barrier."

This isn't the first barrier built by Ben-Eliezer. At the end of the 1970s, when he was a colonel, Ben-Eliezer, who speaks perfect Arabic and who could easily pass for a Lebanese man on the streets of Beirut, secretly traveled three times to Lebanon to meet with Christian leaders. He was there to evaluate their readiness to fight, their arsenal, and to determine the best way to help them combat the thousands of Palestinian fedayeen who had been expelled from Jordan in the aftermath of Black September.[8] When the Christians from the south of Lebanon found themselves under attack by Islamic combatants in their border "pockets," Eliezer responded by building the "good border" between Israel and Lebanon. Consisting of two high fences with electronic intrusion detectors, the "good border" was frequently patrolled by the Israeli army, who from time to time conducted armed incursions into south Lebanon whenever the command post deemed necessary. The border was so effective that, out of 262 Fedayeen attacks reported by the Israeli army in 1980, only 8 were led by combatants who had infiltrated from Lebanon. Two years later, Sharon would nonetheless invoke the frequency of attacks against Galilee as reason for invading Lebanon.

KNOWN FOR HIS DIRECTNESS, BUT ALSO FOR SOMETIMES GETTING CARried away with himself, Ben-Eliezer is the Labor Party "hawk" incarnate, a general whose ascendance through the ranks seems to exemplify the legendary history of the Israeli army. Born in Iraq—hence the nickname Fouad—he traveled via Iran to Israel in 1950, thirteen years old and alone. It was at the Merhavia kibbutz, near Afula, then in a transition camp in Pardesia, to the east of Netanya, where his parents were housed upon their arrival three years after him, that he learned Hebrew. But he never forgot his Arabic, and it later became a major asset for him in the army. He joined the Israel Defense Forces in 1954, two years before the Suez War. He had spent his entire career in infantry combat units before moving up to the rank of general, thirty years later, on the

eve of the "War of the Stones."[9] He has been consistently reelected to
the Knesset since 1984. Scrappy and jovial, but prone to angry out-
bursts, he has a ravenous appetite, and an authoritative voice that one
could easily imagine booming through the chambers of the turbulent
Knesset. He seems to know the rocky hills of the West Bank better than
his own gentrified neighborhood of Tel Aviv, and claims to understand
the Palestinians better than most Israeli leaders because he was born in
an Arab country, he speaks their language, and he has never stopped
talking and fighting with them. After commanding the Israeli forces in
south Lebanon, then serving as military commander of Judea-Samaria
[the West Bank], he was government coordinator of activities in the Occupied Territories. In 1992, before the Oslo Accords, he was discreetly
sent to Tunis by Prime Minister Rabin to ascertain Arafat's intentions.

"The problem," he thunders, "is that we have spent too much time
trying to understand what is happening with the Palestinians. When I
was minister of defense, I went to the prisons several times to talk
with suicide bombers we had succeeded in capturing. They're not idiots. Several of them were highly educated and had graduated from Bir
Zeit University. I even met a young woman from Bethlehem who had
a degree in computer technology and who seemed to have a brilliant
career ahead of her. With people like this, who have a profound desire
to die, you can't just pull out your gun and say, 'Stop, or I'll shoot,'
like you would with any other terrorist. They *want* to die, that's what
they're waiting for. Our arsenal of F-16s, Apaches, and Merkavas—
our whole combat strategy—can do nothing against people like this.
All we can do is prevent them from getting to us. In other words, build
a wall. But once you have said this, you need to address the political
dilemma of the wall. The Right, the National Religious Party, and the
settlements were against it because they didn't want a separation between Judea-Samaria and Israel. The Left, many of my friends in the
Labor Party and the Meretz, were against it because they only would
accept a border following the 1967 line, or the Green Line. Sharon
himself sometimes refused to listen to me, to hear what the Security Service people were saying. It was a long time after he took office, maybe
a year, before he accepted the idea of a barrier.

"As for me, I knew, through my conversations with the army chief of staff and with military intelligence, that the suicide bombings were going to continue, that we had entered into a new cycle of terrorism and that there was only one way to make it stop: block it. When the Security Cabinet of the government had a meeting, on April 14, 2002, nearly three weeks after the Netanya attack, I proposed to Sharon that we put the minister of defense in charge of studying and building this separation line, and he agreed. The basic idea was to put up a permanent barrier to reduce response time and improve the operational capacity of the security forces.

"A pilot inspection commission, presided over by the prime minister, was created. A cell was put in place at the Ministry of Defense and we asked Dany Tirza to study the best system and the best layout. He's from the Right, the far Right, but for this project, which required a very refined knowledge of the terrain, he was excellent. After having examined the situation with him, I proposed that a first section of the wall or barrier be constructed in the center of Israel near the road from Jerusalem to Tel Aviv, where the infiltrations had been more numerous. In the end, the government decided to construct three sections. The first, to protect Highway 65, which connects Hadera to Tiberiade, was to be around sixty miles long; the other two would be to the north and to the south of Jerusalem."

Listening to him today, one would think that Binyamin Ben-Eliezer never had a doubt about the need to build a security barrier, let alone about its ethical implications. However, when the question of the barrier was brought back to the table in the end of the 1990s, Eliezer was in fact opposed to it, perhaps for substantive reasons, but especially because his party rival for the candidacy of prime minister, Haim Ramon, supported it. Ramon rallied for the wall in the spring of 2002, and six months later left the Sharon government with other Labor Party ministers, just as an increase in suicide attacks was stoking widespread anger among Israelis. It seems Eliezer was also in disagreement with the military on the course of the barrier, in particular with his successor at the Ministry of Defense, IDF chief of staff Shaul Mofaz,

A WALL IN PALESTINE   43

a protégé of Sharon. Whereas the first projects conceived by experts at
the IDF at this time show a barrier generously snaking through the interior of the West Bank—nearly 420 miles long—in order to avoid the
settlements, Ben-Eliezer had made a case for a path 220 miles, hardly
longer than the Green Line (195 miles). This was still his position on
Friday, June 14, 2002, when he attended the groundbreaking of the first
phase of the project near the Givat Oz kibbutz, to the north of Jenin,
and explained to journalists his ideas on the security barrier:

"The Netanya attack succeeded in convincing the main political
players that we should change how we fight terrorism, but I would not
say that it meant a definitive change in position for Ariel Sharon on
the question of the barrier. This took place, I might mention, not as a
sudden about-face but gradually over time. In reality, it was the increase in attacks that caused the prime minister to lean in favor of the
barrier. They were too deadly to go on unanswered."

At the time, Avi Dichter was head of Shin Bet, and he claims to have
encouraged Sharon's change by bombarding him with presentations
and memos on the advantages of a fixed obstacle. "I don't know how
many times I told him that we could no longer combat terrorism with
patrols and ambushes. And that he needed to think about the number
of illegal Palestinian workers who were coming into Israel from the
West Bank, even through closed-off areas. Ninety-nine percent of them
were coming only to work, but one percent could be terrorists."[10]

A former member of the famous, yet covert, reconnaissance unit
of the IDF, Sayeret Matkal, Dichter spent his whole civil career in Shin
Bet. Having directed several key departments, including the protection of VIPs in the wake of the assassination of Yitzhak Rabin, he took
the helm in 2000 at the request of the prime minister, Ehud Barak,
and would undoubtedly have been asked to serve another five-year
term in 2005 if he had kept his reservations about the Sharon-prepared
project of the unilateral retreat from Gaza to himself. Disappointed,
he left Israel in September 2005 for a stint at the Brookings Institution,
but then, when he returned a few months later, he supported Olmert's
plan for unilateral withdrawal from the West Bank. Ultimately he took

up the political gauntlet and was elected deputy of the Kadima Party—
that of Sharon and Olmert—where his concerns with security remained unflagging.

"The first time that I imagined the construction of a barrier," he
says, "was right after the Oslo Accords. At the time, I was the head of
the south division of Shin Bet. My counterpart in the army was Matan
Vilnai, who commanded the southern military zone of the Israel Defense Forces. We were both in charge of the Gaza Strip and we shared
the belief that a barrier around the Autonomous Palestinian Territory
was indispensable. I believed, and I still believe, like Vilnai, that high
fences make for good neighbors. I had spoken about this with two of
my colleagues in Shin Bet, Gideon Ezra and Israel Hasson, who are
also now in the Knesset. I didn't understand why they hadn't suggested
the construction of a barrier around the new future border of the
Palestinian Authority. I was convinced that even if we were committed to
a peace process with the Palestinians it was important, for them as well
as us, to avoid terrorist attacks in Israel which could cause this historic
project to fail. In my view, a barrier between Palestinians and us wasn't
only dissuasion; it was a very effective prevention tool. I was well enough
versed in counterterrorism efforts to know that there is no silver bullet,
but that by combining several approaches—intelligence-gathering, inspections—we could destabilize the terrorists, make them more vulnerable, change their way of life. This is what I repeatedly said to my
superiors and to members of the government whenever I had access to
them, but it was all in vain. They were reticent, even hostile, not because they couldn't appreciate my arguments, but because they felt
that this barrier, if it were to be built one day, would hold too much
political significance. And, for sometimes contradictory reasons, they
feared it.

"With Sharon, when he became prime minister, and with Fouad
[Ben-Eliezer], his minister of defense, I put the question back on the
table at every meeting we had following terrorist attacks. I think that
my arguments in the end had an effect. I live in Ashkelon, not far from
Sharon's farm in the Negev. So sometimes we see each other, just the

two of us. We even dedicated, if I remember correctly, two discussions almost entirely to the barrier. So, in fact, I'm not exaggerating when I say that I played an influential role in convincing him after the Netanya tragedy."

Sharon responded to the Netanya attack by giving Uzi Dayan and his minister of defense orders to build the first section of the barrier and to begin a study on a "separation plan." He also asked Shaul Mofaz to redeploy units to all West Bank towns ceded to the Palestinian Authority in 1995 under an intermediary agreement, "Oslo 2, called Operation Rampart." Numerous brigades of Reserves and hundreds of armored vehicles and tanks were mobilized in the most intricate military operation undertaken by the Israeli army since the Six-Day War. Within a few days, Nablus, Jenin, and Bethlehem were under lockdown by the Israeli army, and Palestinian combatants took refuge in the Church of the Nativity in Bethlehem. In Jenin, after a battle that left fifteen Israeli soldiers and fifty-three Palestinians dead, the army sent in armored bulldozers to demolish many of the houses in the refugee camp. On June 6, in Ramallah, Arafat's compound, the Mouqata, was attacked by tanks and bulldozers as well. Arafat and his colleagues were confined to a few rooms in the damaged building. Sharon briefly considered expelling the Palestinian president, but on the advice of Shin Bet, Mossad, and military intelligence, he decided against it—the old "rais" would be more trouble in a foreign country than in the ruins of Mouqata.

The assassination of the Tulkarem head of the Al-Aqsa Martyrs' Brigade, Read al-Karmi (which had been called "an unfortunate act"[11] by general Yitzhak Eytan, commander of the central region, and denounced as "a grave error" by Ben Eliezer), and Operation Rampart a few months later, marked the end of a period of relative calm that had been respected by the Palestinian towns. Sharon and his colleagues—special advisor Dov Weisglass, Shaul Mofaz, and representative of the settlements and old friend Ze'ev Hever—were now considering new political and strategic options, and a very different outline of the barrier than the one for which Sharon had previously argued. Even Ben-Eliezer, who was never considered one of the "dear souls" on the Left so detested by Sharon and his followers for their naïveté and weakness regarding the Arabs, approved Sharon's military operations and, in particular, his "targeted attacks," so as not to appear soft.

But with the peace process languishing in a two-year stalemate, and the growing political influence of the settler lobby, Ben-Eliezer was paid less attention than ever before. The national economy teetered at the edge of bankruptcy, and his political future was now threatened by competition from within the Labor Party (particularly from the mayor of Haifa, Amram Mitzna). Ben-Eliezer began to worry. Several high-ranking officers in the Labor Party resigned on October 30, and brought about the end of a unified national government.

Meanwhile, the barrier project had become an actual construction site. Nine days before the June 23, 2002 meeting at which the government officially approved Decision 2077, "Phase 1" of the plan, the bull-dozers were already in place to the north of the West Bank, between the Palestinian village of Zbuba and the Arab-Israeli village of Salem, separated by the Green Line. On property "requisitioned for military purposes" from their Palestinian owners, the Public Works Department had begun to clear a ribbon of land 180 feet wide in the middle of orchards, greenhouses, and plowed fields, intended, according to Ben-Eliezer, for an enclosure to protect Route 65.

In principle, the owners of this requisitioned land have a right to damages. But the majority refused to collect, often at the request of the Palestinian Authority, so as not to reclassify the requisition of their land into a simple case of expropriation. They could also seek recourse with the legal advisor to the Civil Administration and, if their case is rejected there, bring it before the Israeli Supreme Court. In principle. But few of them, assisted by lawyers or human rights advocates, have gone that far, and when they did, it was always with mixed results. For the moment, under the stupefied gaze of the farmers, the bulldozers advanced, protected by soldiers from a private militia armed with Uzis, who guard the construction sites day and night. When the Cabinet definitively approved the route of Phase 1 of the barrier, on April 14, 2002, the bulldozers had already been at work for a month and the site's long and dusty scar stretched on for miles to the west along the Green Line. For the moment.

"When I received the order from Sharon to launch Phase One, and to conduct a study of the route of the barrier, I had three objectives in mind," recounts Uzi Dayan. "First of all, I had to furnish Israel with the best security possible. Second, on the west side of the barrier, I had to include the least number of Palestinians and the greatest number of Israelis. Last, I had to try to disrupt the daily life of the Palestinians as little as possible."

This seems to correspond with the official priorities of the barrier. Indeed, it effectively responds to Israeli concerns about security. And one may even accept its humanitarian intent with regard to the Palestinians. But from the start, the barrier was built to meet multiple purposes. While Dayan advanced its security justifications—using the very real trauma caused by terrorism in order to manipulate Israeli public opinion, often through credulous media sources—he neglected to mention the other controversial functions of the barrier: Dayan's "technical" rationale for the barrier while presiding over the National Security Council coincidentally *also* serves the ideological beliefs of his political movement, Tafnit—namely the annexation of large blocks of settlements in Judea and Samaria to Israel, and making the barrier a border between Israel and a future Palestinian State.

The man whom, in the spring of 2002, Ariel Sharon placed in charge to direct the construction of the barrier—one of the biggest public works projects in Israel's history—doesn't recall things exactly as Uzi Dayan does. Rather, he has a more brutal way of telling the same story. Netzah Mashiah is as cold and functional as the office building in which he works, the new Ministry of Defense building in Tel Aviv, a cube of concrete and glass cut through with a cylinder of steel. All visitors are eyed up and down from the moment of their arrival, and must surrender their cell phones, computers, and BlackBerrys at security. Mashiah, whom I interviewed in the presence of a ministry spokesperson, is a civilian man with a soldier's qualities, or perhaps a soldier with civilian qualities. At fifty-two years old, this civil engineer has spent close to half of his life—twenty-three years—in the army's construction department. At Sharon's request, he quit a managerial post at Solel Boneh, one of Israel's giant construction contractors, in order to return to the Ministry of Defense and take over as head of the Security Barrier Project.

Not exactly the most expressive person, he does, however, get worked up when reminded that the barrier will divide Palestinian territory into separate municipalities. "That's just propaganda!" he says.

Mashiah is responsible for selecting by competitive bid the companies for excavation, construction, and security. The security contractors are also approved by the army. For the first-phase construction site, the list of selected contractors included twenty or so Israeli companies, among them Magal and Elbit, as well as manufacturers of security systems, and even a U.S. security hardware manufacturer, Detektor. Mashiah is also in charge of supervising the cartographers. They produce digitized topographical profiles from aerial photos of a given zone, then convert them into mathematical models, which are then stored in the army's computers. The army then uses this information to determine the route of the wall, and how best to serve the security imperatives as determined by the government and the IDF.

"The politicians," Mashiah explained, in a voice that was not quite serene, "couldn't stop arguing over the outline of the barrier.[12] That's why the prime minister [Ariel Sharon] and the defense minister [Binyamin Ben-Eliezer] decided to hand the job over to the army, telling them that there was one objective: to prevent Palestinian terrorists from crossing over and getting into Israel. The problem wasn't *where* the barrier would be placed—on which land—but its purpose, and, what path would best serve its purpose. These were the instructions that those put in charge of the project, all military personnel, were given when they went to work. The barrier that you see today on the ground is what was recommended by the army, approved by the director-general of the Ministry of Defense, the head of the armed forces, the defense minister, and the government. The next phase consisted of making it all legal by requisitioning the land for security reasons. This didn't mean we became owners of the land in question. We are only holding on to it for the duration of the barrier's mission, which is to get rid of terrorism. We are working from the principle that this barrier is temporary. And that the length of time it stays up depends on how the Palestinians work toward peace. So, it can stay here five minutes or five decades."

The barrier at the Bir Nabala enclave. *Courtesy of MachsomWatch/Judith Spitzer*

CHAPTER 4

THE DAYAN CAMPAIGN

Sharon still was not completely on board, even though large sections of the barrier in the northwest of the West Bank had been completed and deemed effective by the army and security services.[1] He no longer doubted the security value of a physical separation between Israelis and Palestinians, but he remained concerned about the unplanned long-term consequences of the barrier, particularly as an impediment to his dream of a Greater Israel, spanning from the Mediterranean to the Jordan River. "The Netanya attack had finally convinced him to break ground on this first construction site in June 2002," remembers General Uzi Dayan (Reserves), who had supported Sharon in the elections but later had found himself disappointed in his leadership. "Those of us who were responsible for security, in Shin Bet and Mossad, never stopped showing him—with statistics, maps, and aerial photos—that the construction of the barrier was vital for Israel.

"The truth is, I didn't understand why, at the political level, and in particular with Sharon, there was still hesitation. I knew, of course, the general reasons for this hesitation, on the Left and on the Right. But in my opinion, those reasons did not outweigh the benefits of the barrier. And, anyway, did we have a choice? For Israel, there are only two solutions: Either we keep the whole Promised Land, from the Mediterranean to Jordan, in a binational state—which no one wants, because we're here to live in a Jewish state—or we disengage from the Territories, separate from the Palestinians, and wait for a more favorable climate for negotiating an accord, while protected from terrorism by the barrier.

"The best starting point for those who believe an agreement is possible *and* who want to hold on to a major part of the Territories, is unilateral disengagement and separation. Otherwise, we are creating an unprecedented form of state, one that has no equivalent on earth: In terms of security, it would be like south Lebanon; the political system would be that of South Africa under apartheid; and the regime would resemble a sort of Latin American–style military dictatorship—it's a cocktail that I don't like at all."

"The only way to get the politicians past their hemming and hawing and to accept the idea of separation—in other words, the barrier—was to mobilize public opinion. That's why, in June 2002, I quit my post as president of the National Security Council and, along with other military and security specialists, politicians, and representatives from civil society, formed an association called the Public Council for a Security Fence for Israel. There weren't many of us, but we worked hard. We wrote up a list of the communities along the Green Line that were directly exposed to terrorism, and we divided them into four geographical groups: north, south, center, and Jerusalem. Then we sent out delegations to meet with every mayor and every city council. Everywhere we went, we found that people were exasperated by terrorism and extremely worried. We explained to them that it didn't have to be that way, and that if officials on the local level couldn't guarantee security to their constituents, the government could; there was a way that had been proven effective to protect everyone. As we had hoped, this encouraged most of them to put pressure on the Ministry of Defense to build a barrier in their region.

"Our commission's next target was the Knesset. We undertook a huge lobbying project, writing proposals and sometimes even draft legislation for the deputies of the commissions of defense and security. Finally, and most effectively, we mobilized the media. Our argument was simple: Where there is a security barrier, it is very effective; but along most of the Green Line, there is no security barrier; and the man responsible for this is Ariel Sharon. If a bus explodes tomorrow in Jerusalem, who will be to blame?

"At radio and television stations, we didn't talk to political journalists or editorial writers; instead we approached debate and talk show hosts, interviewers. There aren't many of them, so it was easy. We explained our position, and gave them questions that they should ask over and over each time they had a politician or military guest on their shows: Why is something that worked in Gaza not in other places? What are you doing, exactly, to prevent this wave of terrorism? How many miles of security barrier has the army built? What would you do if there were an attack in a zone without a barrier? I also went to see the people whom I considered most influential at the three major newspapers, *Yedioth Ahronot*, *Maariv*, and *Haaretz*, and I asked them to keep in mind two questions for all of the politicians they interviewed: One, do you think that the barrier is an effective means of fighting terrorism? And two, who is responsible for the fact that there is no barrier?"

Uzi Dayan and his Public Council for a Security Fence for Israel found that many Israelis, weary of escalating terrorism, were receptive to their campaign. The fear of suicide attacks had become omnipresent among Israelis. In the two years after the beginning of the Second Intifada, Palestinian attacks had killed 649 Israelis—337 in Israel and 312 in the Occupied Territories. More then two thirds of those killed—445—were civilians.[2] Surveys and opinion polls across the Israeli media showed that nine out of ten Israelis were "worried" or "very worried" about their security.

While the Camp David and Taba summits fell apart, Uzi Dayan's campaign was going strong. Ehud Barak and his entourage successfully used the media to foster the belief, in Israel and beyond, that Yasser Arafat had deliberately resorted to violence in September 2001 during the Second Intifada, and that his intransigent attitude had stalled the peace process. The old Palestinian president, accused of duplicity and of being complicit with terrorists, was no longer to be trusted, and it was time to give up the hope of living as good neighbors with the Palestinians.

The work of a number of journalists and researchers—notably that of Charles Enderlin[3] and Clayton E. Swisher[4]—suggests that this version of history is simplistic and biased. It is true that there were grave errors in how the Palestinians engaged in the peace process negotiations; their objectives may have been impossible, and they had poorly prepared their people for concessions, while at the same time preserving old myths of Palestinian nationalism. At the very moment when the Palestinians should have seized their historic responsibility, they withdrew from the process. But Barak and his supporters were also to blame. The Israeli prime minister, who at one time was a general and commander of elite army units, had difficulty applying his militaristic mode of thinking to diplomatic objectives. By refusing to withdraw any troops from the West Bank, and by continuously delaying the transfer of villages on the outskirts of Jerusalem to the Palestinian Authority, he reneged on crucial commitments he had made to the Palestinians. Barak's delegation, whose goal it seemed was to demonize Arafat, disastrously mismanaged the negotiations, and the Palestinians concluded that they had been wrong to believe the Israelis were sincere. Arafat and his people were also disillusioned by the U.S. delegation, which had not played the role of an honest broker, as expected. Poorly prepared, Bill Clinton and his advisors had neglected to come with backup positions in case of a stalemate, and seemed to act as a tacit support system for the Israeli delegation.

"The Americans turned their back on us," confides Ahmed Qurei (Abu Ala), then president of the Palestinian Legislative Council and a member of the Palestinian delegation at Camp David.[5] "Shortly before Camp David, I went to see Bill Clinton. I explained to him that we would participate in the negotiations because he had invited us, but that we would be cautious, because during the preparatory meetings with the Israelis we had not seen any decisive change in their position, or any new opening. I had feared that a summit under those conditions would end in a historic failure from which we would all have trouble recovering. Then and there I asked Clinton to promise that he would not make it look like Arafat was responsible for such a potential failure. He promised me this, and he didn't keep his word. We had hardly turned our backs after the fiasco of Camp David when he already pointed to Arafat as being mainly responsible for its failure."

Confirmed by a member of the U.S. delegation at Camp David, Clinton's broken promise was considered treason by the Palestinian leadership, proof that the United States, once again, had taken Israel's side. At the same time, the Palestinians found themselves, once more, in the role of ungrateful enemy of peace. Arafat and the Palestinian Authority have never, in fact, shaken this image of themselves as evasive and defiant.

While Arafat was called by the Israeli political class "the man who could, but who didn't," he was succeeded by Mahmoud Abbas, "the man who wants to but who can't." Fundamentally, nothing had changed. "This legend in which Barak offered almost everything at Camp David and then Arafat responded with terrorism is, today, one of the principal obstacles to reaching a peaceful solution," observes Colonel Shaul Arieli (Reserves), who is now a prominent member of the Council for Peace and Security, and was head of the Peace Administration under the Barak government.[6]

"The wall of concrete and metal that you see today on the ground is the product of the mental wall behind which the Israelis have hidden themselves, in particular after the failure of Camp David,"[7] explains Menachem Klein, professor of political science at the University of Bar-Ilan. After serving as advisor to Shlomo Ben-Ami, the minister of foreign affairs under Barak, Menachem Klein, a devoutly religious Jew, was one of the architects of the informal accord signed on October 12, 2003, and made public two months later in Geneva, by a group of Israeli and Palestinian politicians, military personnel, and intellectuals. He sharply disagrees with the version of Camp David relayed in his former boss's book, *What Future for Israel?*, a version he calls "a shameful distortion of the facts, and crushing for Arafat."[8]

"The problem for a lot of Israelis who were aligned with Sharon, including those from the 'peace camp,'" he says, "is that they have never tried to put themselves in the shoes of the Palestinians. In the end, they are not ready to pay the price of peace, which is to say, to give up land. The Palestinians, on the other hand, have already paid this price with their blood." In other words, the Israelis are cloistered in a kind of moral superiority, living in a "walled" society in which the aspirations of other peoples are cropped out of view, and in which they can live in peaceful denial of their role as oppressors.[9]

It is a society in which the citizens are particularly receptive to military rhetoric, where generals often become politicians, or even prime minister (as Moshe Dayan, Yitzhak Rabin, Ehud Barak, and Ariel Sharon have shown); a society in which security imperatives dictate politics and ultimately determine relations with those dangerous creatures, the Palestinians. It was Ehud Barak who called Israel "a villa in the jungle."

"To be strong and to perceive oneself as weak is an enormous temptation," remarks the writer David Grossman. "We have dozens of atomic bombs, tanks, and planes. We confront people possessing none of these arms, and yet, in our minds, we remain victims. This inability to perceive ourselves as we are in relation to others is our principal weakness."[10]

The diagnosis of David Grossman and Menachem Klein, which is shared with many other intellectuals—such as the former president of the Knesset, Avraham Burg, the writer Batya Gour, and the historian Shlomo Sand—is supported by public opinion polls. A study by the Center for Strategic Studies at the University of Tel Aviv[11] showed that in 2002, 68 percent of Israelis felt that peace with the Palestinians was impossible (in comparison to 56 percent in 2001), 80 percent approved of the use of tanks and combat planes in the Occupied Territories (in comparison to 71 percent in 2001), and 56 percent held the Palestinians solely responsible for prolonging the conflict. Above all, in an eloquent disavowal of their own hopes, only 45 percent said that they had approved of the Oslo Accords in 1993, while questionnaires from the time show approval of at least 65 percent.

When he was elected prime minister in February 2001, Ariel Sharon obviously understood how terrorism had struck at the heart of Israeli society. Although he did not share Menachem Klein's indignation about Israel's metamorphosis into a "military state," he also clearly did not agree with the "doves" in the peace camp, either. He knew that he was now leading a country traumatized by terrorism, and demoralized by the failure of the peace process, and he had built his campaign on the anguish of his fellow citizens—it worked; he won with 62.39 percent of the vote. His Labor Party adversaries rallied behind him without a struggle, and he found himself the head of a national unity government that included Orthodox Sephardic Jews from the Shas Party, the Russian-speaking Yisrael Ba'Aliyah (Israel on the Rise) Party of Natan Sharansky, and the extreme right of Rehavam Ze'evi and Avigdor Lieberman. Without any real internal opposition, he dedicated himself to what he considered a task of the first order: consolidating their alliance with the United States, which was key to Israel's security, and resuming the negotiations begun under the Clinton administration, which provided for the establishment of a Palestinian State on 94–96 percent of the West Bank and Gaza.

The election of George W. Bush, and his response to the terrorist attacks on the World Trade Center and the Pentagon, worked somewhat to Sharon's advantage. At first the tragedy of 9/11 shook up the diplomatic and strategic priorities of the new administration. During the last months of 2001, and until spring 2002, Bush's advisors, obsessed with isolating Osama Bin Laden's terrorist network, combating anti-U.S. sentiment in the Arab world, and reinforcing the moderate regimes of the Middle East, seemed to place most of their hopes on an urgent revival, however painful, of the Israeli-Palestinian peace process. But this implied that they would have to distance themselves from Israel, which at that time had stepped up military operations and targeted attacks in the West Bank and Gaza. Washington had formerly condemned Israel's expansion into the West Bank and Gaza, and Bush, whose aversion to Yasser Arafat was well known, personally intervened and asked Sharon to send his minister of foreign affairs, Shimon Peres, to meet the president of the Palestinian Authority. The meeting took place, after several delays, at the end of September. The following month, Bush went so far as to say that he was in favor of a Palestinian State.

But the Bush administration's hardened stance toward Israel would not hold up to a vigorous challenge in Congress. On November 16, 2001, eighty-nine senators, mobilized by the pro-Israel lobby in Washington, sent a letter to Bush commending his promise in late October not to meet with Arafat until he had done more to stop terrorist violence against Israelis, and requesting that his administration firmly proclaim U.S. support of Israel.[12] By the beginning of December, Bush and Sharon were no longer quarrelling. Two months after he had compared Bush to Neville Chamberlain, and had accused him of "appeasing the Arabs at Israel's expense," Sharon visited the White House for a meeting in early December, and the president was cordial. He issued no criticism of the Israeli military strikes that had pummeled Gaza through the month of November. Accused of "appeasement" by an ally who owes its security largely to U.S. military aid, perhaps Bush deserved at least an apology? In any case, he didn't get one. Sharon knew that his loyal and influential allies in Washington had defended him, and that with the help of both the fundamentalist Christians and the Likudnic advisors who surrounded Bush, he had won a decisive diplomatic victory. Sharon had succeeded, in convincing Bush that the conflict in the West Bank and Gaza was part of the global war on terrorism and that Arafat, like Bin Laden, was a threat to the stability of the Middle East. The Palestinian claim of independence was swept aside; Palestinians' legitimate aspiration to statehood, long recognized by the international community, was forgotten. Whether they were Islamists or not, they had all been drafted into the cabal of worldwide terrorism. Eclipsed by the global fight against Al Qaeda, the Israeli occupation and the endless suffering of the Palestinians were erased from international conscience, at least for the time being.

SHARON TRIUMPHED. BUT IN THE MONTHS AND YEARS THAT FOLLOWED, relations between Israel and the United States would have both highs and lows. In April 2002, Bush's national security advisor, Condoleezza Rice, would ask in vain for the withdrawal of the Israeli army from the West Bank. Meanwhile, the head of the State Department, Colin Powell, would return empty-handed from a tour in the Middle East during which he had attempted to renew Israeli-Palestinian negotiations.

Fourteen months later, in June 2003, while meeting with Mahmoud Abbas and his advisors in Ramallah, Rice responded angrily when shown a map of the barrier and its meandering path into the interior of the West Bank. After presenting the map, Stephanie Khoury, legal advisor to the Palestinian Authority's Negotiations Affairs Department, claimed to have been "stupefied" by Rice's outburst: "she was furious, as if she had just discovered that she had been fooled."[13]

But these incidents were minor. For Sharon and his U.S. allies, the overall picture was generally positive. Relations between Israel and the United States had not been so strong in years. Between 2000 and Sharon's hospitalization at the end of 2005, the Israeli prime minister took eleven trips to the United States. Whenever he was unable to leave Jerusalem, he sent his loyal colleague Dov Weisglass in his stead. Between May 2002 and August 2004, Weisglass had twenty or so meetings with Condoleezza Rice, each at least an hour and a half long, and they became such good friends that they now call each other "Condi" and "Dubi."

Ehud Olmert, Ariel Sharon's successor, also maintained close relations with the U.S. leadership; he often consulted advisors in the Bush administration on critical matters before broaching them with his own ministers. "On more than one occasion," confides a former advisor to a Labor Party minister, "Olmert has discussed an important decision with Bush, and rendered it public, before having talked about it with Ehud Barak and Tzipi Livni, two of his most important ministers. He thinks of them more as competition than colleagues." Washington's indulgent attitude toward Israel is further illustrated in how the United States has allowed the Israeli government to take multiple liberties in administering the terms of the Roadmap for Peace. For example, the Roadmap requires a freeze on settlement activity in Gaza and the West Bank, which obviously has not gone into effect. By contrast, the United States has rigorously insisted that the Palestinians follow the terms of the Roadmap, to the letter.

A man in his olive grove after the bulldozer. *Courtesy of Nick Marcroft*

CHAPTER 5

HOW MANY OLIVE TREES?

Under pressure from a public traumatized by terrorism, and from the politicians and media outlets methodically mobilized by Uzi Dayan and the Public Council for a Security Fence for Israel, Ariel Sharon would eventually overcome his doubts about the barrier. But other concerns that were perhaps less explainable to the international community also moved the prime minister to change his mind. According to Ron Nachman, the mayor of Ariel, one of the largest settlements in the West Bank, and an old friend of Sharon's, "it was the route chosen by Dany Tirza that finally convinced him. It connected to Israel the major settlements—Ma'ale Adumim, Ariel, Gush Etzion, Modi'in Illit—but it also suggested what would become the long-term plan for the region." In other words, Sharon finally accepted the barrier not only because it would contribute to Israeli security, but also because it annexed the vast majority of settlements in the West Bank, along with land rich in agricultural potential and water reserves vital to the future of Israel. It might even create an obstacle to the birth of a Palestinian State. It was a plan that disregarded international law and several UN Security Council resolutions, as well as previous accords between Israel and the Palestinians, and formal and informal commitments made to the United States, the United Nations, the European Union, and Russia as a part of the Roadmap for Peace. But who would bother to point this out, besides the Palestinians and their "biased" allies? To the majority of Israelis, not to mention their numerous foreign supporters, protecting Israel from terrorism was a perfectly credible justification for the security barrier.

After a terrorist attack on a voting station where Likud primaries were being held on November 28, 2002, which killed six and wounded more than forty, the Sharon government gave the green light to begin construction on the second part of the "north barrier." This thirty-mile section of the barrier, which would span from Salem to Tirat Zvi in the northeast corner of the West Bank, was essentially the finishing touch on the "zone of separation" at the edge of the Jordan Valley. Here, the barrier follows closely to the Green Line through the Jezreel Valley, around the ancient fortified Palestinian city of Megiddo (where the first kibbutzes broke ground), before verging along the ridge of Mount Gilboa, known by hikers and campers for its freshwater sources and iris fields.

In the meantime, Sharon carried the legislative elections of January 28, 2003, which had been brought on when Labor Party ministers quit en masse the previous October over Sharon's generous budget appropriations for the settlement communities. Though it was still a coalition government, the media would brand it, in fact, "totally right." It was now composed of not just Likud, but also members of the secular Shinui Party, the National Religious Party, the usual supporters of the settlements, and some hard-liners from the Far Right, such as Binyamin "Benny" Elon, who was in favor of the "transfer" of Palestinians to Jordan. Sharon put him in charge of tourism.

As the prime minister admitted at the time, his coalition of supporters did not necessarily share the same vision for the peace process (or what remained of it), but they were very much united by their belief in the separation barrier, even if some were growing concerned about its long-term effects.

During the summer of 2003, there was much heated debate among the Council of Ministers; while some of them expressed their reservations about the barrier, its ardent supporters complained that construction was taking too long. Twice in the space of a few weeks, the minister of health, Dani Naveh, a Likud member, asked Sharon about the barrier's timetable. "It's important," he insisted, "to complete its construction. It would be a terrible mistake to stop midway: the stream of terrorists will just go around it." Sharon agreed with Naveh, without necessarily formally approving the barrier. The minister of finance, Binyamin Netanyahu, asked Uzi Dayan the same question when they met in Netanyahu's office at the Knesset on July 7. Dayan was accompanied by four of his colleagues from the Public Council for a Security Fence for Israel. "We will need a year to build it," Dayan had said. But Dayan and his colleagues were surprised to find that Netanyahu could not explain why only part of the barrier had broken ground when, in principle, the government had approved the construction of the entire barrier. Convinced that something was holding up construction, Uzi Dayan shared his concern with Netanyahu.

Ultimately Dayan could get only a general timetable of the barrier construction, passed down to him from Matan Vilnai of the the Labor Party and Avshalom Vilan of Meretz, who had received it from the vice-minister of defense, Ze'ev Boim: Section C, from Elkana to Jerusalem, was scheduled to be completed by 2004; Section D, from Jerusalem to the Arad Valley, was projected to be finished in 2005 or 2006. They had no further details.

Who, besides Sharon himself, could be delaying the barrier's construction? The finance minister? "No," states Uzi Dayan, "there were no budgetary constraints on anything concerning the construction of the barrier." This was confirmed by military and government personnel in charge of the project. Was Sharon under pressure from the Bush Administration? During her visit to Jerusalem at the beginning of July 2003, Condoleezza Rice had asked the prime minister not to include the Ariel settlement, in the central West Bank, among the areas protected by the barrier, and requested that the wall avoid the Palestinian neighborhoods in and around Jerusalem. But Sharon did not take heed of these requests, especially since they came with no specific conditions. At no time, for example, did the United States threaten to cut off or limit aid to Israel if it ignored its advice. In fact, in his address to the Likud parliamentary group the day after his meeting with Rice, Sharon reassured the barrier's supporters that he had not given in an inch to the United States. "When I met President Bush in Aqaba,[1] he asked us not to build the barrier. I told him that it was impossible not to do so. That's what I repeated to Ms. Rice. I explained to her in no uncertain terms that it was a question of security. I gave her examples of places where the barrier has reduced the number of terrorist attacks." No one whom I interviewed for this book, whether involved in the design or the construction of the barrier, recalls receiving even the slightest suggestion to modify the path of the barrier after Rice's visit.

Incidentally, the pace of the wall's construction may have been held up by disagreements within Sharon's "total Right" coalition. Of course, all his ministers, from Avraham Poraz of Shinui to Avigdor Lieberman of the National Union, were in favor of the construction of the barrier as a "security mechanism," but some, such as Rabbi Benny Elon, director of the Beit Orot Talmudic school and resident of the Beit El settlement, were afraid to see it one day become a real border, and they grew more outspoken about this concern. Others bombarded the prime minister with suggestions for the ultimate route of the barrier. Though Sharon usually forged ahead like a tank, this time he needed to move with political tact—to listen to, consult with, and reassure others, even if he disregarded what he'd heard once the time had come to act. For example, he could not ignore the opposition he faced when the wall crossed into property owned by Christian communities; it is perhaps more difficult to send bulldozers into the orchards of priests than into the olive groves of Palestinian villagers, especially while negotiating with the Vatican.

But these delays, which worried supporters of the barrier and exasperated Uzi Dayan, did not truly hinder the barrier's progress. While supervising construction in the northwest of the West Bank, where the first section of the barrier was determined operational and handed over to the army in August 2003, Dany Tirza was pursuing his work on a "separation line" composed of barriers and walls that would pass by Jerusalem and extend, to the south, to the shores of the Dead Sea. The cartographer of the IDF confirmed that his drafting pencil was guided solely by the objectives defined by the National Security Council and approved by the government, namely to circumscribe a space that provides the tightest possible security, with the least number of Palestinians and the greatest number of Israelis on the western side of the barrier, and to find a balance between Palestinian rights and Israeli security imperatives. Most of the wall's major players, such as Dayan, Ben-Eliezer, and Netzah Mashiah, agreed with this plan, but it remained to be seen whether they would agree on its execution.

Strictly from the point of view of security—in other words, as protection against terrorist incursions—the barrier effectively meets the demands of the IDF. It is between 150 and 180 feet wide, and it stands out against the rocky hills of the West Bank like a highway cutting through scrubland. What would an intruder have to do to cross it? Starting on the Palestinian side, he would first be faced with a six-foot-high pyramid of razor wire. This sits in front of an anti-vehicle ditch eight feet deep and between nine and fifteen feet wide. Then there is a road used by the Israeli army's Humvees and Jeeps to patrol the barrier, and on the other side of the road there is a nine-foot-high fence, anchored to a low wall of concrete, fitted with electronic sensors capable of detecting any infiltration. In the unlikely case that an intruder succeeds in crossing this first series of obstacles to the Israeli side of the barrier, he would find himself confronted with a nine foot wide incursion-detection pathway composed of very fine sand on which the slightest imprint, even that of a bird's foot, is visible. Another patrol route runs along the other side of the incursion-detection pathway, and sometimes a second incursion-detection pathway as well. Along the pathways there are numerous armored observation towers with remote-control cameras that can capture even the smallest incident, day or night, and in any weather. Sensitive radar devices designed to detect any movement approaching the barrier complete the picture, and military sources confirm that there are plans to implement sensor networks to prevent underground intrusions as well.

According to the Israeli defense minister, every mile costs $3.25 million. Every mile displaces 85,000 cubic yards of earth and rocks, requiring 6,000 cubic yards of backfill, and is paved with 5,000 square

yards of asphalt; over each mile, there is an average of about 300 concrete poles holding up 40 detection lights, 2,500 square yards of fencing,
and 8 miles of barbed wire. According to United Nations observers,
since September 2004 the separation zone has also had, by order of the
army, a buffer zone between 500 and 2,500 feet wide on the Palestinian
side of the barrier. Palestinians are not permitted to build or do anything on this land. Wherever the barrier follows the Green Line, the
buffer zone is on the Palestinian side of the barrier. When it snakes into
the West Bank, onto Palestinian territory, there are two buffer zones:
one on each side of the barrier. The military order that authorized this
buffer zone does not forbid Palestinians from traveling across it, but
according to a report published in March 2005 by the United Nations,[2]
the buffer zone freezes more than 12,300 acres of land in the largely
Palestinian towns of Tulkarem and Qalqiliya and in the forty or so
villages that line the barrier's path.

The first slice of the separation zone is eighty-seven miles long, and
for five of those miles the barrier becomes an actual wall. Drivers on
Highway 6 might not notice it, because it is hidden behind a mound
of land covered with bushes, but where the Trans-Israel Highway runs
parallel to the Green Line, near the Palestinian towns of Tulkarem and
Qalqiliya, this wall—23 to 27 feet high, 17.5 inches thick, and made of
concrete—stands less than 100 yards away from the houses of these
towns. "In the case of Qalqiliya and Tulkarem," explains Dany Tirza,
"we chose to build a wall to protect the highway from snipers. Several
times on this major commercial highway, vehicles had been hit by snipers
hidden in the houses close to the road. We needed to put an end to this
immediately. By building a twenty-seven-foot-high wall with watchtowers, we made sniper attacks impossible. The height of the wall is such
that even a sniper crouching on a roof or in a minaret cannot see the
highway. And I have software on my computer that integrates the relief
and the topography of the area, so if a Qalqiliya resident decides to add
a storey or two to his house, I can calculate by how many inches I need
to raise the wall in order to compensate, and where I need to raise it.

"In Jerusalem, we chose the wall option for a different reason. It's an
urban zone, and there isn't enough space to build a security barrier like

the one in the countryside. We would have to raze hundreds of buildings to do it. The government never intended to go that far.[3] That being said, the wall costs substantially more than the barrier. It is made up of concrete bars twenty-seven feet high and four feet wide. They are manufactured in Negev, transported to the construction site by a convoy of trailers, and put into place by cranes. It is much more complicated than marking out the pathways and laying down barbed wire and fencing. So we will build as little as possible. I have calculated that of the four hundred and forty miles of the separation zone, the walled part will represent only five percent when finished."

You read that right: 440 miles. This is, in fact, the length of the barrier Dany Tirza proposed in October 2003, and again the figure he would quote in August 2005, although the Negotiations Affairs Department of the PLO claims that it is 422 miles, and the United Nations says 420 (adjusted from its previous assessment of 386 in the spring of 2004). The length of the barrier is twice that of the Green Line (195 miles).

How to explain the meandering path of the barrier? Why does it follow the Green Line for only 20 percent of its path, and veer off course sometimes for more than three miles into the West Bank? The answer is clear from looking at the first part of the separation line, completed in July 2003. Its route follows the Green Line very closely to the southwest of Salem, but then makes a wide loop into the West Bank, around the settlements of Hinnanit (700 residents), Shaked (500), and Reihan (148), enclosing some 5,000 Palestinians east of the large village of Barta,'a Asha Sharqiya in the "closed zone" between the barrier and the Green Line. After this first loop, the barrier curves toward the village of Qaffin, severing a section of its land, and cuts back toward the Green Line, which it then follows to Tulkarem, where it becomes a wall. To the south of Tulkarem, it turns at a right angle toward the east, along Route 557, then heads back south, winding around the Sal'it settlement (440 residents). It then veers back toward the Green Line, leaving the Palestinian village of Falamya (600 inhabitants) untouched on the east side of the wall, before zigzagging around the Zufin settlement (1,000 residents). It then encloses about 45,800 Palestinians from the town of

Qalqiliya behind a section of the wall, and they now have only one road connecting them to the rest of West Bank. The security fence also envelops the Alfei Menashe settlement and its 5,500 residents. This section of the barrier is particularly troubling, because it contains the 1,200 residents of five Palestinian hamlets near the settlement, separating them from the rest of the West Bank and from their larger neighboring village, Habla (5,300 inhabitants), which, like Qalqilya, is encircled by another loop (see insert maps of the West Bank and Qalqiliya/Alfei Menashe).

According to a July 2004 UN document issued by the Office for the Coordination of Humanitarian Affairs, the total surface area of the "closed zones" comprises more than 118,500 acres, or 8 percent of the total area of the West Bank. Two years later, the UN estimated that these zones covered 141,000 acres (or 10 percent of the West Bank), enclosing 60,500 Palestinians between the Green Line and the barrier. As for demolished houses, contrary to Dany Tirza's assurances, the path of the first section of the barrier was strewn with them. According to B'Tselem, the Israeli Information Center for Human Rights in the Occupied Territories,[4] nearly three hundred buildings were destroyed in the Jenin, Tulkarem, and Qalqiliya districts during 2002 and the first three months of 2003. Most of the orders to demolish, issued by the Civil Administration, the branch of the army in charge of relations with the people of the Occupied Territories, targeted houses, stores, and workshops west of the barrier. One hundred and seventy in Nazlat Issa, sixty in Baqa al-Gharbiya, seventy-two in Barta'a Asha Sharqiya, and twenty in Azzun Atma were demolished. The official reason cited in almost all cases was that the owners did not have a building permit. But the Civil Administration based these decisions on land registries dating from the British Mandate, which established the boundaries of the towns and villages as they were before 1948, and had designated most of the West Bank as "agricultural land," or not zoned for construction. These registries do not take into account the increase in population over more than half a century[5] and are considered obsolete by the Palestinian municipalities. But just as Ottoman or Jordanian legislation was applied before and after the British Mandate, these old registries have become a part of Israel's legal arsenal, along with a mountain of military regulations put into effect since 1967. The Civil Administration uses these old laws and regulations to bring a semblance of legitimacy to the ways in which it now controls Palestinian land and people.

The same formalities, though, required the army to post requisition notices (always claiming to appropriate the land "for security purposes") to the trees and electrical poles in each future construction zone before breaking ground. Many of the people who live in areas near the Green Line have kept copies of these documents, stamped with the army's seal, and they readily show them to visitors as evidence of what happened to them. According to the documents, those who live on the route of the barrier have one week to produce titles and proof of ownership for their land, and to present them before a hearing with the Civil Administration. If their request is denied, they have one more week before the start of construction to request a hearing before the Israeli Supreme Court of Justice. During the first months of construction, few Palestinians were able to take these complex and costly measures. Later, committees for the defense of villagers were formed, with the assistance of nongovernmental organizations and Israeli and Palestinian lawyers, and cases began to pile up at the Supreme Court clerk's office. Around Jerusalem and in the Bethlehem region, the construction of miles of wall or barrier was delayed for months while the Supreme Court deliberated, much to the chagrin of Dany Tirza, Netzah Mashiah, and their colleagues. In August 2007, Michael Sfard, one of the Israeli lawyers defending the cause of the Palestinian villagers, estimated that more than eighty cases relating to the route of the barrier had been heard by the Supreme Court.

TO THE NORTHWEST OF THE WEST BANK, WHERE THE FIRST SECTIONS HAVE been operational since the summer of 2003, the Palestinians are trying to make the best of their lives with the barrier, but it is not going well. Simple things have become complicated, ordinary activities impossible, and there are many new constraints and humiliations. On October 2,

2003, a month after the end of construction of the first section, General Moshe Kaplinsky, commander of the forces in the general region, made public order number 378-5730-1970, which declared the area between the Green Line and the barrier a "closed military zone." The document, in which the zone is called a "seam area," states that "no one is to enter or remain in this zone" and that "all persons there must leave it immediately." At the same time, the order specifies that "these restrictions do not apply to citizens and to Israeli residents, including settlers residing in the West Bank." For some five thousand Palestinians living in the closed zones of Jenin, Tulkarem, and Qalqiliya, it was now necessary to obtain a permit of "permanent residency" in compliance with the regulations rendered public on October 7, 2003, and signed by the commander of the Civil Administration, General Ilan Paz, even if they have always lived there. Anyone over the age of twelve who does not live in the zone but who wishes to enter to work on his land or to visit friends must apply to the civil administration for a permit—which is only the beginning of a complex bureaucratic process.

According to the requirements set forth by the army, Palestinians who wish to obtain a permanent residency permit fall into about a dozen different categories. Each category requires a specific form and the presentation of a certain number of documents. Landowners who wish to go to their property must produce a photo ID, a photocopy of this ID, and a certificate of application to the land registry delivered by the District Coordination Office. How does one obtain this certificate? With great patience. After paying the application fee, the applicant must start another application, submitting his or her ID card, a sworn declaration before a Palestinian magistrate certifying that the land in question has not been sold, a photocopy of the will if the previous owner has died, and certification from the municipality verifying the authenticity of the documents provided. Then all that's left to do is wait for the Civil Administration's verdict. Depending on the general political climate at the time the application is being processed, and the geographic zones for which entry is requested, between 25 and 40 percent of the requests are denied. The administration's response is given verbally and in person, or the forms are simply stamped "Refused," and no reason for the rejection is given. Theoretically, it is possible to appeal the decision, but few Palestinians have done so. The authority to grant appeals stems from the Civil Administration, who are also responsible for granting or denying permits in the first place. According to B'Tselem, the Israeli Information Center for Human Rights in the Occupied Territories, these opportunities for appeal are there only for show.[6]

In some zones, the Palestinians who have a residency permit may cross the barrier with their farming vehicles; in others, they need to obtain yet another special permit in order to cross. Theoretically, the permits are valid from sunrise to sunset and allow entry through a single "agricultural gate." When the permits expire, though, depends on the type of work to be done: greenhouse keepers, who work daily, may receive a permit for two months, while farmers employed for an olive harvest, which occurs only during October and November, may obtain permits for six months; the permits are issued on a basis that seems at once arbitrary and obstructive.

According to a report published in March 2005 by the United Nations Office for the Coordination of Humanitarian Affairs in the Occupied Palestinian Territory (OCHA/OPT), a number of Palestinian farmers now face economic ruin because the barrier has made it so difficult for them to harvest their olives and tend to their livestock. To make matters worse, many Palestinians are cut off from schools, universities, and regional hospitals, and are isolated from local social assistance networks because travel restrictions have fragmented village communities. And these problems are only going to get worse over time. A report by the UN, made public in January 2006, shows that the permit system has become more stringent since it was put into place.[7] The number of permit requests denied went from 27 percent in December 2004 to 38 percent in July 2005. At first, the army's reason for the increased number of rejections was largely security concerns. Now the requests are more often rejected due to issues of land ownership. In July 2005, 65 percent of denied requests were from Palestinians who could not produce land ownership titles in time, or could not prove a direct family link with the owner. As land in rural

Palestinian society is usually cultivated by members of one extended family—spouses, children, grandchildren, nieces, nephews—this tightening of the permit system makes it difficult, if not impossible, for the cultivation of certain crops. It could also put an end to the secular tradition of the community olive harvest.

For those who manage to obtain a permit, there remains the problem of finding a place that will allow them to cross. According to UN inspectors, in October 2005 only half of the forty-two agricultural gates planned for the municipalities of Salfit, Qalqiliya, and Tulkarem were open to Palestinians in possession of a permit, and they were open only three times a day, for about twenty minutes to an hour.[8] When the gates will be opened or closed is at the sole discretion of the checkpoint soldiers, and they can change those hours at random. If there is a "security incident," they may close a gate for several days with no warning. Farmers face harassment from the checkpoint soldiers, and often are not allowed to go through the agricultural gate with their tractors or trailers. This forces many of them to transport their tools and their crop yields in donkey carts.

A network of Palestinian nongovernmental organizations[9] have underwritten an investigation, and found that fifty-one Palestinian towns and villages in Jenin, Tulkarem, and Qalqiliya were directly affected by the construction of the barrier. The separation zone consumed 3,700 acres of their land, destroying more than 100,000 trees and isolating more than 24,700 acres of cultivated land—olive, orange, and lemon trees, and pastures—on the other side of the barrier. Half of these fifty-one towns, home to more than 165,000 people, were cut off from their land, most of which no longer has irrigation systems. Near Nazlat Issa, to the north of Tulkarem, centuries-old olive trees were torn down by the builders of the barrier. The affected Palestinians lament not only the loss of their primary means of earning a living, but also the loss of what is, essentially, their ancestral heritage. "The oldest olive trees are the most profitable," explains Ahmad Assad, a distraught old villager. He can't take his eyes off of the anti-intrusion track, a ribbon of dusty earth among his trees, many of which have been flattened by bulldozers. "A fifteen-year-old tree brings in seventy

dollars a week. A one-hundred-year-old tree, ten times that amount."
How many olive trees were torn down? Tens of thousands, according
to the Palestinians; the exact number is unknown. But the Israeli daily
Yedioth Ahronoth confirmed that in July 2003 one of the companies in
charge of building the barrier had put "an unlimited quantity" of olive
trees up for sale in Israel at the price of 1,000 shekels ($265) each.

According to the Israeli Ministry of Defense, specific "humanitarian" arrangements were set up to help villagers whose olive trees had
been torn down to make room for the barrier. These arrangements were
particularly important in areas crossed by Phase 1, areas such as Jenin,
Tulkarem, and Qalqiliya, where the local economy is dependant upon
agriculture. To the villagers of this region, desperate from the loss of
trees sometimes several centuries old, the army offered to transplant the
uprooted olive trees to other areas in the same zone or to provide compensation. But this idea of compensation was disregarded by most
Palestinians—sometimes at the request of the Palestinian Authority—to
avoid legitimizing the expropriation of their land. As for transferring the
olive trees, it was rarely possible, due to a lack of available land.

"I know construction of the barrier created countless problems for
the Palestinians," responds Netzah Mashiah when confronted by these
statistics, or by reports issued by the UN OCHA team. "But the expe-
rience gained from the first phase has helped us to conceive a plan
called 'Living with the Barrier,' which should allow us to smooth out
some of these difficulties in the next steps, particularly those concerning travel and how they cross at authorized points, where we are going
to use technology to make inspections simpler and faster. When it is all
finished, the Palestinians will even have better roadways than before."

Whatever its political or humanitarian problems, Netzah Mashiah
can hardly contain how proud he is to be the Pharaoh-like head of
this construction site, which extends for hundreds of miles and is the
largest public works project in Israeli history, a project that employs
more than 6,500 workers (among them many Palestinians) and whose
total budget is expected to reach $2.2 billion.

Palestinian youths throw stones at an Israeli army vehicle during a protest against the barrier at Qaffin, near Tulkarem, June 5, 2008. *Courtesy of REUTERS/Mohamad Torokman*

CHAPTER 6

THE KIBBUTZ MONTENEROS

When the military arrived at the Metzer kibbutz in the northwest region of the West Bank near Tulkarem in the spring of 2002, they already had a strong sense of where they would draw the route of the barrier. The Green Line is equidistant from the kibbutz and the Palestinian village of Qaffin, and yet they would ultimately decide that the barrier would diverge from the Green Line and make a sizeable loop around the kibbutz. It would run very close to the houses of Qaffin, and ultimately cut the village off from much of its arable land. Naturally, the military had assumed that the people of Metzer would happily accept this plan: not only would it leave their land completely untouched, but it would also establish a wide security zone—a veritable no-man's land, in fact—between them and their Palestinian neighbors. How poorly they understood the residents of Metzer.

Founded in 1953 by a hundred or so young Argentine immigrants, most of them activists in the Socialist Zionist movement who had fled the Perón regime, the Metzer kibbutz today remains loyal to the mission of its founders, namely to build on this rocky terrain a humanist Jewish community that can live in harmony with its Arab neighbors. What was once an inhospitable Jewish border outpost surrounded by Arabs has become a welcoming and prosperous village of five hundred residents. Over the years, more emigrants fleeing Latin American dictatorships have joined the kibbutz: Uruguayan Tupamaros, Argentine Monteneros, followers of Che Guevara, and others who have fled their respective battles abroad to come and reconnect with their Jewish roots in this biblical land—and have done so without giving up the humanitarian convictions of their native political movements.

Today, a hundred houses have sprung up under the cool shade of the cypress, pine, filaos, and jacarandas trees planted by the founders of the kibbutz. The people of Metzer have comfortably made their living as farmers—raising cattle and practicing organic dairy farming; growing bananas, persimmons, and avocados—and, most profitably, from the manufacture and sale of Metzerplas-brand irrigation systems. The company was started by just a handful of kibbutz members in 1970, and it now employs 130 people. Their patented product is a drip irrigation system designed specifically to irrigate the roughest and driest of terrains. Metzerplas is the fourth largest manufacturer of these systems in the world, and the company provides the kibbutz with 70 percent of its revenue. "We're a good old-fashioned private company," explains Dov Avital, a sturdy fifty-year-old man with salt-and-pepper hair who is president of Metzerplas as well as secretary of the kibbutz. "At this moment the only shareholders are the two hundred members of the kibbutz. A long time ago we decided to get rich together, and that's what we're doing today."[1]

Dov Avital's family is originally from Bukovinia, a region of the Carpathian Mountains that runs along Romania and Ukraine. His grandfather fought in the Austrian army during World War I. Years later, in 1940, his parents fled anti-Semitic persecution and immigrated to Uruguay. In the wake of the Uruguayan military coup on June 27, 1973, he left Montevideo for Israel. He married the daughter of one of the founding members of the Metzer kibbutz and settled there eighteen years ago. "At the beginning, I worked in the manufacturing plant of Metzerplas and then in the Export Department, before becoming president of the company and vice-president of the Kibbutz movement." Despite their economic prosperity and successful integration into Israeli society, the beliefs and convictions of Metzer's residents have not fundamentally changed. The children no longer live in separate dormitories, and members of the community are now permitted to keep part of their earnings, rather than contributing all of them to a

communal pot, but the principles of the founding members of the kibbutz remain the same. Metzer still has no synagogue, and the only
yarmulke-covered heads are those of visitors. The kibbutz is tradition-
ally left-leaning, and in the elections held on March 29, 2006, a historic
46 percent of its members voted for the Meretz Party. The rest voted
for Labor (32 percent), the Green Party (10 percent)—who, at the national level, did not obtain the required minimum votes for a seat in
the Knesset—and Ehud Olmert's Kadima Party.

Over the years, and through sometimes bloody political upheavals
in the region, the kibbutz residents have maintained good relations with
their neighbors. Indeed, the very history of the kibbutz is tied to that of
the two neighboring Arab villages: Meisar on the Israeli side, and
Qaffin, on the other side of the Green Line, in the West Bank. "When
the founders arrived," recounts Dov Avital, "there was nothing here
but the rocks, brush, and mosquitoes. The pioneers lived in tents. It was
thanks to the villagers of Meisar, who lent them pumps, that they had
any water. In exchange, the nurse from Metzer took care of their sick."
After the Arab-Israeli War of 1948, Meisar, a tiny agricultural village
built around a single minaret, found itself on the Israeli side of the
Green Line. Many of the older residents of Meisar remember how they
had given water to "those young Jews from America," but their memo-
ries are also tinged with bitterness, because some of the land on which
the young Jews settled had belonged to Arab families of Palestine before
the war. Over time, however, relations between Meisar and Metzer
improved and even became friendly. In 1967, when the men of Metzer,
called to duty, left to fight the Arab armies in the Six-Day War, the peas-
ants of Meisar came with their tractors to help the women of the kibbutz farm their land. In the 1970s, Meisar and Metzer even sponsored a
team together in the Israel Soccer Federation. And today the kids from
Meisar still come to Metzer to play basketball and to swim in the kibbutz's communal pool. The kibbutz and the village share farming equipment, and even visit one another on religious holidays.

Relations with the Palestinian village of Qaffin, however, have been
more complicated. "Before 1967," explains Dov Avital, "it was a West
Bank village annexed by Jordan. Since 1967, it has been a Palestinian

village of the West Bank occupied by Israel. We share the struggle of
our neighbors in Meisar for their civil rights—in principle, our fellow
citizens. But it is different with Qaffin. As Israelis on the Left, we are
willing to fight against the occupation for peace and for the creation of
a Palestinian State. But the people in Qaffin are also struggling for national rights. We support them, but because they are Palestinians and
we are Israelis, we cannot really take part in that."

Until the construction of the barrier, however, none of this had
stopped Qaffin and Metzer from enjoying relations that were rather
rare between Israelis and Palestinians. Children from Qaffin would
use Metzer's sports facilities; volunteers from Metzer would help out
with the olive harvest; if there was a fire in Qaffin, the kibbutz would
send its fire trucks. They would exchange gifts and boxes of sweets
across the Green Line during holidays and religious celebrations. If
ever there was tension between the kibbutz and the town, or if it was
necessary for them to work together on something, such as building a
common water pipe or sharing medical facilities, the mayor of Qaffin,
Taisir Harashi, and Dov Avital would simply call each other on their
cell phones and talk it through.

"For us, the first barrier the army proposed was unacceptable," recounts Dov Avital, while reading emails in his tiny office at the kibbutz. "At the beginning, we did not even like the idea of a barrier. We
were used to moving between our banana trees and their olive groves
however we pleased. If we ended up supporting the barrier on principle, it was because of the increase in suicide attacks. But, in our minds,
it could only be built on the Green Line, so as not to compromise the
creation one day of a Palestinian State. Now, the way that the barrier
passes right under the windows of the houses of Qaffin, seems to me
completely useless and unjust. It cuts the village off from its olive groves,
and, above all, it doesn't address any actual security issue. It was totally arbitrary how they built it, and that's what I explained to the military. I told them that maintaining friendly relations with our neighbors
in Meisar and Qaffin was essential; that, up until then, our ties to them
had allowed us to live in peace, and we did not want to be complicit in
any plan that our friends in Qaffin would rightly see as aggression. So

the secretariat of the kibbutz and I proposed that the barrier be built precisely on the Green Line. This would mean that the strip of land requisitioned for the barrier would be equally shared between us and Qaffin. This seemed fair. I then called the mayor of Qaffin, explained our position, and proposed that from now on we conduct a united campaign to have the barrier moved west. Later I found out that our proposition had prompted a heated discussion at a town meeting in Qaffin. Some residents were suspicious of our motives; they thought it was a trap. But the mayor won them over, and we worked together to persuade the army to change the path of the barrier. In the fall of 2002, we thought we were finally close to our objective, and on Monday, November 11, we had a meeting scheduled with the leaders of the Defense Ministry to present our case and that of our friends in Qaffin."

But the meeting never took place. On the night of November 10, shortly before midnight, an armed Palestinian entered the kibbutz. He broke into a house and killed a thirty-four-year-old woman, Revital Ohayon, and her two sleeping children, Matan, five, and Noam, four. He then killed two more people—Yitzhak Drori, a kibbutz leader, and Tirza Damari, a visitor from nearby Moshav Elyachin—before fleeing. The next day, the Al-Aqsa Martyrs' Brigade, an armed group tied to Arafat's Fatah Party, claimed responsibility for the attack.

"They did that *here*!" says Dov Avital. "We just couldn't understand it." Three years after the attack, it is still difficult for him to revisit the memory. "There aren't a lot of us in Metzer. Everybody knows everybody. The residents of the kibbutz were now incredulous; the sorrow and the anger were so strong that I didn't have the nerve to raise the question of the barrier again. They would have stoned me.

"We knew the killer wasn't from Qaffin: the police told us right away that he was from the refugee camp in Tulkarem. I just kept telling myself that the crime of one Arab is not the crime of all Arabs, that the blind hate of this terrorist was not shared by all Palestinians. And Arafat condemned the attack in a statement through the Palestinian Authority, saying that targeting civilians, whether they were Israelis or

Palestinians, was 'shameful.' Many people from Meisar, Qaffin, and other Arab villages in the region shared our pain.

"This is what I talked about when Sharon came to visit a few days after the attack. No one here wanted to see him exploit this tragedy for political gain. I assured him that we were not Quakers, and that I fully expected the army to find and to kill the terrorist. But the government must remember that the majority of Palestinians are not terrorists, and that it is essential to ensure that they have a political future. I added that even if the hunger for revenge was understandable after what had happened, we had to remain true to our convictions and continue to live in peace with our neighbors. This is why we asked Sharon to make sure that the route of the wall was moved west. He promised to do what he could."

However, the designers of the barrier do not recall any effort from Sharon to intervene, and the request of the villagers and the kibbutz was seemingly ignored. Standing upon a path that runs between Metzer's banana trees and Qaffin's olive groves, virtually on the Green Line, Dov Avital points to the barrier about two kilometers away. It runs right to the edge of Qaffin, where the army had originally proposed building it.

"So there you have it," he says, "we lost, and so did they."

On October 4, 2003, less than a year after the attack, a special army unit succeeded in finding and killing the man responsible: Sirhan Burhan Hassin Sirhan, an Islamist living in the Tulkarem refugee camp. During the operation, a seven-year-old child, Muhammad Aiman Youssef Ibrahim, was caught in the crossfire and killed by the Israeli soldiers.

"NOW, IF YOU WANT TO GO TO QAFFIN, YOU HAVE TO TAKE AN EIGHT-MILE detour through Baqa al-Gharbiya, Nazlat Issa, and the agricultural gate." Showing me the route of the wall on a folded map, Dov Avital draws a loop that starts in Metzer, generously circles around the kibbutz to the south, then comes back almost to its starting point.

The mayor of Qaffin, Taisir Harashi, speaking to me via cell phone, offers a detailed description of the barrier's route, and how I must navigate around it in order to reach his office in Qaffin. "After the Baqa al-Gharbiya checkpoint," he says, "head toward Nazlat Issa, then to Baqa al-Sharqiya. Take Route Five-eighty-five east for almost two miles, until the road splits, then bear north. Once you've cleared the security checkpoint, call me. I'll come and get you."

With a cell phone, a full tank of gas, at last, and a good road map issued by the United Nations Office of Humanitarian Affairs detailing the locations of the barrier checkpoints, I found the ten-mile trip from Metzer to be simple enough, even though there are not many road signs. But nothing is ever simple in an occupied territory; most of the roads are obstructed by cement blocks, ditches, or mounds of earth; the roads that have not been blocked are open to some but closed to others, and passage is determined by your ID card, or sometimes by the mood of the checkpoint soldiers.

On the morning that I present my ID at the checkpoint outside Qaffin, I am greeted by a red-haired soldier in a slightly rumpled uniform who seems weighed down by his M-16. The soldier decides after looking at my passport and my journalist ID card marked "Visitor" that I cannot travel to Qaffin because the village is "closed." His counterpart, a female soldier with somewhat better language skills, translates all of this into basic English for me. So how can I get to Qaffin, I ask? "He doesn't know," the female soldier replies, "we need to find out," and the grumpy red-haired soldier picks up a military field phone on one of the cement blocks nearby to make a call.

Nearby, a Palestinian dressed in a beige suit and tie, who has walked across the barrier with an old woman in a traditional embroidered dress, has overheard our conversation.

"It's like this all the time," he says to me. "I've just been to Qaffin; it's not closed at all. They're just having fun with you, wasting your time because you're a journalist." The man is a professor at Baqa al-Gharbiya, and an Israeli citizen who speaks Hebrew and English, as well as Arabic. He offers to help. When the female soldier returns holding a piece of paper, he tells me, "Here is our answer. The officer says that you need to go though Barta'a and the Daher al-Abed entrance." Barta'a? Daher al-Abed? The professor traces my new itinerary on the

road map with his finger. It will be a twenty-five-mile detour down
Routes 574 and 65, bringing me to Qaffin from the north. Bear in mind
that I can see the houses of Quaffin right here in front of me, not even a
kilometer away.

"It's market day in Barta'a, so it'll take you more than an hour to
drive through that," says Taisir Harashi when I call him to tell him of
my problems with the soldiers. Harashi's news is not very encouraging,
but he seems resigned to patiently wait for me. Contrary to what one
may assume about a people living under occupation, the Palestinians
are infinitely patient. Waiting at checkpoints, at vehicle pull-overs and
verifications, at barrier doors; waiting at the Civil Administration office
for travel permits; waiting for the release of prisoners; waiting for the
creation of a Palestinian State. Their lives consist of endless waiting.

It took me nearly two hours, including a twenty-minute stop at the
barrier, to reach Qaffin, a large village on the side of a hill. A flood of
uniformed schoolchildren running through the narrow streets led me to
the town hall. After hours of driving, missed turns, and traffic jams under the burning sun, it felt good to finally sit inside this dark, cool building. "We turn off the electricity during the day to save money," says the
mayor. "We haven't paid our bills in eleven months." Qaffin's mayor is a
slender man with short hair, a narrow face, and a thick gray moustache.
He is seated in his office under a portrait of Yasser Arafat, and is surrounded by half a dozen villagers who have come to air grievances.
"This village is ruined," Taisir Harashi explains, as a young woman in a
long gray dress, her hair covered by a beige scarf, brings us tiny cups of
coffee flavored with cardamom.[2] "Out of the nine thousand residents of
Qaffin, about twenty percent used to make their living from farming,
and about eighty percent worked in Israel, usually for construction
companies, while farming a small plot or harvesting their olive trees.
The First Intifada didn't change our lives much. The second one caused
more problems because of the clampdowns and the road closings. It was
impossible to get anywhere by car; you had to walk across fields and stay
off the roads. People were able to keep their jobs in Israel only by walking there, and they had to take hidden paths so as not to be caught by the
Border Police. Once they reached the other side of the Green Line, their

employers would pick them up in trucks. But the barrier put an end to all that. There's no possibility of going to work in Israel, and a good part of our land is now on the other side. Out of the ten thousand dunums[3] owned by the village, more than six thousand are on the other side of the barrier, and at least six hundred were swallowed up by the separation zone—a four-mile strip of land one hundred and eighty feet wide. More than twelve thousand olive trees were uprooted, most of the irrigation pipes cut. Our joint proposal with the people of Metzer never went anywhere, and that has proved disastrous.

"What happened was horrible. Horrible for them, of course, but horrible for us, too. Even though they knew that we had nothing to do with the attack, something has been broken between us. And we know that they didn't want the barrier to be built as it stands today.

"We don't see much of each other anymore. If the barrier had been built along the Green Line, as we had wanted from the start, we would have lost perhaps two or three hundred dunums[4] and saved the rest, and we could at least have been able to work our land. Today, if we want to work in our fields or olive groves, we have to request a special permit good for only one entry point, and only for a few months. This year, nearly two thousand permits have been requested, and only seven hundred granted. Largely they are given out to women and the elderly. For those who have a permit, an 'agricultural gate' is open for one hour in the morning and one hour in the evening. That is, if the soldiers in charge say so. Sometimes they change the schedule; or grant a permit that allows entry only at a point that is far away. The villagers need to travel miles to reach their land, and sometimes the soldiers are not even there to let them in. Also, in principle, the farmers cannot go through the agricultural gate with their tractors and trailers. And so, for example, in 2004 the olive harvest was only a quarter of what it used to be. This was once a prosperous village. We now have eighty percent unemployment."

Seated in a corner of the room, an old peasant wearing a keffiyeh asks the mayor if he may speak. "I'm Abu Ismael," says the old man, as the mayor translates for me. "I'm seventy-two and I have eight children. I own sixty dunums[5] of land divided into three parcels, two of which are on the other side of the barrier. I wanted to say to our visitor that working the land is not only how we make our living; it is a way of life we inherited from our fathers. It is what we have always done. It's what tells us what time of the year it is. In January, we prepare the ground for planting wheat, barley, and vegetables. In February, we prune the olive trees to protect them from insects, and we pull out the weeds from the wheat and barley fields. In May and June, it's the harvest. In July and August, in the heat of summer, we rest and repair our houses and farming equipment. In September, we need to pull out the brambles around the olive trees to prepare for the harvest again. From the end of September to November, we gather the olives. In the mornings, the whole family is in the groves picking olives, and then in the afternoons we sort them. This is also the season when we make our preserves. We rest for about a week or two following the olive harvest and then we go back to tending the trees again. It has always been this way. We have never harmed anyone. Why do they take our land, uproot our trees, and keep us from taking care of what remains?"

"I have a hard time explaining to my people that we, the municipality, are as poor as they are," confides Taisir Harashi, "and that the only way we can help them is to intervene for them through the Palestinian Authority so that the Israelis don't cut off our electricity." Although the establishment of the Palestinian Authority in 1994 was seen here as a victory, a first step toward independence, it was also seen as the birth of a benevolent power that would protect the Palestinians, a gurantee that they would not be left to face the Israeli army alone. One can imagine their frustration, their weariness and desperation, when they discovered that the Palestinian Authority does not have a single dollar to help them, and that it is powerless when Israel takes their land. Everyone here understands perfectly well that the main purpose of the barrier is to steal land from the Palestinians. In two months, there have been five fires in the olive groves on the other side of the barrier. The army forbade the firefighters from Tulkarem from entering. Only Israeli military vehicles were allowed to go through the barrier. The Israeli firefighters were positioned there, ready to protect the kibbutzes and neighboring settlements, but they did nothing to save our olive trees, our carob trees, our almond trees. We're not idiots; we understand what happened: It's true that the olive groves are not maintained as well as they once were because it is difficult, if not impossible, to get to them and do so. There were weeds and shrubs everywhere; but fires don't start all by themselves. And we know the old Ottoman law that all land not worked for a period of three years can be confiscated and declared 'state property.' "

In the mayor's office, we are served cups of hot tea, and then glasses of orangeade and plates of fruit. Taisir Harashi smokes one cigarette after another as he listens to his visitors tell him about their worries. Some of them bring him crumpled documents covered in official stamps. It is not until all of his visitors have left that Harashi, still smoking, finally talks a little about himself. "I was born in Qaffin," he says, "but I lived for a long time in other countries. After studying engineering in Egypt, I worked for a shipping company in Kuwait for several years; I was in charge of machines and containers on cargo ships. After the first Gulf War, when life for Palestinians in Kuwait became unbearable, I found another job in another shipping company in Jordan. I was well paid. I was even able to put money aside. In 1994, when I saw that Palestinians were going home to take part in the thriving new Palestinian economy, I decided to come back to Qaffin. I ran as an independent in the municipal elections. At the time, I was convinced that the Olso peace process would lead us to the creation of our State and to independence. It seemed to me that, given the geographic location of Qaffin, our ties with neighboring Arabs and Israelis, and our economy, which was based on both employment in Israel and agriculture, we had a lot to look forward to from peace, and I could even imagine Qaffin attracting tourists. I founded my campaign on these ideas, while touting my qualifications, my education, and my personal experiences abroad, and I was elected.

"But the end of the peace process and, especially, the construction of the barrier turned all these hopes to dust. I was going to get married, but my fiancée and I decided to put off the wedding because it would have been indecent to throw a party while our village was suffering. For the people here, the land is as essential as water is to fish. If you take a fish out of water, it dies. If you deprive a Palestinian of his land . . ."

Ruth Kedar, Rafik Mrabe, and Yassin Younes on a hill outside the village of Ras a-Tira. *Courtesy of the author*

CHAPTER 7

THE GREAT LIE

Ruth Kedar, an elderly woman in a white sunhat· and a blue-and-white plaid shirt, swerves her old Toyota through traffic on Highway 5 toward the Green Line. She looks like a charming old woman on her way to a family picnic in the hills, but this morning she is not on a leisurely outing. She has left her cool and comfortable home in Ramat HaSharon to drive in the hot sun down Qalqiliya Road—a route many Israelis consider rife with terrorists—to the West Bank village of Ras a-Tira. Like her husband, Paul Kedar, a retired colonel who was once head of the Israel Defense Ministry delegation in Europe and a Mossad official, Ruth Kedar dedicates much of her free time to a small humanitarian organization, Yesh Din[1] (There Is Justice), which fights against human rights violations committed by the Israeli army and police in the Occupied Territories.

Ras a-Tira is a tiny village of about three hundred people, stretching out along a rocky ridge some five hundred yards to the south of the Alfei Menashe settlement. Along with four other villages—a-Dab'a ·(250 residents), Arab a-Ramadin (250), Wadi a-Rasha (120), and Arab Abu Farda (120)—Ras a-Tira was included, against the will of its citizens, in the barrier loop that surrounds the Alfei Menashe settlement. Part of the land that belongs to these villages was requisitioned for the barrier, which here is about sixty yards wide, and another large portion of their land simply ended up on the Israeli side of the border. As with other enclaves in the region, in October 2003 Alfei Menashe was declared a "closed military zone." Palestinians over the age of twelve who wish to continue living in villages in the closed military zone must obtain a permit from the Civil Administration, which is valid for two years. On the back of this document is a troubling note stating that the permit in no way guarantees the property rights of its bearer. The Palestinians must also obtain a permit, good for between three months and two years, if they wish to travel outside the enclave for work on the other side of the barrier, or to tend their land, which they also must adequately prove they own. The permit clearly states that its holder may not enter Israel. Their neighbors in the Alfei Menashe settlement, however, are not required to obtain permits to live near and travel across the barrier, and this is a constant source of bitterness and resentment among the local Palestinians. Like all Israeli citizens, the settlers can come and go as they please, so long as they follow the army's orders.

The situation is even worse in the tiny Arab villages nearby, which are too sparsely populated to attract much commerce. These villages have always been dependent on the larger Palestinian communities of Habla, Ras Atiya, and Qalqiliya for their food, education, and health services; the only hospital in the region is in Qalqiliya. In Habla, there are only two doctors, two pharmacists, and one dentist, but to get there the villagers must now spend a great deal of time standing in line at a barrier gate, which is open at variable hours, showing their permits and submitting to searches by the soldiers. The Habla entrance is open three times a day for only one hour. Qalqiliya can also be reached via the Habla entrance through a connecting tunnel that runs under Route 55, and since June 2005, the Ras Atiya entrance to the south of Habla is open from 6:00 a.m. to 6:00 p.m. The only vehicle approved by the Civil Administration to pass through these gates is a bus for transporting children to the four schools in Habla and Ras Atiya; residents of the enclave are forbidden to transport any goods across the line. So it is rather difficult for villagers from Ras a-Tira to sell their fruits and vegetables in Habla as they used to, or to bring home provisions purchased in town, especially if they wish to do so by car. In the Occupied Territories, vehicles, like people, need the proper authorization to travel anywhere, and as a general rule, commercial vehicles are preferred to those licensed for personal use. Those who seek to obtain authorization must prove that their vehicle is duly licensed, and that the vehicle is in top condition—no broken headlights, faulty blinkers, or tires that are low on air. There is only one entrance at Qalqiliya through which Palestinians carrying merchandise may enter or leave the enclave. And according to the villagers, the checkpoint police inspect each Palestinian vehicle with great scrutiny, issuing heavy fines for even the smallest infraction. It is also illegal to lend one's car to a family member or a friend; only the vehicle's owner may drive it across the barrier.

The Qalqiliya checkpoint, which the soldiers call Intersection 109, forces the residents of the Arab villages to the south of the enclave to make a long, time-consuming nine-mile detour to Habla. Before the barrier was built, the same journey took a matter of minutes. Because this same road leads to the Kedumim and Karnei Shomron settlements, the checkpoint is actually open at all hours, with soldiers on duty day and night, but for this very reason—namely that there is so much Israeli traffic—the merchandise being transported by Palestinians on this road is subject to more Draconian inspections, which can escalate into harassment and humiliation. The villagers of Ras a-Tira often tell the story of a cattle breeder who had to unload then reload a ton of fodder in his truck by himself so that the checkpoint soldiers at Intersection 109 could verify that he was not hiding anything in it.

The villagers of Ras Atiya recall a much more serious incident. In February 2004,[2] a two-year-old child suffering from a high fever and convulsions did not make it to Qalqiliya Hospital in time because the Ras Atiya barrier gate was closed. His parents and the doctor who was with them had to take an hour-long detour through the villages of Izbat Salman, Kafr Thulth, and Azzun to get to Qalqiliya. The child died on the way.

"When I look back, I see that my generation made many errors," admits Ruth Kedar while we wait at a checkpoint near the Green Line.[3] "We were perhaps too arrogant, too proud about building up the country. I am not ashamed to be Israeli, but I am disappointed, maybe even a little sad, despite my natural optimism. It's because of this malaise that I threw myself into activism for the Palestinians. There comes a time in life when you have to let your conscience and your sense of justice speak. So I started by surveying the checkpoints with volunteers from Machsom Watch.[4] We observed the checkpoints to make sure that the soldiers and the border guards weren't abusing their authority, or using violence against the Palestinians. It was a small endeavor, but the soldiers behaved better when we were there, and that counts for something. Then, in March 2005, my husband and I helped to found Yesh Din. Our long-term mission is to improve the human rights situation in the Occupied Territories. We work to collect information on current violations, while using the law and public opinion to put pressure on people in power. Our organization is made up of volunteers, but we have a team of human rights experts, lawyers, and communications consultants. Whenever it seems that legal action is needed, we find the financial means to take it."

Many new immigrants stepping off planes from Brooklyn or from Nice lose their heads whenever there is a critique of Israel or a defense of Palestinian rights; by contrast, Ruth Kedar's civic engagement reveals a more nuanced understanding of the conflict in the Middle East. She is, in many ways, the embodiment of several chapters of Israel's tumultuous history. She is descended from Russian immigrants who founded the city of Rehovot, south of Tel Aviv. Her mother was born in Palestine in 1892, and her father, a British officer from a Jewish family from Manchester, came to Palestine in 1917 to fight the Turks with General Allenby's army. He was killed in July 1946, along with ninety others, in the bombing of the King David Hotel, which was carried out by an Irgun commando under the authority of the future prime minister Menachem Begin. The hotel, which today hosts the guests of Israeli dignitaries, was at that time the seat of the British Mandate's administration and military intelligence services. Coincidentally, Irgun, which according to the British Mandate was a terrorist movement, was also the first militant group that Paul Kedar, Ruth's husband, had joined.

A member of the executive board of the Museum of the Jewish

Diaspora, of which he is one of the founders, Paul Kedar is a cultured, multilingual man in his eighties. He speaks with a kind of nonchalant irony, common in former intelligence agents accustomed to keeping state secrets. Dressed in shorts, he sits in his garden enjoying a slice of Ruth's pecan pie as he talks to me. I was surprised to hear this son of Jewish revisionists,[5] who was raised on the conservative nationalist Zionism of Ze'ev Jabotinski and Menahem Begin, speak of "these Israeli leaders who don't have the courage to make peace." Paul Kedar took part in the clandestine fight against the British, then joined the air force of the young Israeli state and its intelligence services. From his youth as a soldier in the ranks of Irgun, to his activist retirement in Yesh Din, Paul Kedar's life, and the lives of his family, is a reflection of the complexities and torments of modern day Israel. He worked with Mossad in the air force and in the diplomatic corps. His three sons served in the First Lebanon War at the same time that their father was the Israeli army's press secretary. His oldest son, Alexander (Sandy), now teaches law at the University of Haifa, he is a specialist in property law and he shares the liberal beliefs of his parents. The middle child lives and works in the United States and France. The youngest works in the restaurant business in Israel. Paul also has a daughter who works at a biotechnology firm in Nazareth, "the only Arab-Israeli company in Israel," her mother says proudly.

As Ruth and I talk, our car approaches a checkpoint soldier verifying IDs. It is clear that he is not fond of the idea of an Israeli visiting a Palestinian village, and even less thrilled with his orders to prevent her from entering. His sentiments are amplified by a yellow sign planted at the side of the road: "No Israeli citizen may enter this village, by order of the IDF, The Region Commander." Ruth is unfazed by this little obstacle and pulls out her secret weapon: a telephone full of indispensible contacts. With only two quick phone calls, we are allowed to pass through the checkpoint, and to continue on the narrow, rocky road toward Ras a-Tira.

The first thing we see on the other side of the barrier are rows of greenhouses in Habla and Ras Atiya. On the barrier's barbed-wire fences hang threatening red signs that read: "Danger—Military Zone.

Any person crossing or attempting to damage the barrier is putting his life in danger."

This is obviously not the first time Ruth Kedar has been to Ras a-Tira; the villagers come out to greet her as she rolls down her window and asks in basic Arabic where to find Yassin Younes, the village's council president. They direct us to meet him at his home.

Younes is a bearded fifty-year-old man wearing a white forage cap, whose expression may be described as severe and a little stiff, a common demeanor for notable Islamists when they are among strangers. But he does crack a smile as he welcomes us with the traditional "*Ahlan wa sahlan,*" ushering us through the gate to his property. He walks us into a private courtyard surrounded by high walls that protect us from being seen by onlookers, if not from the heat of the high noon sun. We sit at a little table under a lemon tree with two other residents of the town, and Yassin Younes, who speaks neither English nor Hebrew, asks them to act as our interpreters. One of them, an out-of-work chicken farmer named Nasser Moussa, knows some Hebrew and basic English; the other, Rafik Mrabe, also bearded and wearing a short-sleeved shirt and fine-woven wool slacks, works for the government and is president of the local committee against the wall. His English is much better; he will be the one who translates for us here in the courtyard and later, as we walk through the village streets to the rocky promontory across from Alfei Menashe. Rafik's anger is evident as he translates Younes's account of what the barrier has done to his village.

"First of all, we had nearly forty dunums[6] confiscated for the barrier.[7] Then we lost two hundred more, along with greenhouses, olive trees, and five wells that are now on the other side. Before the barrier, everything we needed came from Qalqiliya, and almost everything we produced—fruits, vegetables, eggs, chickens—went there or to Habla for sale. They were only about twenty minutes away. Today it can take anywhere from an hour to as long as half a day to get there, depending on the line at the checkpoint and the mood of the soldiers, and only those with a permit are allowed to go through. If someone from the village needs to be hospitalized or operated on after six p.m.— that is, after the Ras a-Tira entrance is closed—we must take the patient to Qalqiliya Hospital. That would involve calling the District Coordination Office to obtain an ambulance authorization from the Israeli army, which takes time.

"Lately, I spend a lot of my time negotiating permits. I have to go to the Civil Administration office in the Kedumim settlement, twelve miles away, and drop off the required papers. Sometimes it takes about half a day for them to respond, sometimes several days. Just a few years ago, most of the villagers worked in Israel or in Alfei Menashe, but those days are over; three quarters of them have lost their jobs. As for myself, in the last three months I've been able to work on my land for only ten days. The barrier changed everything. It has killed all our hope here, just as it has in the other villages of the Alfei Menashe enclave; we all have the same problems. It's as if the Jews"—Rafik Mrabe actually translated it as "the Israelis"—"want to make our lives as difficult as possible. They don't let anyone pass through [the checkpoints], even for weddings or funerals. The truth, you see, is that they want to make us leave. They want the land, not the people."

"It's true," says Rafik Mrabe, "they're doing everything they can to destroy social ties. I have a sister in Habla, not two miles away, and another in Ras Atiya, even closer, and I haven't seen them in more than three months. The telephone is our only way of communicating. And all of this has nothing to do with the fight against terrorism, or the security of the Israelis—that is the great lie."

This "great lie" is the reason why Ruth Kedar has come to Ras a-Tira. After traveling from village to village, combing through land registries and urbanization plans, activists from Yesh Din have concluded that, contrary to local officials, security imperatives were not what ultimately determined the route of the barrier here. Yesh Din supported a petition brought before the Supreme Court by the villages in the enclave to have the barrier moved to the foot of the Alfei Menashe settlement.

"Come," Rafik Mrabe says to us as we get up from the table and he leads us out to the narrow road that runs through Ras a-Tira. "I am going to show you why the barrier makes such a big loop around Alfei Menashe, why we are prisoners, and why they are lying to us."

At the edge of the village, where the old gravestones blend into the rocky terrain and the thorny bushes, he stops and points to a hill about fifty feet southwest of Alfei Menashe, where there is construction under way. "Israelis call this hill Tal; it's where they're going to build hundreds of houses to extend Alfei Menashe. Another extension is planned for Ras a-Tira. The people who are building the barrier know very well about these projects. That's why the separation barrier doesn't pass between our villages and Alfei Menashe, but *around* our villages, enclosing them with the settlement."

Approved by the minister of public works and housing in 1998 and now accessible to the public, the expansion and urbanization plan for Alfei Menashe shows that, in fact, more than a thousand residences, 1,406 to be exact, are to be built on the approximately 250 acres of Project 115/8, the official topographic name for the Tal Hill expansion. Project 115/8 leaves enough room for the local Israel population, now at 5,700 residents, to double, and will include public buildings, businesses, tourist sites, and a zoo. Construction will be carried out in three phases. The first phase will be a crown of small five-story buildings with 288 apartments at the top of the hill. According to the Alfei Menashe municipality, about 100 of them have already been sold. The same plan shows that three other urbanization projects in the region are in various stages of development. Project 115/9, called Ilanit or Qaniel, covers fifty-two acres to the south of Ras a-Tira and a-Dab'a. It has not been submitted to the minister. Project 115/16/4, or Nof Hasharon, which was approved in 2003, covers almost 10 acres and runs to the east of the Green Line through the Israeli settlement of Nirit. Project 115/10 is an extension of 115/16/4 and includes the construction of 1,200 apartments over its 185 acres. It is still in the early planning stages. But as recent aerial photos of the region show, the sinuous path of the barrier in the regions of Alfei Menashe and Qalqiliya is clearly designed to enclose not just the settlement but its future extension as well. "One of the primary considerations in determining the route of the barrier around Alfei Menashe was to put the extension zones on the Israeli side of the barrier," write the authors of a report titled "Under the Guise of Security."[8] Published in December 2005 by Bimkom (Planners for Planning Rights) and the human rights organization B'Tselem, this document shows, with many examples, that the path of the barrier was designed not only to protect Israeli citizens from terrorism, but also, and perhaps especially, to annex nearly seventy West Bank settlements to Israeli territory, and the land necessary for their extension.

The town council of Alfei Menashe makes no effort to conceal the true intentions of the barrier design around the settlement; when they agreed to talk with me about it they were clearly proud of their successful negotiations. "Would you like to know how we got the barrier loop to go around us?" says Eliezer Hasdai, the mayor of Alfei Menashe and a member of the Likud Central Committee. Hasdai freely admits that his municipality discussed the barrier's path with the army, and will even direct anyone who wants to speak about the matter to the office of the head of security for the settlement. "Ask Zissman. He knows more about it than I do, and his English is better."

"What do you think? Of course we discussed the path of the barrier with Dany Tirza," says Arie Zissman, secretary of the Alfei Menashe municipality, who also serves as head of security for the settlement. "Of course we had our development projects, and those of our neighbors, in mind. That was the whole point." Zissman has a stocky build and a strong handshake, and even though he immigrated to Israel from the United States some twenty years ago, he still has his New York accent. In his office, he keeps three combat helmets, three loaded magazines—two for a pistol, one for an M-16 assault rifle—a bulletproof vest, and two walkie-talkies. The office is also decorated with protest signs from the settlement rallies that had resisted evacuating the Gaza Strip in August 2005. He does not accept what he calls "the strategy of giving gifts to the Arabs," and generally does not seem like the kind of man who takes life lightly. "It was people like me who put Sharon in power, and they betrayed us with their Labor Party ideas. What's worse is that Bibi [Binyamin Netanyahu] is no better than Sharon." Zissman is obviously furious over the withdrawal from Gaza.[9] Nonetheless, he laughs when I ask if he haggled with the army over the placement of the barrier.

The Alfei Menashe administrative center combines the town hall, the police station, the post office, and several other public service offices into one building. It is a beige, arc-shaped building facing the horizion, built at the highest point of the settlement, like the wheelhouse of a ship. From here, there is a sweeping view of the coastal lowland that extends all the way to the towers of Tel Aviv. The Mediterranean is about 12.5 miles away as the crow flies, and the Ben-Gurion Airport about 15.5. "In clear weather," says Zissman, "you can see north to Haifa and south to Ashkelon. Imagine what a strategic position we hold."

Today, the settlement, located at the summit of a 900-foot hill, is home to 6,500 Israelis, according to Zissman (although www.peace now.org reports the population at 5,500). The list of towns and villages at Israel's Central Bureau of Statistics reports that Alfei Menashe, which became an autonomous municipality in 1987, has welcomed 1,500 new residents over the last eight years. Many of the people who chose to live there do not necessarily come for religious or ideological reasons: this "dormitory settlement" allows its residents to live in the countryside, only a twenty-five-minute drive away from Tel Aviv, while enjoying the financial incentives intended to attract Israelis to the Occupied Territories. Even if rents in Alfei Menashe have increased between 25 and 30 percent since the construction of the barrier, they are still well below those of Petah Tikva, not to mention Tel Aviv. "Our real problem," admits Zissman, "is that we have no jobs here. Most of the residents work on the other side of the Green Line, in Tel Aviv."

"At first," says Zissman, "we didn't think we'd be to the west of the barrier. Originally it had been drawn precisely on the Green Line in this area, and it ran close to the first houses of Qalqiliya in order to protect the Trans-Israel Highway from snipers hiding in the town's minarets. When the mayor discovered the route of the barrier, he was furious. Why? Well, look at the map. Route Fifty-five, which connects us with Kfar Saba, the Trans-Israel Highway, and the coastal plain, passes exactly between Qalqiliya [45,000 residents] and Habla [5,500 residents]. These two Arab villages are a little more than half a mile away from each other, which could quite easily cut us off from Tel Aviv and leave us isolated in the middle of hostile Arab villages. This was unacceptable. Our mayor held an important position in the Likud; he was on the Settlement Committee, and so he was able to talk to the right people. Ben-Eliezer and Sharon came to see the situation for themselves, and we started negotiating. We joined forces with the town council of Matan, which faces Habla on the other side of the Green Line, and this helped in our negotiations with the military.

"The Matan town council had learned that in order to maintain secure access to Alfei Menashe and to the settlements in the Ma'ale Shomron region," Zissman continued, "the army planned to build a new road that would circle around the south of Habla and Ras Atiya and converge with a road linking [the Israeli villages of] Kfar Saba and Kfar Qasem. This road would so ruin the view of Matan residents that the Left-controlled municipal council of the town vigorously opposed it. The people of Matan had also stressed, like us, that it would be crazy not to separate Qalqiliya and Habla with a physical barrier. In August 2002, they had even written a letter to the Labor Party's Central Committee asserting that these two Arab towns might lead others in the area to gather force and form a single collective community of one hundred thousand Arabs, which would constitute a danger to the region. Their letter must have hit home: at the end of September, Amos Yaron, director-general of the Ministry of Defense, and Haim Ramon, Labor Party representative and president of the Defense Committee in the Knesset, came to Matan with military personnel, and concluded that, indeed, it would be a mistake to maintain the territorial continuity of Qalqiliya and Habla. From that point forward, things moved very quickly. The barrier would no longer be built along the Green Line. Dany Tirza started to draw plans for the new barrier, which would isolate Qalqiliya and Habla by looping around them. Perhaps inspired by the expansion plans in Alfei Manesh, Tirza designed the barrier that exists today, which loops around our current expansion construction.[10] We won."

Confronted by the demands of elected officials from Matan and Alfei Menashe, the political-military bureaucracy of the State of Israel, so often deaf to the petitions of the Palestinians, performed a miracle: Only a few days after their visit at the end of September 2002, Amos Yaron and Haim Ramon received a letter from Amikam Sivirski, the prime minister's settlement advisor, stating that their petition had been accepted and that the path of the barrier in the Qalqiliya–Alfei Menashe region would be redrawn according to their requests. The additional expense to the Ministry of Defense was estimated at 130 million shekels (€25 million). Eliezer Hasdai welcomed the news, proclaiming to the media, "We have moved the Green Line!" Hasdai was being modest; he and his comrades had not only moved the Green Line, they had in essence moved the security barrier, and likely the border of the future Palestinian State.

The mayor of Alfei Menashe would later say that his colleagues from the Settlement Committee were envious of his success, and had spread rumors that it was his position in the Likud Party, and not his negotiating skills, that had closed the deal. Nonetheless, he firmly believed that his €25 million project was awarded not because of his political orientaion, but because he was able to effectively illustrate that Alfei Menashe, which is located on the first mountain chain next to the coastal lowlands, was, like a fortress wall, of strategic importance.[11]

Looking back, this debate seems moot. The people who wanted the barrier to follow the Green Line, such as Ben-Eliezer, had lost the fight before it began. At the same time, given the final path of the barrier, from the north to the south of the West Bank, and the events that inspired its location, the role of Eliezer Hasdai seems minor. Here, as elsewhere, the barrier, designed in principle to "prevent terrorists intruding from Judea and Samaria [from] commit[ting] attacks in Israel"[12] had a very different objective. It was also conceived and constructed to protect the settlements, to give them room to develop

and grow, and to create territorial integrity with Israel. The meanderings of the barbed wire and concrete that protect Alfei Menashe, and
its satellites, while choking off Qalqiliya and Habla, serves this function very well.

A tractor lays down barbed wire as part of the separation barrier between Qalqiliya and Tulkarem. *Courtesy of B'Tselem*

CHAPTER 8

QALQILIYA IN THE NET

The barrier isn't expected to make everyone happy."

This rather cruel understatement is one of the favorite phrases of Uzi Dayan, former chairman of the National Security Council. No one in Qalqiliya would disagree. Alfei Menashe and Matan's successful campaign to move the separation line came at considerable cost to the town of Qalqiliya: not only did they lose a significant amount of arable land, but also a piece of their heritage. Their situation today exemplifies the unspoken strategy of the Sharon and Olmert governments, put into effect by Dany Tirza, not only ensure the security of the Israeli settlements, but also to annex land for their expansion, regardless of the toll on neighboring Palestinians.

Apart from the Jerusalem Envelope—the name given by the government to the section of the barrier in the Jerusalem area—no section of the barrier is as confusing and labrynthine as the route that runs through the Qalqilya–Alfei Menashe zone (see map). Over this twenty-five-square-mile area between Jayous to the north and Jalud to the south, the separation zone, which alternates here between a barrier and a twenty-four-foot high wall, meanders in three loops that almost twist back onto themselves, forming little islands of Israeli and Palestinian territories, each totally isolated from others. Since the summer of 2003, Qalqiliya has been closed in by this cement-and-barbed-wire net. To the west, a wall was constructed in the middle of tomato and eggplant gardens. This wall, which separates the town from the Trans-Israel Highway, is almost two miles long, with watch-towers placed approximately every three hundred meters. The highway, the only toll road in the country, runs right next to the wall; and on the Israeli side, it is neatly concealed behind a mound of earth covered with greenery and bushes. To the north and south of Qalqiliya, the wall joins a separation barrierer not unlike that which runs through most of the West Bank, composed of barbed wire, anti-intrusion lanes, an electronic fence, a patrol route, and numerous optical and electro-magnetic detecting systems. The barrier around Qalqiliya loops approximately four kilometers east of the Green Line, and skirts very close to the houses in the city.

"They want to starve us, make us leave. Or turn us into terrorists so that they can kill us." As she serves cold drinks on the patio of her new house, Nuhaila Awaydat speaks with frustration and anger about the treatment she and her husband have received under the Israelis. Pushed to the brink of financial ruin, they've seen their dream of raising their children in a big house with a yard crushed. Since the Second Intifada, Nuhaila's husband's business, an auto shop, which made most of its money from Israeli customers, has been in serious trouble, due to the blockades that have isolated so many Palestinian villages. They are now almost bankrupt. "He's wondering if he should sell everything now. He's in town, talking to someone about it," explains this young woman wearing a long brown dress, her hair under a scarf, as is the custom in a traditional Islamic home.

Their recently completed house, into which Nuhaila's husband had put most of his savings, has become dreary. The cement wall stands less than nine hundred feet away from their front door, and even from the second-story terrace, their view of the nearby fields and woods of the Israeli countryside have been blocked out, along with the sunset.

"WE USED TO EXPORT OUR LEMONS, OLIVES, AND GUAVAS AS FAR AS SAUDI Arabia and the Emirates. Now I can't even sell them in Nablus or Jenin." With a basket in hand, Assad Atalla stands in the middle of a trampled patch of tomatoes, courtesy of the daily wall patrol. This small plot, squeezed in between the road and the wall, is all that remains of his family's land. The rest lies buried under cement or is inaccessible on the other side. "But the worst part," says this fifty-year-old vegetable farmer, "is that they uprooted eight thousand olive trees. Right before our eyes, they loaded them onto their trucks, and when we asked the soldiers what they were going to do with them, they said that they couldn't tell us, for security reasons."

That was in July 2003. Ma'arouf Zahran, Qalqiliya's mayor, had invited me to accompany him in his pickup truck on the bumpy road that runs alongside the barrier. "They've turned our city into a prison," he said. "You need to see it to believe it."[1] Formerly a college professor, Zahran went into politics post-Oslo and, running on the Fatah Party line, was elected mayor in 1996. "How could they have come up with this? How could they sever all the ties woven over the years between our two communities? And how could the international community allow one country to unilaterally draw its borders on its neighbor's territory?" Clearly overwhelmed by what had happened to his town, he stopped his car to greet the neighbors of the wall. He showed me now-inaccessible olive trees or a well that ended up on the other side. As we walked together he exchanged a few words with a vegetable farmer working what was left of his plot of land. The mayor's voice was at once indignant and resigned.

"Before the wall, I was convinced that peace was still possible," Zahran says, "that it was only a question of time. Up until the Second Intifada, we had always lived on good terms with the Israelis. Nearly six thousand of our residents worked in Israel, and there were about twenty Israeli-Palestinian businesses. I even had sealed administrative agreements with the municipality of Kfar Saba for water treatment. But the blockades and the ban on traveling in the West Bank hit us hard. Many who worked in Israel lost their jobs. The Israelis are afraid to come to our city. We no longer have the right to leave. Commercial exchanges have come to a halt. Agriculture now represents forty-five percent of our economy, up from twenty-two percent before the wall. More than eight thousand families receive food or financial assistance.

Now the wall is the final blow: we have lost five hundred acres, including dozens of greenhouses and around thirty olive trees, which were confiscated or cleared away by bulldozers to make way for the cement. Almost forty-five percent of our arable land and nineteen of our thirty-nine wells are now on the other side. More than six hundred stores have closed and eighteen Israeli-Palestinian companies have been liquidated. Qalqiliya is left with only one point of entry and exit. Today, people over the age of thirty-five are permitted to enter and leave the city only by foot. All vehicles, including ambulances, need authorization from the army."

As we talked, Ma'arouf Zahran and I arrived at the enormous yellow doors of the barrier gate at the southern boundary of the city. A soldier observed us from his tower as we zigzagged around potholes and cement blocks. Lining the road were closed-up storefronts and abandoned warehouses, many with Hebrew signs. A little farther down, the road ran straight into the wall.

"The Israelis would come here on the weekends, even after the First Intifada, to buy fruits, vegetables, furniture, car parts," the mayor explained. "They'd have lunch here while their cars were being worked on at the garage. They got good deals, and business was good. In Qalqiliya today, unemployment is at sixty-nine percent, and I can see no way out of these crises. I am at my wit's end. When I was elected in 1996, I ran on the futility of armed conflict, on the benefits of peace for our city and the inspiring possibility of a State. Look where we are now. There are no benefits to peace. We are worse off than ever before. The chances of a negotiated solution are less and less probable. The situation is desperate, and my party, like the Palestinian Authority, is far from equipped to handle it all. The Fatah still does not understand that it needs to give up on an armed movement; they need to become a political organization, and to really contribute to the birth of the State. Here in Qalqiliya, more than sixty people have been killed because of rumors that they were collaborating with Israel. Add to that accusations of corruption within the Palestinian Authority, and the construction of the wall—over which we have been completely powerless—and Hamas can easily win the next elections."

MA'AROUF ZAHRAN WAS RIGHT. IN MAY 2005, THE CANDIDATES OF THE Islamic Resistance Movement, Hamas, won fifteen seats on the Qalqiliya city council. They had campaigned for continuing armed resistance and new political ideas, and against the Palestinian Authority's corruption and deal-making with Israel. The mayor-elect, Wajih Qawas, was unable to take office right away, as he had been under "administrative detention" for the previous three years without trial, accused of terrorist activities. After forty-four months in prison, he was finally released, to serve as mayor of a city on the verge of imploding.

Qalqiliya, even when it attracted Israeli weekend shoppers, was never a particularly popular destination, although the souk and the commercial streets were noisy and bustling on market days. Today the city is a disaster area. The center is full of closed-up shops, their iron gates locked down and covered with posters and flyers memorializing the "martyrs" killed by the Israeli army or blown to pieces by their own bombs in suicide attacks. Nearly four thousand residents have left, to look for work in the West Bank or abroad. About two thousand people continue to live in Qalqilyia but work elsewhere. Of the four "agricultural gates" into the enclave, which in theory are open to those with a permit, one to the northeast has been condemned and covered in barbed wire; two others, to the northwest and southwest, are reserved for Israeli military vehicles; and the last one, to the south, was closed in August 2004, after a suicide attack.[2]

Today it is almost impossible for Qalqiliya residents to access their greenhouses and farmland on the other side of the barrier. More than forty years after the Israeli army almost demolished it during the War of 1967—diplomatic pressure had stopped the bulldozers in extremis— the city is now slowly dying, suffocating. Qalqiliya's location, overlooking the Israeli coastal lowlands at their narrowest point, has given it an unintended air of menace, as though it were seated above vulnerable territory, like an enemy fort. And not only did their elected Hamas leaders and their "new ideas" produce no miracles, they also accepted kickbacks and succumbed to nepotism, and lost many supporters.

In the January 2006 legislative elections, Qalqiliya's residents, having ousted Ma'arouf Zahran and replaced him with an Islamist municipal team, would now turn against Hamas. While the Islamist movement won an absolute majority in the Palestinian Legislative Council and ran the party of Yasser Arafat and Mahmoud Abbas out of town, Qalqiliya, along with Rafah and Jericho, elected the Fatah Party for all deputy seats. It took only eight months for the inhabitants of Qalqiliya, who are as passionate about politics as any Palestinian, to understand the true nature of Hamas's power. Their brief taste of Islamist rule was enough to dissuade the voting population of Qalqiliya from again throwing their support behind Hamas. By contrast, at the same time, many other Palestinians throughout the West Bank, who were suffering under similar conditions, ousted Fatah and voted Islamists into power.

COULD PALESTINIAN CITIES OR VILLAGES EVER SEE THE THE SEPARATION barrier moved, as it was for the Israeli settlement of Alfei Menashe? "Impossible," says Ma'arouf Zahran, who, after his defeat, left Qalqiliya for Ramallah and took a high post with the Palestinian Authority. "We have been under Israeli occupation for almost forty years. Their policy of colonization openly violates international humanitarian law, with complete indifference to the global community. Why would a government that mocks the Geneva Conventions and relevant United Nations resolutions with impunity respect the petition of a single Palestinian citizen or of a Palestinian town council?"

Aggressively optimististic Ruth Kedar disagrees. "That could be changing," she says. "To encourage soldiers, police, and settlers to respect human rights and to obey the law in their daily encounters with the Palestinians; to have the State of Israel ensure the protection of populations in the Occupied Territories, as international law requires . . . these are some of the objectives of Yesh Din and other organizations we work with. Look at what happened with the residents of the five villages imprisoned in the Alfei Menashe enclave. That is progress. It should even be considered a small victory, for them and for us."

———

THE MAN RESPONSIBLE FOR THIS VICTORY IS MICHAEL SFARD, A THIRTY-four-year-old Israeli lawyer who specializes in the defense of Palestinian victims of "injustice and attrocity committed in the Occupied Territories," as he puts it. An activist attorney, and proud of it, this son and grandson of Polish immigrants does not look like a man fighting a desperate cause. His chubby face, delicate round glasses, and outspoken manner lend him an air of a serious student, an upperclassman. Surrounded by a team of young colleagues, he has given his law practice the exuberant feel of an academic research center or the newsroom of a daily paper, and at its center, Michael Sfard is confident of his cause and his ability to fight for it. Born in Jerusalem, he chose to live in Tel Aviv to escape the religiosity of the Holy City. He opened his own practice in 2004, and since then he has worked out of the fourth-floor office of a nondescript building on Rothschild Boulevard, toward the south of the city. He has one room. The walls are decorated with a poster from a Picasso exhibit and some caricatures of his fellow lawyers and judges. Across from him are shelves of law books in English and Hebrew. Bound copies of the four Geneva Conventions of 1949 and 1977 are within reach of his desk.

The neighborhood, filled with Bauhaus-inspired cement buildings from the 1930s and '40s, is being renewed and has taken on a California feel, with cafés, terraces, and a shaded pedestrian lane on which weekend cyclists and Rollerbladers speed by. The stock exchange is two blocks away. Glass-and-steel towers line the boulevard; restaurants, art galleries, and fashionable clothing and furniture stores attract a rich clientele, young and apparently carefree. The separation barrier, the checkpoints, the daily confrontation between Israeli soldiers and Palestinian villagers, and the threat of suicidal terrorism all seem to exist on another planet, even though the Green Line is only about twenty miles away.

"When I began studying law," Michael Sfard confides, "I was interested in cases of political import.[3] I belong to a generation that has known only one side of Israel: that of the occupier. I grew up in a country where a small group of Jewish fundamentalist settlers benefitted from a level of political power out of all proportion with their modest number, where both the Right and the Left supported settling in the Palestinian territories—and, for this occupation, for this colonization, Israel pays a very high moral price. Our code of ethics is degraded. Even our culture has been affected. This place was founded on values of humanism, pluralism, and democracy; the idea of the State of Israel to which I am attached no longer exists. I do have a problem with my Israeli identity; everything that is being done today on the other side of the Green Line—the settlement expansions, the house demolitions, the wall, blockades, arrests, humiliations, targeted executions—are being done in my name. And the Israeli system of justice, both civil and military, justifies all of this in the name of security. We know what is going on, and we let it happen. That's why I refused to do my required Reserve service. I belonged to an infantry unit in the Occupied Territories. I even did three weeks in prison some years ago for refusing to serve in Hebron. And I am not the only Israeli who thinks this way. In 2002, four hundred and fifty Reservists, most of them between twenty-five and thirty-five years old, signed a petition that was published by the Israeli press, declaring that they refused to participate in the Israeli occupation or to serve on the other side of the Green Line. I was one of the signees, and I served as legal aide for several of the others. I defended them when they appeared before the judges and visited them when they were in prison.

"They had not necessarily witnessed or participated in atrocities. They made the choice because they could no longer tolerate daily life in the Occupied Territories. I don't know whether people abroad, or even within Israel, can understand the significance. Hundreds of soldiers and officers, many of them members of the most elite units of the Israeli army, used to risking their lives for the State of Israel, were, at the same time, questioning the morality of their presence in the Occupied Territories. People from all backgrounds suddenly realized that the order to go and dominate another people inevitably brings about human rights violations. They understood that the occupation established inequality between Israelis and Palestinians and sowed the seeds of true anti-Arab racism.

"The first time someone asked me about the barrier, it didn't exist," Michael Sfard tells me. "I was working at the law office of Avigdor Feldman, one of our most famous Israeli lawyers—known for his work on big criminal and political cases—when Hamoked and B'Tselem[4] came and asked us to explore possible legal measures for opposing the wall. We agreed to help, and in December 2003, we presented a petition to the Supreme Court. It was based on three principal arguments. One, the wall is not a vital military necessity for the State of Israel; it was not even constructed on Israeli territory, but rather on Palestinian territories, and its path is designed to protect Israeli settlements. Two, in constructing the barrier, Israel illegally annexes the territories located to the west of this separation. Three, in its essence, the barrier is an integral part of the West Bank settlement plan. This settlement is illegal, and therefore so is the barrier.

"Meanwhile, the northern part of the barrier was built. The judge concluded that in certain aspects, our case could be heard, and in others, not; that it was not possible for him to render judgment on the whole path of the barrier, and he could review requests pertaining only to particular segments of the wall. With no discussion, our general petition was put on the back burner.

"When I became interested in the affair of the enclave of Alfei Menashe and the five Palestinian villages," Michael Sfard continues, "I quit the offices of Avigdor Feldman and opened my own practice. Volunteers from Yesh Din, for which I serve as legal advisor, had gathered firsthand accounts of the difficulties facing the villagers. We also studied the plans for the development of Alfei Menashe. And we concluded that the route of the barrier, as it had been drawn, was designed to guarantee the extension of the settlement rather than to ensure the residents' security, in violation of the rights of the Palestinians, who, against their will, were locked up in the enclave."

IN AUGUST 2004, A YEAR AFTER THE COMPLETION OF THE FIRST SECTION
of the barrier, six residents of the Palestinian villages of the enclave,
supported by the Association for Civil Rights in Israel (ACRI), presented a petition to the Supreme Court demanding that the barrier,
which had cut them off from the rest of the West Bank, be declared
illegal and dismantled. Three of the villagers, Zaharan Younis Muhammad Mara'be, Mourad Ahmed Muhammad Ahmed, and Muhammad Jamil Mas'ud Shuahani, lived in Ras a-Tira. Three others,
Adnan Abd el Rahman Daud Udah, Abd el Rahim Ismail Daud
Udah, and Bessam Salah Abd el Rahman Udah, came from the neighboring village of Wadi a-Rasha. They were represented by three Israeli lawyers, including Michael Sfard. Their petition was addressed
to Israel's prime minister, Ariel Sharon; to the defense minister, Shaul
Mofaz; to the chief commanding officer of the Israeli forces in Judea-
Samaria, Major-General Moshe Kaplinsky; to the local authority re-
sponsible for the barrier; and to Alfei Menashe's municipal council.
On September 12, 2004, less then two weeks after the petition was
filed, the case was examined by the president of the Supreme Court,
Aharon Barak, and the vice-presidents Eliahu Mazza and Michel
Cheshin. The judges' first decision was to adjourn in order to allow
the State to examine the position further. "This adjournment," the
Court stated, however, "should not prevent the addressees of the petition from doing all they can to ease the daily life of the addressers."
The second hearing took place six months later, on March 31, 2005,
once again before three judges, with Judge Dorit Beinisch replacing
Vice-President Mazza, who had retired in the interim. The night before the hearing, Michael Sfard had submitted a letter to the court
from the council presidents of the five affected villages in the enclave;
in this document, the notables affirmed their support for the petition
of their citizens and designated the young lawyer from Tel Aviv as their
representative. But the discussion then came to a standstill. On April
21, 2005, as the impending withdrawal from the Gaza settlements
sparked anger among the Israeli Right, the Court decided that the villagers' petition would be examined by an expanded jury of nine judges
at the same time as two other cases,[5] concerning the construction of

the barrier around the Ariel settlement. The hearing was set for June 21, 2005.

"Our case was solid," says Michael Sfard, who cannot help smiling when he recalls his strategy before the nine Supreme Court judges. "Part of our argument was based on humanitarian issues, the other on legalities. We laid out in detail the damages inflicted on people by the barrier. We showed that every facet of daily life—health, education, familial and social relations, work, commerce, religious practice—had been adversely affected, and that the Palestinians near Alfei Menashe had suffered enormously." The villagers' testimonies were supported by the expert opinion of four architects and urban planners, who had been sent to the court shortly after the petition was filed. Members of the Israeli association Bimkom, which advocates for equality and justice in Israel's spatial planning process, had concluded that the barrier's path seriously compromised the lives of Palestinians living in this area. "The experts determined that the barrier and system of permits associated with it make it very hard to access regional services, and jeopardizes economic potential and existing social structures."

"Our legal argument was based in part on the conclusions of the International Court of Justice (ICJ) at the Hague," Michael Sfard explains. "In its advisory opinion of July 9, 2004, the Court held that, in terms of international law, the construction of the wall was illegal, and they requested that the General Assembly and Security Council of the United Nations examine measures to put an end to the situation created by the Israeli government. Frankly, I found the reasoning of the ICJ rather weak from a legal point of view: not solid enough, vulnerable to appeal. But, at the same time, it was valuable, almost indispensable, because it transformed the issue of the wall from just an Israeli-Palestinian debate into an international one, and that put the State of Israel in a delicate position. Even if Israeli politicians and leaders pretended to ignore this condemnation, even if they blamed it once again on the rampant anti-Semitism of the UN, even if they repeated that the Court had remained silent during the Second World War and the extermination of the Jews, the Court's decision stands. The Israeli judges saw that they could no longer proceed as though this advisory opinion had not been rendered. The president of the Supreme Court had, in fact, acknowledged at the hearing that the decision of the ICJ could not be ignored.

"We thus explained, in the wake of the ICJ," Sfard continues, "that the Israeli prime minister and other leaders and institutions did not have the authority to put up a barrier around the enclave, first because it did not respond to a security imperative and, second, because it led to a territorial annexation to the State of Israel. So, in fact, the barrier was moving the State of Israel's boundaries east, something that is prohibited by laws defining the rights and responsibilities of occupying powers. We also pointed out to the court that, to our knowledge, the wall's route was a direct result of pressure from the residents of Alfei Menashe and Matan. The second part of our argument raised the question of the disproportionate amount of damage caused by the barrier. We showed that the barrier's existence violated the majority of the villagers' fundamental rights—from the right to property and movement to health, education, work, and dignity. However, Israeli law, like international law, states that any infringement on the rights of individuals must be in proportion to the objective being pursued. This is far from the case here, since it is not established that the construction of the barrier along the sinuous path chosen by the defense minister is indispensable for the protection of Israeli civilians. One could even argue the contrary, as many officers have: that a barrier that follows the Green Line and that would thus be straighter and shorter, would better serve the theoretical security objective of its builders."

In order to protect the Alfei Menashe residents, was it necessary to construct a loop so expansive that the barbed wire was as far as fifteen hundred meters from the Israeli houses? Was it necessary also to imprison the five neighboring Palestinian villages in the loop as well?

This was the central question that the judges asked of Colonel Dany Tirza on June 21, 2005, when he presented his maps of the enclave to the tribunal. Confronted with his own documents, the barrier's architect admitted that he had enlarged the loop around the settlement and placed the villages of Ras a-Tira, a-Dab'a, and Wadi a-Rasha inside it in order to protect the extension of Alfei Menashe to the south and the west. He also explained that the two villages to the north of the enclave, Arab a-Ramadin and Arab Abu Farda, were on the "Israeli" side of the barrier because they bordered Highway 55, which linked Alfei Menashe to Israel, and thus had to be on the inside. He stated that this section of Highway 55 posed "security problems" based on a history of sniper fire raining down on Israeli cars from the direction of Qalqiliya. In fact, it had become such a hazzard that at one point Tirza, who considered Highway 55 to be little more than a temporary access road, had proposed shutting it down and bypassing it with Highway 5250, which passes close to Matan and links to Alfei Menashe via the south. Thanks to documents filed by the petitioners, the successful efforts of Matan's residents to cancel this project, which threatened their quality of life, were revealed to the court.

After all the testimony illustrating the humanitarian impact of the wall, not to mention the revelation of Dany Tirza's maps, the judges were quite shaken, and not at all convinced that the extension of Alfei Menashe and the inclusion of the three villages within the barrier's loop were vital to Israeli security. Also they were not convinced of the necessity to maintain an access road to Alfei Menashe inside the loop, along with the two Palestinian villages that bordered it, since there was a safer alternative. "At the end of the hearing, we were pretty optimistic," Michael Sfard remembers. "It seemed clear to the judges that we were in a kind of legal and humanitarian chaos, and that something had to be done. And we were anxious, but confident, about what would be the Court's decision."

The Supreme Court rendered its judgment on September 15, 2005. The president and the eight judges were, in their sixty-six-page decision, unanimous, which is unusual for this level of jurisdiction. "This alone speaks volumes," opines Michael Sfard. "It shows clearly that the tribunal, while expressing its divergence with the advisory opinion of the ICJ, considered the section of the barrier under its consideration in a very bad light. According to them, the separation zone in this area violated, without any possible security justification, the rights of the Palestinians. From this perspective, the Court's injunction addressed to the authorities was inevitable.

"After noting that the human rights of the inhabitants of the five villages were indisputably violated, and having established that the protection of the Alfei Menashe settlement could not justify the chosen path, Aharon Barak, the president, with the approval of his eight colleagues, ordered the State of Israel to reconsider in 'a reasonable time period,' other options for the separation barrier at Alfei Menashe while examining alternative security solutions that would reduce the toll on Palestinian villages. In this context, Judge Barak said, Israel must examine the option of including only Alfei Menashe and a single road to the south within the enclave."

Six months later, nothing had changed. The barrier still stood, the villagers still suffered. "Two projects are being looked at," Michaele Sfard says. "The State of Israel should choose one of them." This time the villagers will be consulted on the path of the barrier. "On principle we said that we would not approve any path that did not follow the Green Line, but we also sent a list of objections to the two projects to the Ministry of Defense. The first project remains very problematic because while it puts the villagers on the Palestinian side of the barrier, it leaves much of their land on the other side. The second is unacceptable because it isolates the villages to make room for the settlement's extension. The army, which for the first time is taking into account villagers' opinions, prefers the first option because they know that there is fierce opposition to the second. However, the government seems intent on approving the first. The Alfei Menashe municipal council, on the other hand, is strongly against the first solution because it would stem the settlement's plans for extension, and they have already solicited expert military opinions to petition the Supreme Court." Sfard continued: "I think that we, too, will go back to court to rectify the new path and to reduce the amount of arable Palestinian land to the west of the barrier. The upside of all of this, of course, is that if the first project goes through, the villages will no longer be separated from the rest of the West Bank. They can renew their traditional social, cultural, and economic life. The downside is that the Supreme Court set no deadline for the implementation of its decision. It speaks only of a 'reasonable time period,' which is open to interpretation. Time, in other words, is not on our side."

Michael Sfard was right to be cautious. Two years after the Supreme Court's first judgment, nothing had changed, and legally, the situation became more complicated. In its judgment of August 29, 2007, the Supreme Court chose the path that excludes the three villages to the south, Ras a-Tira, Wadi a-Rasha, and a-Dab'a, from the Alfei Menashe enclave, but keeps the two villages to the north, Arab a-Ramadin and Arab Abu Farda, with their total residents on the "Israeli" side of the barrier. The judges felt that this solution respected the balance between Alfei Menashe's security imperatives and the humanitarian concerns of the Palestinian population, since it "returns" 472 acres of their land to them. They also decided that the barrier must go around "Tal Hill," where an extension of Alfei Menashe is under way, but that, contrary to the requests of the settlers, it will not envelop other Alfei Menashe expansions currently under development. "The design of the security barrier," the judges ruled, "must not be based on the desire to include land from the Israeli side that had been designated for the extension of the Jewish settlements, particularly when there exists no planning for its development."

As expected, Michael Sfard launched a counterattack, maintaining that the five villages must remain outside of the enclave, and he once again showed that the path of the barrier was designed to appease political considerations and to accommodate the expansion of Alfei Menashe. But time, he knows, is still not on his side.

Sheikh Sa'ad, a Palestinian town just outside Jerusalem. *Courtesy of Checkpoint Monitors Team, B'Tselem*

CHAPTER 9

THE SIEGE OF SHEIKH SA'AD

To demonstrate the strategic qualities of the barrier around Jerusalem, one of its designers, Dany Tirza, likes to drive his visitors to the Richard and Rhoda Goldman Promenade in Talpiot. The promenade, a walkway of shaded terraces to the southwest of the Holy City, facing the southern wall of the Old City and the Dome of the Rock, is frequented by picnickers and tourists who come to take in its panoramic view of the eastern neighborhoods, which span from the Mount of Olives to the ridges towering over the Desert of Judea and Bethlehem. This spot is particularly important to Tirza, a devoutly Jewish man, as it is the site of a significant biblical event. "Right here," he explains, "is where, for the first time, Abraham sees Mount Moriah, and later where his raised arm is stopped by the angel at the moment he is about to sacrifice his son, Isaac. In the Christian tradition, it is on this hill that the Caliph lived, and where it was decided to deliver Jesus to the Romans. That is why in the New Testament it was called "The Hill of Bad Counsel."

Indifferent to this bad omen, and to the neighborhood of the valley of Gehenna,[1] Tirza gazes down upon the thick gray line of the wall snaking among the houses and olive trees along the eastern boundary of Jerusalem, running over hills and through narrow valleys. It looks as out of place in this biblical landscape as a gas station in front of the Angkor Wat moat. And it is quite clear from this perch over East Jerusalem that the wall does not pass in between Israelis and Palestinians, as it should if it were truly designed to ensure the security of the former and to block terrorists hidden among the latter. Between El-Azariyeh and, to the south, the agglomeration of Abu Dis, are steeples and minarets on both sides of the wall, which can be seen on the very detailed maps Tirza has brought with him to the promenade. "For the route of the barrier in Jerusalem"—he uses the word "barrier" even though here it is a wall—"I had three options: One, build the barrier between the Jewish and Arab sections of East Jerusalem. Impossible in a democratic country; it would have been considered racist. Two, we could attach to Jerusalem some Palestinian areas on its border, like Abu Dis, El-Azariyeh, and Al-Ram, all of whose cultural, economic, and social activity is strongly linked to Jerusalem's. This would have opened up Jerusalem to almost one hundred thousand Palestinians holding orange cards, residents of the Occupied Territories. Also impossible. Our third option: to build the wall so that it follows as closely as possible the boundary of Jerusalem. This solution also had its disadvantages. Some families have members living in Jerusalem, while others are in the West Bank. There are also Palestinian families living in the West Bank who work or send their children to school in Jerusalem. Depending on the area, I did my best to minimize any inconvenience for the Palestinians. I know I did not always succeed, but I had to carry out first and foremost the mission assigned to me by the government—to protect Israelis—and this is what I did."

Tirza does not mention it, but surely he is aware that five minutes from the belvedere where we are looking at his maps, the residents of the village of Sheikh Sa'ad are in revolt against his planned path, which has completely isolated them. In order to reach this angry little village, one simply has to take a left off the Richard and Rhoda Goldman Promenade toward Talpiot and the southern neighborhoods of Jerusalem. Just before it plunges toward the Valley of Cedron, the road becomes narrow and passes in front of the Government House, where, above the pines and cypress, the blue United Nations flag flies. Inaugurated in 1930 by Sir Arthur Wanchope, the British high commissioner in Palestine, this big octagonal building served as the offices of Her Majesty's proconsuls under its mandate by the League of Nations in 1922. The British were here until 1948, but for more than half a century now, the building has housed military observers of the UN, in charge of supervising the cease-fire imposed on Israel and the Arab states by the UN Security Council in May 1948. The invisible demarcation between the Jewish and Arab neighborhoods runs somewhere between the UN parking lot and a police station protected by fencing and blocks of cement. The station stands like a fort watching over the Arab suburbs down below.

About a half kilometer from Government House, I come to a small shop. A Palestinian greengrocer is sitting in the shop reading a newspaper in English, so I ask him for directions. "Sheikh Sa'ad is at the end of this road, just across from Jabel Mukaber, where you see an Israeli watchtower. You can't miss it," he explains. "But you should leave your car here and enter the village on foot."

In fact, that is part of the problem. Sheikh Sa'ad, a village of less than two hundred houses, built on a rocky spur across from Jabel Mukaber, sits at the foot of one of the wall's enormous cement watchtowers, and all roads into the town have been closed to cars and vehicles since 2002. A one-hundred-foot-long ramp links the main road and the road bordering Jabel Mukaber. The ramp is blocked by a stone-and-cement guardpost, which, on the day of my visit, was manned by three soldiers from the Border Police. The soldiers are chatting and listening to the radio, protected from the oppressive summer sun under a camouflage canopy, their assault rifles within reach. As I approach, they clearly are not pleased to see me, and their mood does not improve when I show them my passport and an ID card issued to me by the press office of the Israeli government for visiting journalists.

"This is a closed zone," one of the soldiers tells me. "Only residents have the right to come and go."

"But there's no sign saying this," I reply. "Do you have a military order you could show me?"

"Security reasons. The village is dangerous."

About fifty feet from the roadblock, four villagers are sitting on plastic stools in front of a minimarket, deep in conversation—they seem about as threatening as a group of boule players. Nonetheless, I have to negotiate for ten minutes with the only English-speaking blockade soldier as he examines my papers, before he agrees to call his superior officer. He is on the phone for another ten minutes before finally they allow me to enter the village, advising me to "be careful."

Of course, none of this is lost on the villagers, who have been watching the whole scene. "Welcome," says the owner of the minimarket, offering me a straw and a cold Coca-Cola. "You've seen how they are with you. Imagine how it can be with us. A man named Mohammad is on his way. He speaks English well. He's going to explain to you what is happening here."

Mohammad Abdu, a solid, sixty-year-old man with a mustache, arrives. Once the receptionist at the Lawrence Hotel, he came to Sheikh Sa'ad to live out his retirement in his family house. Lately, though, he finds himself serving as an impromptu press secretary for the village. He speaks good English and even some French, which he picked up visiting a friend in Sartrouville. Like many Palestinians, he deals with the stress of daily life by chain-smoking, and as soon as we begin to talk, he lights up. "Since 2002," he says, "I think it was near the end of September—the army barricaded the only entrance to the village. No vehicle could cross. Before the bulldozers set down the blocks of stone and cement, the soldiers asked the people here who had cars to make a choice: either they could keep them in the village and never take them out, or they could drive them around the barrier, on the road's shoulder, and never take them back into the village. Since then, everything we need must be unloaded from our cars at the blockade and then carried into the village on foot. For people who kept their cars in the village, gas is delivered to them in jerricans. Our consumption of gasoline is almost nothing, since we don't get around much in the cars that are still here. Those who leave for good—and many have [left] since the village was closed up—must hoist their furniture, refrigerators, and washing machines over the blockade before loading them on to trucks on the other side. Sick people or pregnant women going into labor have to be moved on stretchers or chairs over the stone blocks and then met by an ambulance. Can you imagine all the problems this situation causes? What's going to become of us? We cannot live like this, iso-

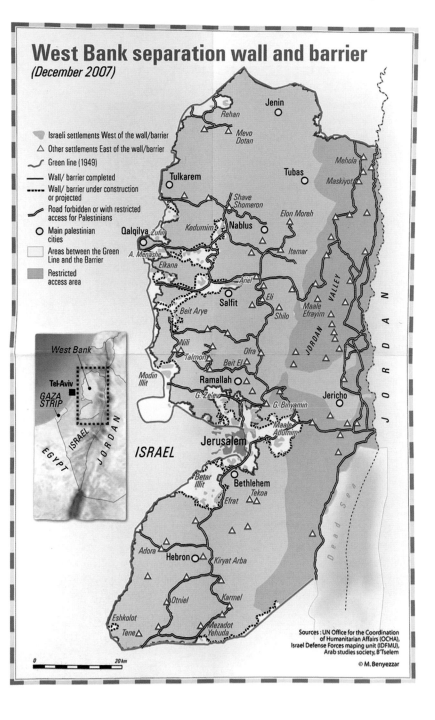

West Bank separation wall and barrier
(December 2007)

Jenin ○

Rehan

△ *Mevo
Dotan*

Mehola

Tubas ○

Maskiyot △

Legend:

- 🏵 Israeli settlements West of the wall/barrier
- △ Other settlements East of the wall/barrier
- ∿ Green line (1949)
- ⎯ Wall/ barrier completed
- ▪▪▪▪ Wall/ barrier under construction or projected
- ∿ Road forbidden or with restricted access for Palestinians
- ○ Main palestinian cities
- ☐ Areas between the Green Line and the Barrier
- ▨ Restricted access area

Tulkarem ○

*Shave
Shomeron*

Elon Moreh

Qalqilya ○ *Zufin*   *Kedumim* △   Nablus ○
△

A. Menashe   *Itamar* △

Elkana

Ariel

Salfit ○   *Eli*   *Maale
Efrayim* △

Beit Arye   *Shilo*

J O R D A N   V A L L E Y

Nili   *Ofra*

Talmon   *Beit El* △

*Modin
Illit*   Ramallah ○△

G. Zeiev   Jericho ○

G. Binyamin

*Maale
Adumim*

West Bank

Tel-Aviv ■

**GAZA
STRIP**

ISRAEL   *JORDAN*

EGYPT

ISRAEL   Jerusalem ○

*Betar
Illit* ○   Bethlehem ○

Tekoa
Efrat   △△

D e a d   S e a

△   △

Adora   Hebron ○△   *Kiryat Arba*

△

Otniel   *Karmel*

Eshkolot

Tene △   *Mezadot
Yehuda*

J O R D A N

0 ⎯⎯⎯⎯ 20 km

Sources : UN Office for the Coordination
of Humanitarian Affairs (OCHA),
Israel Defense Forces maping unit (IDFMU),
Arab studies society, B'Tselem

© M. Benyezzar

Jerusalem area
wall and barrier

Ramallah

Beituniya

Rafat

At Tira

Givat
Ze'ev

Beit Duqqu

Givon
Hadasha

Al Jib

Bir Nabala

Beit Iiza

Al Qubeibeh

Har
Shmueil

Nabi Samuel

Qatanna

Biddu

Har Adar

Beit Surik

Beit Iksa

Ramot

West Bank

Tel-Aviv

GAZA
STRIP

ISRAEL

ISRAEL

JORDAN

EGYPT

Old City

West Jerusalem

Sharafat

Beit Safa

Gilo

Al Walajeh

Battir

Beit Jala

Bethler

Husan

Al Khader

Ad Dawha

Betar Illit

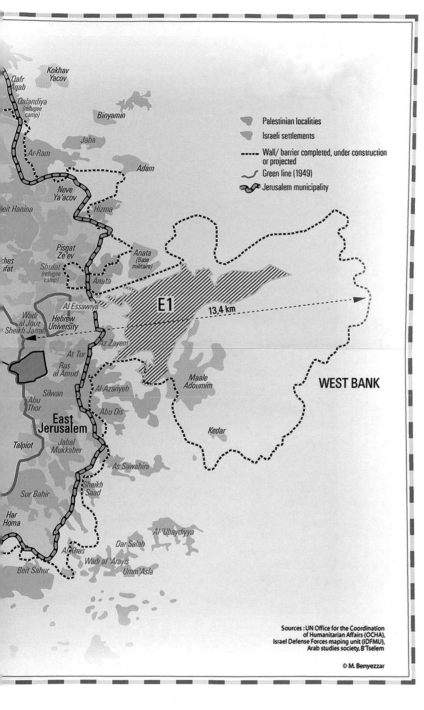

Qafr
'Aqab
Kokhav
Yacov
Qalandiya
(refugee
camp)
Binyamin
Jaba
Ar-Ram
Adam
Neve
Ya'acov
eit Hanina
Hizma
Pisgat
Ze'ev
Anata
(Base
militaire)
ches
rfat
Shufat
(refugee
camp)
Anata
E1   13,4 km
Al Essawiya
Wadi
al Jouz
Sheikh Jarrah
Hebrew
University
Az Zayem
At Tur
Ras
al Amud
Al-Azariyeh
Maale
Adoumim
WEST BANK
Silwan
Abu
Thor
Abu Dis
East
Jerusalem
Talpiot
Jabal
Mukkaber
Kedar
As Sawahira
Sur Bahir
Sheikh
Saad
Har
Homa
Al 'Ubaydiyya
Dar Salah
Al Khas
Wadi al 'Arayis
Beit Sahur
Umm 'Asla

Palestinian localities
Israeli settlements
Wall/ barrier completed, under construction
or projected
Green line (1949)
Jerusalem municipality

Sources : UN Office for the Coordination
of Humanitarian Affairs (OCHA),
Israel Defense Forces maping unit (IDFMU),
Arab studies society, B'Tselem

© M. Benyezzar

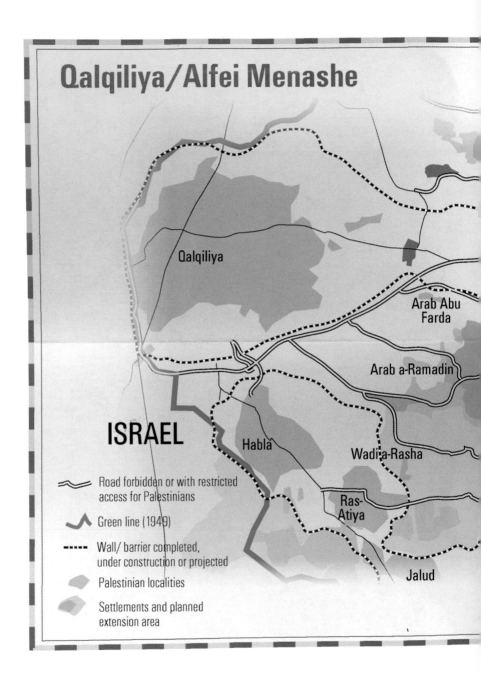

Qalqiliya/Alfei Menashe

Qalqiliya

Arab Abu Farda

Arab a-Ramadin

ISRAEL

Habla

Wadi a-Rasha

Ras-Atiya

Jalud

Road forbidden or with restricted access for Palestinians

Green line (1949)

Wall/barrier completed, under construction or projected

Palestinian localities

Settlements and planned extension area

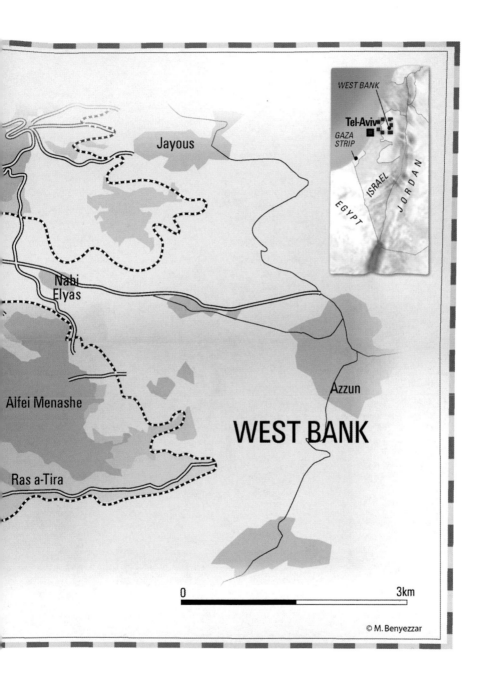

Jayous

Nabi Elyas

Alfei Menashe

Azzun

Ras a-Tira

WEST BANK

WEST BANK

Tel-Aviv

GAZA
STRIP

EGYPT

ISRAEL

JORDAN

0   3km

© M. Benyezzar

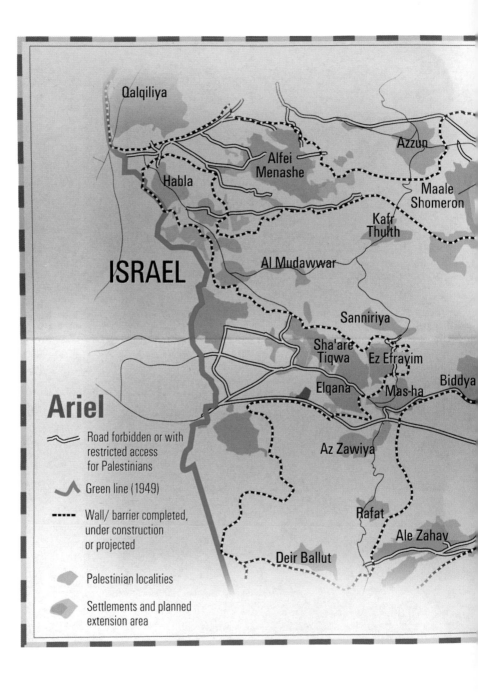

Qalqiliya

Azzun

Alfei
Menashe

Habla

Maale
Shomeron

Kafr
Thulth

ISRAEL

Al Mudawwar

Sanniriya

Sha'are
Tiqwa

Ez Efrayim

Biddya

Elqana

Mas-ha

Ariel

〰 Road forbidden or with
restricted access
for Palestinians

⋀ Green line (1949)

----- Wall/ barrier completed,
under construction
or projected

◗ Palestinian localities

◗ Settlements and planned
extension area

Az Zawiya

Rafat

Ale Zahav

Deir Ballut

Al Funduq

Immatin

WEST BANK

Tel-Aviv

GAZA
STRIP

ISRAEL

JORDAN

EGYPT

Karnei
Shomeron

Emmanuel

WADI QANA

Notim

Yaqir

Deir Istya

Jamma'in

Qarawat
Bani Hassan

Revava

Haris

Qira

Marda

Barqan
Sarta

Barqan
(industrial zone)

Ariel

Ariel West
(industrial zone)

Khirbet
Susa

Salfit

Bruqin

Farkha

afr ad Dik

0   3km

Sources : UN Office for the Coordination of Humanitarian Affairs (OCHA),
© M. Benyezzar   Israel Defense Forces maping unit (IDFMU), Arab studies society, B'Tselem

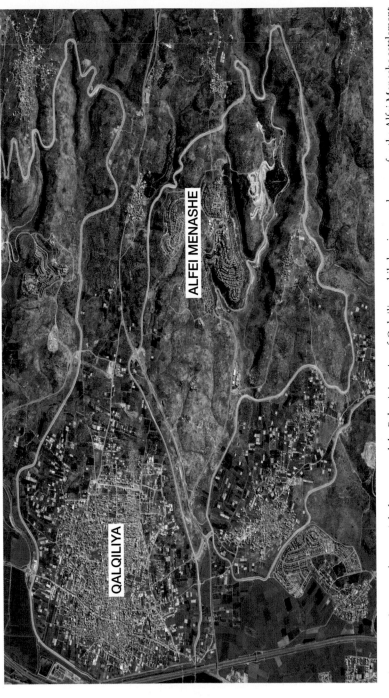

QALQILIYA

ALFEI MENASHE

The West Bank Barrier draws a tight loop around the Palestinian city of Qalqiliya, while leaving ample space for the Alfei Menashe settlement to expand. *Courtesy of DigitalGlobe and eMap*

lated, cut off from everything. We have two primary schools, but no middle school. Our children go to the high school in Jabel Mukaber or Jerusalem. There is a medical office in the village for basic care and vaccinations, but for tests, consultations with specialists, births, and operations we have always gone to Jerusalem. Jerusalem is also where we used to do most of our shopping and where most of our residents worked. There are no jobs here. There's not even any land to work, the inclines are too abrupt. Cutting us off from Jerusalem is like depriving us of air, suffocating us. Maybe that's what the Israelis want."

Two years after the installation of this blockade, almost eight hundred residents—25 to 30 percent of the population—have left the village. Most of those who stayed are out of work, living off their savings or off assistance from their families. A report issued by B'Tselem in February 2004 deemed the living conditions in Sheikh Sa'ad "intolerable." "Israel is authorized to limit the movement of the local population in order meet military requirements," wrote the author of the report, Yehezkel Lein. "However, the harshness of the seige on Sheikh Sa'ad and its indeterminate timeframe illustrate an utter indifference to the suffering it has caused in the village, and are a flagrant violation of international law."[2] And the worst was yet to come.

"At the beginning of the summer of 2006," continues Mohammad Abdu as his pack of Marlboros is passed among the villagers assembled in front of the minimarket, "the Israelis decided to post three or four soldiers of the Border Police here day and night. In principle, they are charged with verifying that no one crosses the blockade without authorization. But they are also here to make it understood that it would be best for us to leave. They can make our lives impossible, for example, by throwing deafening grenades into the village in the middle of the night, jolting everyone awake. The presence of the soldiers doesn't change much for people with blue identity cards, technically 'permanent residents' of East Jerusalem. They can cross the blockade by foot and then take a bus, taxi, or even their own car, if it is on the other side, to go to Jerusalem. But this scenario has become rarer, as those with blue cards who had some savings or relatives to help them have already left. For people with orange identity cards, which means that they are officially residents of the West Bank, things are more complicated. They can still travel regularly to Jabel Mukaber or even Jerusalem by slipping between two patrols and avoiding blockades and checkpoints, but it is risky: if caught by the police, you are escorted back to your home and made to sign a document saying that you will no longer leave the village; if you are caught a second time, you could face a fine of one thousand shekels [about €200] and even prison."

There is, in fact, another way to travel in and out of the village without going through the guarded blockade, but it is not for everyone. Upon entering Sheik Sa'ad, you find a little street that runs straight through the village; it becomes a dirt path that then runs out of the village, down a rocky hill, to the bottom of a ravine, then back up the ravine and toward the town of Sawahira a-Sharqiya, where it links up with another road leading to Abu Dis. The ravine is so steep for a few kilometers, and the path so narrow, that it is quite dangerous. The villagers claim to have seen four-by-fours from Bethlehem successfully drive this treacherous route, but no one in Sheikh Sa'ad owns a four-by-four, so they must walk. The terrain is dry and rocky, and the expedition takes at least an hour. It is considered too strenuous for children, pregnant women, the elderly, and anyone in poor health. In the hot summer, the hike is a challenge even for those in good shape, because one must also look out for deadly snakes along the path. In winter, rain turns the dirt into mud, and the journey is just as perilous. This is the path that orange card-carriers of Sheikh Sa'ad must take if they wish to go to the headquarters of the Civil Administration, near the Ma'ale Adumim settlement, to request a permit for entering Jerusalem. Once they have obtained this permit, they must take the same path to get to the Hazeitim terminal, north of Abu Dis, one of the new gates of Jerusalem for visitors coming from the east.

Sheikh Sa'ad is one of seven satellite villages of Jabel Mukaber, which itself became a Palestinian neighborhood of Jerusalem following the Six-Day War. After the occupation of the West Bank and the annexation of East Jerusalem in 1967, the Israeli government unilaterally redrew the boundaries of the Holy City to its liking. The area of the municipal territory grew five times larger, annexing the land of

thirty or so neighboring Palestinian towns and villages. Virtually overnight, many Arab localities on the edge of Jerusalem found themselves to be part of the city, which is what happened to Jabel Mukaber.
Though they were not Israeli citizens, the residents of this big village
were issued blue identity cards, like the Palestinians of East Jerusalem,
and were considered "permanent residents" of Israel. This gave them
access to Israeli schools, health care, and social security, and as with
Israeli citizens, it allowed them to drive with yellow license plates, which
are invaluable for getting around Jerusalem and Israel. All of the smaller
villages bordering Jabel Mukaber were also annexed to Jerusalem,
with the exception of one: Sheikh Sa'ad. Home to almost two thousand Palestinians, why was it not included in the annexation? No one
knows, not even the village's mukhtar,[3] Hussein Eiwisat. Born here in
1939, and today living in an immense shaded house built in a style
common among prominent locals, Eiwisat says that he has never received a convincing explanation for why the village was excluded. He
was director of a hotel under Jordanian administration, and then an
administrator with the Board of Education of Jerusalem, before becoming, since his retirement, a volunteer social worker. Eiwisat prefers
to greet visitors in his living room, and to surround himself with his
sons, sons-in-law, and grandchildren. He explains that for more than a
quarter of a century, the difference in stature between Sheikh Sa'ad and
the neighboring villages was not very important. "Some residents had
blue ID cards, some orange cards from the Occupied Territories. But
who paid any attention to this bureaucratic detail? Everyone came and
went as they pleased and traveled to Jerusalem with no problem. For
us, Sheikh Sa'ad and Jabel Mukaber were the same place, with only a
road between the two." The two villages were actually quite close, and
even had some cultural exchange. For example, just like Jabel Mukaber
and the surrounding villages, Sheikh Sa'ad had adopted the tradition
of hanging white flags from windows and balconies to celebrate local
weddings. The neighboring villages of Jerusalem were all interdepen-
dant for their hospitals, schools, and retail stores. Even the Sheikh
Sa'ad cemetery was in Jerusalem.

The border existed only on paper, until 1991, when it became brutally real on the ground. That is when the trouble started for Sheikh Sa'ad. In its fight against the First Intifada, the Israeli government decided to forbid Palestinians of the Occupied Territories from entering Jerusalem unless they had a permit from the Civil Administration. Then, in March of 1993, six months before the Oslo Accords and the signing of the "Declaration of Principles" in Washington by Yasser Arafat, Yitzhak Rabin, and Shimon Peres, restrictions were greatly tightened. Blockades and checkpoints guarded by the army or Border Police were set up along all roads leading from the West Bank to Jerusalem. All vehicles and passengers were divided into two categories— those with permits and those without—while footpaths, alleyways, and gardens were regularly patrolled to snag people trying to get around the military blockades.

Later, after the explosion of the Second Intifada in September 2000, the bureaucratic requirements for attaining a permit grew ever more byzantine—it was like entering a lottery in which winners were increasingly rare. The Israeli army rejected nearly all permit requests by Palestinians from the West Bank who worked in Jerusalem, citing reasons of security that were never fully explained to the applicants, many of whom lost their jobs. As for the number of permits granted for medical reasons to orange card holders, it has continually decreased since 2000, and the few that are approved are rarely valid for more than twenty-four hours, even if the patients require tests and care over several days.

The residents of Sheikh Sa'ad faced this bureaucratic persecution with a resignation common among Palestinians. "Those who could, moved," says Mohammad Abdu. "As for the rest of us, getting around the blockades and avoiding the patrols day and night has become routine." It was not until September 2002, two years after the blockade was set up at the entrance of the village, that the first stones were thrown at the soldiers. In August 2003, upon learning that the government had approved the construction of a ten-mile wall between Beit Sahour and El-Azariyeh, and that this wall would pass between their village and Jabel Mukaber, the villagers agreed to take nonviolent action to stop it. With the assistance of their lawyer, Ghiath Nasser, a specialist in disputes between Palestinians and the Israeli administration, the village committee of Sheik Sa'ad decided to bring their case against the State of Israel before the District Court of Tel Aviv.

They were surprised to find several residents of the nearby Jewish neighborhoods among their first allies. Outraged by the arbitrary route of the wall, some of the residents of Talpiot, Arnona, Armon, and Hanatziv made financial contributions to the committee and shared their contacts with the Sheikh Sa'ad legal team. They got involved for a range of reasons: political, humanitarian, civic, and personal. Sami Nahmias, who was and born in Talpiot seventy-one years ago and still lives in his childhood home, believed that this was the perfect moment to repay an almost eighty-year debt to the residents of the village. "During the Arab riots of 1929," he explained at a meeting I attended with Sheikh Sa'ad notables, "my grandparents had to abandon their home. Some Arabs from another village were pillaging it when the people of Sheikh Sa'ad called the British police. Everything that had been stolen was returned to my grandfather. Since then, my family has always been on friendly terms with the people of Sheikh Sa'ad."

Despite these acts of solidarity, the odds were very much against the villagers. At the time they filed their case, the courts had heard only two petitions concerning the path of the wall. Both cases were ultimately appealed to the Supreme Court. Neither of those petitions, though, concerned the path of the wall around Jerusalem.

The case was scheduled to be heard before Judge David Gladstein in March of 2006. In the meantime, the Israel Supreme Court heard the case of another Palestinian village to the west of Jerusalem, Beit Surik, whose residents were also supported by their Israeli neighbors, and on June 30, 2004, a historic decision was rendered in that case. Judges Aharon Barak, Eliahu Mazza, and Mishel Cheshin declared the route of the barrier between Beit Surik and the Israeli neighborhood of Mevasseret Zion to be illegal and requested the Ministry of Defense to propose another route that would better balance the "demands of security" and "the legitimate needs of the residents." "Our committee had obviously studied this decision," Hussein Eiwisat recounts, "and our case seemed at least as solid as that of Beit Surik."

At the hearing, Dany Tirza, speaking on behalf of the Ministry of Defense, held to the official line of his administration: that only security considerations had determined the path of the wall in Sheikh Sa'ad. He added that Sheikh Sa'ad is an independent village, and that it never had any legitimate tie to Jerusalem. But then the Sheikh Sa'ad legal team called Amir Heshin as one of their expert witnesses, a retired colonel, like Dany Tirza, and a member of the Council for Peace and Security, an association of former Israeli officers. He was the advisor to the mayor of Jerusalem for Arab affairs from 1984 to 1994, he knew the situation of the village inside and out, and his testimony significantly challenged Dany Tirza's claims. "Sheikh Sa'ad is not an independent village," Heshin explained. "For the municipality of Jerusalem, it has always been considered part of the city. The families are the same, the clans are the same, and anyone looking at a topographical map would immediately see that the village is not tied to any other locality outside of the borders of Jerusalem."

The defense then called its own military man, Colonel (Ret.) Yuval Davir, who also happened to be a member of the Council for Peace and Security. Former commander of the Gaza and North Sinai zones, Davir was known by his colleagues at the Ministry of Defense to be reliable and honest. In response to the security argument, Davir explained that "according to the army's plans, the path of the wall in the region of Sheikh Sa'ad crosses the valley below the village, exposing the soldiers in charge of its protection to threats from above. This is a disastrous choice . . . the residents of Sheikh Sa'ad could bombard the soldiers with eggs from their windows." Confronted with these technical arguments, Dany Tirza was forced to back down. "A wall constructed below the houses is a wall in danger," he ultimately admitted before the judge. "Here we find ourselves confronted by a very problematic weak spot in the path of the wall."

Judge David Gladstein rendered his decision on March 19, 2006: "Sheikh Sa'ad is part of Jabel Mukaber," he wrote, "the center of life for the residents is undisputably Jerusalem. This cannot be arbitrarily changed. As for the route of the wall, it is far from being the most judicious path in terms of guaranteeing security. After we noted the vulnerability of this route and its impact on the residents, we then examined the report on the military and humanitarian impact of the wall and noted that several other routes could have more effectively fulfilled the security imperatives, but that the one chosen was the most damaging to the residents of Sheikh Sa'ad. I advised the Ministry of Defense to choose a new route to the east of Sheikh Sa'ad, one that does not cut ties between the village and Jerusalem, one that allows for the construction of a more efficient and less vulnerable wall."

"More than one hundred and fifty Israelis and Palestinians came to the small party we organized to celebrate the victory," remembers Hussein Eiwisat. "We told each other that this was a good sign. That we were still capable, despite everything, of living side by side in peace as good neighbors. And also that we had to remain vigilant and mobilized, because we had carried the day, but the battle was not finished. The army had decided to go, if necessary, right up to the Supreme Court."

While the army appealed the decision, the siege of Sheikh Sa'ad continued. A labyrinth of iron blue barriers guarded by the police replaced the blockade of cement blocks. A permanent guardpost was put into place, perhaps to impress upon the villagers that this was an uneven fight, one they had no hope of winning.

Graffiti on the wall at Al-Ram in the Jerusalem Envelope. *Courtesy of Mach-somWatch/Tamar Fleishman*

CHAPTER 10

SPARTHEID

The Jerusalem Envelope is a combination of walls and barriers enclosing the Holy City and much of its surrounding territory in a huge clover-shaped agglomeration. When it is finished, it will span ninety-three miles, covering more than nine square miles, and will effectively isolate Jerusalem from the Occupied Territories. "This giant metropolis, which is open to Israel but completely cut off from its Palestinian back country, was in fact part of a plan set forth with the conquest of East Jerusalem in 1967,"[1] says Khalil Toufakji, director of the Map and Survey Department of the Arab Studies Society, a research center with ties to the Palestine Liberation Organization. Toufakji showed me a map of Israel and the West Bank on his wide computer monitor. With the mouse, he traced the Green Line, which has separated Israel from the West Bank since 1949, and which, theoretically, cuts Jerusalem into two parts. Toufakji knows the twists and turns of the wall and the barrier around Jerusalem perhaps almost as well as Dany Tirza, but from a Palestinian point of view. Born in Jerusalem in 1950 and educated in Syria and in the United States, he has tirelessly observed and documented the process of settlement. From 1992 to 2001, he was the cartographer of the Palestinian delegation during its periodic negotiations with representatives from the Israeli government. In 2003, he was one of the architects of the Geneva Accords. Currently he resides in a shaded house in the middle-class neighborhood of Wadi al-Joz, with his wife, Joumana. He would like to see his four

successful children continue to live in Jerusalem as citizens of an independent Palestinian state. At the same time, though, he fully understands the strong temptation for them to one day emigrate to Canada
or Australia.

While the peace process initially ignited his optimism, lately his
mood has soured. It has been difficult for him even to keep the Arab
Studies Society offices open because the government has forced him
repeatedly to relocate, which illustrates the absurd, almost comic degree of bureaucratic entanglement and outright harassment endured
by residents of Jerusalem with ties to the Palestinian Authority or
the PLO. When it was founded in 1983, the Arab Studies Society was
based in a wing of the Orient House, a stone building erected in 1897
(the year of the First Zionist Congress in Bale) by the rich and powerful Husseini family. In 1988, Yitzhak Rabin, then defense minister,
ordered the Orient House, which had become a political and diplomatic
symbol of Palestinian presence in Jerusalem, to be closed. Toufakji
moved the organization to a building that was still under construction
in the Sheikh Jarrah neighborhood. But when the Jerusalem Envelope
broke ground, his colleagues found it increasingly difficult to travel to
the new office, and they were forced to move again, this time near the
intersection of Al-Ram, to the north of town. The front door of his office now opens upon an endless wall of cement that cuts the Jerusalem-
Ramallah Highway in two (half of the highway is in the West Bank,
and the other half is in Israel). "Getting out of Jerusalem is very easy;
getting back in has become a challenge," Toufakji says. "In the morning, it takes me fifteen minutes to get to the office, but then two to
three hours to get back home at the end of the day, because of checkpoint delays.

"Since they took the city, the Israelis have not stopped expanding
the municipal boundaries, at the expense of the Palestinian territories
on the outskirts of the city. The city has grown from approximately
twenty-four square miles in 1967, to sixty-six square miles today. In
other words, more than twenty-six square miles of the West Bank have
been annexed. On this land, the municipality has constructed a dozen
clusters of residential buildings that the Israelis call 'Jewish neighbor-

hoods,' but are defined under international law as 'settlements,' because they were built east of the Green Line. These settlements, where more than one hundred and eighty thousand Israelis live, have broken up the Palestinian part of the city into fragments, and have paralyzed its development. There have been a slew of regulations aimed at discouraging Palestinian residents from buying, constructing, or renovating their homes in East Jerusalem, while at the same time, West Jerusalem and Israeli settlements in East Jerusalem have fruitfully developed thanks to a steady flow of municipal credit loans." The Jerusalem daily *Kol Ha'Ir* compared the city's Arab neighborhoods (185,000 residents) and Jewish neighborhoods (460,000 residents) in 2005. According to their study, the Jewish neighborhoods have access to six times as many social workers, twenty-four times as many green spaces, fifteen times more playgrounds, and ten times the number of public benches than the Arab neighborhoods. As for the budget outlays for social services, $3.5 million has been allocated for Jewish neighborhoods, as opposed to $530,000 for Arab ones.[2]

"The guiding principle of those responsible for the 1967 annexations was simple," surmises Menachem Klein, former advisor to Ehud Barak and a political science professor at Bar-Ilan University: "it was to add territory to the city while keeping the Palestinian population as low as possible—the objective was to maintain a Jewish majority in Jerusalem."[3] Menachem Klein is a specialist on the question of Jerusalem, but not one of the so-called peace-loving "dove" intellectuals afraid to actually venture into East Jerusalem. A longtime supporter of negotiations with the Palestinians, Klein is a devout Jew who is equally at ease in trendy cafés in the German Colony and Palestinian bars in Sheikh Jarrah. He has eagerly thrown himself into politics whenever he felt that he could contribute to building peace. An advisor to the minister of foreign affairs, Shlomo Ben-Ami, and to Prime Minister Ehud Barak during the Camp David and Taba negotiations, he became one of the architects of the Geneva Accords. "We are in this current situation because every government for the past forty years has pursued the same 1967 strategy," he insists. "One of the results has been a chain of settlements designed to contain the growth of the

Palestinian population. When Sharon was prime minister, he further destroyed the urban coherence of East Jerusalem by cutting off this part of the city from the West Bank—in other words, from its natural Arab environment. However, contrary to those who came before him, Sharon didn't want to change the demography of the city; he simply wanted to control the Palestinians, to impose the superiority of the Jewish Jerusalem over the Arab Jerusalem by force. The most appropriate name for this policy could be 'Spartheid,' apartheid achieved with Spartan tactics! If this plan is carried to completion, two hundred and fifty thousand Palestinians of East Jerusalem—one in ten residents of the West Bank—will be cut off from their social, political, economic, cultural, and linguistic 'hinterland.' "

RETIRED COLONEL SHAUL ARIELI, DIRECTOR OF THE ECONOMIC COOPeration Foundation and of the Council for Peace and Security, has also studied at length the possible "final status" of Jerusalem. "The strategy since 1967," he says, "consisted essentially of annexing Palestinian territories to Jerusalem to ensure the city's development, to separate Jerusalem from the West Bank, and to push back the municipal boundaries beyond the hills that encircle the city. The real objective was to make any future division of Jerusalem impossible."[4]

Seven years before Binyamin Ben-Eliezer broke ground on the first section of the barrier to the north of the West Bank, B'Tselem had already denounced the "policy of discrimination" pursued by the Israeli government in Jerusalem. In the conclusion of a well-documented report edited by Eitan Felner, B'Tselem outlines its indictment of the policies of the municipal governments of Jerusalem since 1967, policies that have had the unequivocal support of the State. "A single objective has guided Jerusalem's urban planning," writes Felner, "namely to strengthen Israeli control over the whole of the city. This goal is manifest in the creation of a demographic and political reality that has established Israeli sovereignty in East Jerusalem. While the Israeli authorities launched massive construction programs, invested an enormous amount of money in the Jewish neighborhoods of East Jerusalem, and encouraged Jews to move into those neighborhoods, they choked off, by act or omission, urban development programs for Palestinians—perceived as a 'demographic danger'—threatening Israeli control over the city. The Israeli authorities use all legal and administrative means at their disposal to advance policies that are in flagrant violation of international law and fundamental principles of democracy, and these policies have had serious consequences for human rights."[5]

"East Jerusalem could one day become the capital of a Palestinian State," says Khalil Toufakji, "and that idea is unacceptable to the majority of Israeli politicians. Consider from that angle the development of city policy, urban planning, and, today, the path of the wall. Even if the Oslo Accords were no more constraining on this point than on many others, successive governments, along with the municipality of Jerusalem, have done everything they can to eliminate this risk. With the wall and the barrier, they must think that they have at last achieved their aims. They don't seem to realize that Jerusalem is the center of *our* political, cultural, religious, and economic life, too. A sacred and symbolic place, it is as important to us as it is to them."

In 1950, the Knesset had issued a resolution proclaiming Jerusalem the capital of Israel. Two years later, upon the death of the first president, Chaim Weizmann, his successor, Yitzhak Ben-Zvi, one of the founders of the Labor Party, moved the presidential residence to Jerusalem. In July of 1953, the Ministry of Foreign Affairs also moved to the Holy City. Today, all primary state institutions—with the exception of the Ministry of Defense—are located in Jerusalem. However, because the United Nations Security Council rejected the "reunification" in a 1980 resolution, the embassies of countries with diplomatic ties to Israel have remained in Tel Aviv.

The bizarre shape of the Jerusalem Envelope, as drawn by the Ministry of Defense, is in many ways a reflection of Israel's annexation and settlement policies over the last forty years. To the northwest, about six miles from the heart of Jerusalem, the barrier makes a large loop around the Givat Ze'ev settlement and its satellites, where more than thirteen thousand Israelis live. This pocket annexes eighteen square miles of Palestinian land for the extension of Greater Jerusalem (already expanded by thirty-two square miles in 1967 at the expense of the West Bank), and is aimed at making room for the future development of the settlements it contains, as shown in the blueprints of Ze'ev and Givon Hadasha. Nabi Samuel, a "metropolitan park" to be built on the edge of Highway 437, is one of these projects. The annexed pocket is also home to the huge Ofer military base at the edge of Ramallah, and a long section of Highway 443 that links Jerusalem to Tel Aviv by the West Bank. The barrier cuts off eight Palestinian agricultural villages located west of the pocket from part of their land.

In the beginning, more than twelve square miles of this land—43 percent of the cultivatable land of the villages—was located on the "Israeli" side of the barrier. But following legal action taken by the residents of Beit Surik, the Supreme Court ordered on June 30, 2004, that eighteen miles of the barrier must be redrawn to accommodate the Palestinian petitions. Seven months later, on January 30, 2005, the Israeli army proposed a path that annexed "no more than 6.5 square miles" of their land, and then quickly sent in the bulldozers. Encouraged by the success of their first legal endeavor, the residents of Beit Surik took the State back to court, but this time in vain. On March 6, 2005, the judges rejected their petition, and the bulldozers once again took over the hills.

TODAY, THE GIVAT ZE'EV POCKET MAKES UP A LARGE A PART OF THE "SEcurity reinforcement" between Jerusalem and Ramallah, and establishes territorial continuity between the annexed lands in the northwest of Jerusalem and the city center, via the "urban settlement" of Ramot Allon and Golda Meir Boulevard (see map of Jerusalem). According to many Palestinians, it is a glaring example of the multiple land thefts for which construction of the barrier has served as a pretext. Local officials and human rights activists also note that inside this meandering barrier, which encloses not only settlements but also Palestinian villages, the roads are reserved for Israelis and not accessible to Palestinian travelers. According to the military, the close proximity of Palestinians gives the settlers an "insecure feeling." So the army has created this enclave, surrounded by a wall approximately nine miles long, between nine and fifteen feet high. The enclave contains five villages with a total population of approximately fifteen thousand Palestinians. A number of them hold Jerusalem "permanent resident" cards, which, theoretically, guarantee them open access to the city. The people of "the ghetto of Bir Nabala," as a brochure from the PLO Negotiations Affairs Department calls it, are, in fact, completely cut off from the majority of their land, and from the surrounding Palestinian cities as well, notably Ramallah and East Jerusalem.

Bir Nabala, itself a sizeable town of more than 6,000 Palestinians, with 350 artisan shops and small businesses, is slipping into widespread bankruptcy because travel outside its bounds is considerably interrupted or delayed. The residents also fear the disastrous consequences the closure of the enclave will have on their educational system. Some teachers from Bir Nabala come from neighboring villages and East Jerusalem, and nearly all students are registered in the universities of East Jerusalem. To the south of the enclave, the village of Beit Hanina Al-Balad (1,400 residents) will be cut in two by the wall—the girls' school will be on one side, and the boys' school, along with the rest of the village, will be on the other. The same problems are expected in terms of health care: once the barrier is completed, the only accessible hospital will be in Ramallah, which is already overcrowded and incapable of offering the same quality of care as the big hospitals in East Jerusalem. The Israeli army announced that it had planned to build two access routes to the enclave, one to the north, toward Ramallah, and the other to the southwest, toward the neighboring Palestinian villages of the Givat Ze'ev pocket. But these roads cannot be built without two tunnels being dug under Highways 45 and 437, and the construction of three bridges. The road toward Ramallah is open. The other, which will cost tens of millions of shekels,[6] will apparently not open anytime soon.

FOLLOWING THE PATH OF THE BARRIER ON THE GROUND, AS IT SNAKES through the rocky hills of the West Bank, is not easy. On the Israeli side, the patrol routes along the finished sections are off-limits to civilians, and access to them depends largely on the goodwill of the guards. Suffice it to say that they do not inspire one to commit acts of disobedience or to trespass. Any section where the barrier is under construction is usually considered a "military zone," even when construction sites are guarded by Druzee or Arab-Israelis rather than Israeli soldiers. Here there is no possibility of negotiating passage. The dogs are even more menacing than the soldiers' Uzis.

It is equally difficult to follow along the wall on the Palestinian side, again due to the heavily guarded construction sites. Reaching the barrier itself is difficult. After the suppression of the Second Intifada, the Israeli army erected several clay-and-cement roadblocks, or dug ditches across most roads. A number of villages are now accessible only by a single road, and many others are cut off. Traveling by foot, with a good road map and a local guide, is the best way to take in the barrier. This allows one to compare the maps provided by the Israeli army's cartography department with those of the United Nations Office for the Coordination of Humanitarian Affairs, and to examine the real reasons for the detours and zigzags of the barrier's route.

First, the loop around Givat Ze'ev annexes more than eighteen square miles of Palestinian land. Then, to the east, the barrier forms another loop designed to keep Kafr Aqab and the Qalandiya refugee camp outside of Jerusalem—since the First Intifada, these areas have been considered "difficult" by the Israeli military. South of the Qalandiya camp, the wall runs parallel to the municipal boundary of Jerusalem and effectively cuts off the towns of Al-Ram and Dahiyat Al-Barid (sixty-three thousand residents) from the city, and thereby from Jerusalem, even though half of the population of this area holds permanent residency cards for Jerusalem.

"To cut us off from Jerusalem is to suffocate our city," says Mohammad Aslan, executive director of the town council of Al-Ram, whose office is filled with irate shop owners and parents. "We no longer have any space for development, especially since the Israelis forbid construction less than nine hundred feet from the wall. And where are the fifteen thousand students from Al-Ram who have registered at schools or universities in Jerusalem supposed to study? At least twenty percent of our citizens with blue cards have moved to Jerusalem, or plan on moving soon. What's going to become of this city?"[7] .

"More than five hundred and fifty shop owners are on the verge of closing, says Assad Maslamawi, director of the Al-Ram Chamber of Commerce. "And to go where? With what money? Stores that were worth one hundred thousand dollars are now lucky to sell for thirty thousand!" In 2004, representatives from Al-Ram presented a petition to the Israeli Supreme Court requesting that the wall be moved east in recognition of Al-Ram's multiple ties with Jerusalem. On June 28, 2004, the judges ruled that the army must find another route for the section of the wall surrounding Al-Ram and Dahiyat Al-Barid. Construction immediately came to a halt, and Al-Ram had won what seemed like a historic victory. But the following August, at the Qalandiya checkpoint, two Palestinians were killed and six Israeli Border Police soldiers injured by the explosion of a thirty-three-pound bomb hidden in the baby carriage of a suicide bomber. We were back to square one, and a few days later, the bulldozers returned and construction began on the wall along the original path. Two years later, representatives from Al-Ram and Qalandiya joined a petition to the Supreme Court filed by the villagers of Bir Nabala and three other towns requesting a suspension of the wall's construction—again, the petition was rejected. On April 18, 2006, the Court determined that the Palestinian freedom of movement in the region had been ensured by this last version of the path, and that the state could continue with the construction of the barrier and of the wall.

To the south of Al-Ram, the wall's path wanders again from the municipal boundaries of Jerusalem and loops around land set aside for the expansion of the Neve Ya'akov settlement, before it returns to the border of Greater Jerusalem, leaving the Palestinian neighborhood of Hizma to the east of the wall. Then, south of the Givat Ze'ev settlement, the wall makes a deep three-mile loop into Jerusalem territory. Why the detour? Clearly, to exclude Anata and Dahiyat Al-

Salam from East Jerusalem, keeping them in the West Bank. The section also keeps the small town of Shufat on the western (Jerusalem) side of the wall, but places Shufat's refugee camp on the eastern (West Bank) side. More than ten thousand Palestinians, officially registered by the United Nations as refugees, live in Shufat. The oldest among them were chased out of their villages by the Israelis in 1948, and found refuge in Jerusalem; then, when the city was taken over in 1967, they were placed in the Shufat camp. The youngest refugees are now confronted with a difficult choice: either stay in Shufat and lose their 'resident' rights in Jerusalem, or leave and attempt to find affordable housing in East Jerusalem. To facilitate travel in and out of Shufat, the Israeli army has expanded and modernized the checkpoint at the camp. In February 2005, a requisition order for 7.5 acres was presented to the owners of the neighboring properties to accommodate the expansion. In spring 2006, it was opened to Palestinian pedestrians and drivers with blue identity cards, and to West Bank Palestinians with permits issued by the army.

According to the United Nations, in Spring 2007, a total of thirteen passage points controlled the movement of people and goods from one side of the barrier to the other. Only four of these points around Jerusalem were accessible to Palestinians holding proper permits. Seven were reserved for Israeli citizens. Three other passage points were under construction or in the planning stages. In January 2008, the OCHA released a statement, reporting that the number of passage points had not changed: eleven of these passages, which resembled regular border crossings, were open to Palestinians and humanitarian workers; five others served as commercial terminals, equipped with X-ray mechanisms to inspect vehicle content, and were reserved for trucks carrying goods from one side of the barrier to the other. A sixth commercial terminal was under construction in Mazmouria, to the southeast of Jerusalem.

The wall and the barrier had made it nearly impossible for the majority of Palestinians to travel between the West Bank and Israel, and Jerusalem—the historical heart of Palestine and the Holy City for both Christians and Muslims—was all but completely out of reach.

At the end of September 2008, a United Nations document stated that 60 percent of the Palestinian population was not authorized to go to the al-Aqsa mosque in Jerusalem during Ramadan. Entry for Friday prayer was restricted to men over 50 years old, women over 45, and children under 12. Special permits, valid for the four Fridays of Ramadan, were issued, but only available to men between 45 and 50 years old and women 30 to 45 who were married with children and had been approved by security services. Everyone else was denied access to Jerusalem.

The proliferation of checkpoints, barriers, and diverse obstacles inside the West Bank, along with the permit system imposed on Palestinians—all of which are a direct result of the barrier—have ravaged the Palestinian economy. The unemployment rate in the West Bank jumped from 16.9% in 2000 to 25.2% in 2007. In addition, the Central Bureau of Statistics of the Palestinian Authority calculated that Palestinian GDP declined by 10% between 2006 and 2007, and 10% more between 2007 and 2008. The situation of the Palestinian economy was so disastrous at the beginning of 2008 that close to 800,000 West Bank residents needed United Nations food assistance.

The Ma'ale Adumim settlement. *Courtesy of Brave New Alps/Bianca Elzenbaumer and Fabio Franz*

CHAPTER 11

THE E-1 FILE

Since 1975, when the Ma'ale Adumim settlement was established by Yitzhak Rabin along a rocky spur about four miles from Jerusalem, the majority of Israeli governments have harbored a desire to unite the heavily populated settlements of the West Bank with the Holy City, making one continuous territory. By 1994, Ma'ale Adumim's population had swollen to more than fifteen thousand, and Rabin, who had returned to power two years earlier, decided to examine how to establish this "continuity" using land within the municipal boundaries of Ma'ale Adumim. He apparently saw no contradiction between this initiative and the Oslo Accords he had just signed with Yasser Arafat, which had required both parties to preserve the "integrity and the status" of the West Bank and the Gaza Strip during an "intermediary period," while the final status of the land was being negotiated.

On November 4, 1995, Rabin was assassinated in Tel Aviv by a young orthodox Jewish fanatic. At that time, the Ministry of Housing and Construction had only just begun to develop a general urban planning arrangement for Jerusalem, in which land to be annexed for territorial continuity, called East-1, or E-1, had been earmarked. Spread out over a dozen square miles around the eastern slope of Mount Scopus and the surrounding highlands, the pieces of land that made up E-1 were not exactly an urban planner's dream. They largely comprised inhospitable rocky hills, escarpments, and ravines. But the architects of territorial continuity had already built 120 settlements on similar terrain throughout the West Bank. In 1997, less than a year after having been elected prime minister, the head of Likud, Binyamin Netanyahu, who, as it happens, was also housing minister, aggressively supported territorial continuity between Jerusalem and Ma'ale Adumim. He asked his people to begin the process of designating the tracts of lands for future use, and to prepare a more detailed outline of the project. Ehud Barak, who succeeded Netanyahu in May 1999, continued in this vein.

The E-1 project was well under way by the time Ariel Sharon took office in February 2001. According to his colleagues, Sharon had traveled high and low throughout the West Bank in his Jeep, and knew the terrain very well. He certainly recognized the political and strategic importance of this project, but also its potentially embarrassing diplomatic implications. Responsibility for the administration of the project rested with the minister of housing and construction, who at that time was former Russian dissident Natan Sharansky, a passionate supporter of the settlements. In reality, the project was directly controlled by Sharon. The plans included an industrial park, a dozen hotels and shopping centers, buildings planned for a possible university, a cemetery, and thirty-five hundred apartments to house the fifteen thousand new settlement inhabitants—all of which would break ground over an area of approximately eight square miles. It would be an impressive feat of landscaping and construction. The police headquarters, which had been located in the Palestinian suburb of Ras al-Amud, would be moved to E-1 and become the centerpiece of the new settlement.

Two years later, the plans had still not been officially approved by the government. Nonetheless, General (Ret.) Effie Eitam, from the National Religious Party, who had succeeded Sharansky as housing minister, authorized construction to begin on an access road and supporting wall, with Sharon's approval. The bulldozers broke ground, and the E-1 project officially became a construction site.

In the meantime, the prime minister had allowed construction of the security barrier to proceed through the spring of 2002. The first maps of the barrier are not explicit about how the land between East Jerusalem and Ma'ale Adumim would be developed, but they do show the barrier making a large loop around the settlement, which is home to more than twenty-five thousand people.

In the opinion of Dany Tirza, who lives in one of the satellite communities of Ma'ale Adumim, the most heavily populated settlements of the West Bank[1] naturally should be integrated into Greater Jerusalem—any other course would be unthinkable. The final route of the barrier is not quite that expansive, but it does annex nearly forty square miles of Palestinian territory to Jerusalem. The Ma'ale Adumim loop is nineteen miles long, wrapping around Kafar Adumim, which is almost five miles west of Jericho and eight miles east of the Green Line. In other words, it runs right through the narrowest section of the West Bank, cutting the territory of the future Palestinian state nearly in two, like a wedge. And it includes, as planned, the E-1 zone.

For Palestinians, welding Jerusalem to Ma'ale Adumim and its satellites via E-1 is a form of aggression, and stands as perhaps *the* major obstacle to restarting the peace process. Geographer Khalil Toufakji affirms: "Not only does this enormous extension of Jerusalem toward the east cut off all the roads joining the north and south of the West Bank, it also deprives us of land that is full of promise for true economic development. If the project is completed, the two halves of the Palestinian part of Jerusalem will be completely separated, with no growth potential, and the viability of the future Palestinian State will be seriously threatened." As the maps discussed in Taba and Geneva show, the Palestinians have not excluded the possibility that some settlements may be annexed to Israel in a future peace agreement. But, according to their principal negotiator, Saeb Erekat, they cannot accept an "annexation that cuts their state in two."[2]

In a scathing November 2005 report on East Jerusalem, the heads of the diplomatic missions of the European Union in Jerusalem and Ramallah dedicated an entire page of their eight-page report to the E-1 project. After noting that the "barrier is not motivated solely by security concerns" and that it "separates Palestinians from other Palestinians," the document's authors confirm that the E-1 project and the barrier together "encircle the city with Jewish settlements, dividing the West Bank into two separate geographical areas." They go on to note that "the economic prospects of the West Bank—where the [per capita] GDP is less than $1,000 per year—are heavily dependant on access to East Jerusalem—where the [per capita] GDP is closer to $3,500 per year. From an economic perspective, the viability of a Palestinian state depends to a great extent on the preservation of organic links between East Jerusalem, Ramallah, and Bethlehem."

The European diplomats concluded that "the prospects for a two-state solution with East Jerusalem as the capital of Palestine are receding" and suggested that their governments clearly reaffirm that "Jerusalem remain subject to negotiation." This document was intended for the ministers of foreign affairs of the European Union. But it did not lead, as some of its authors had hoped, to a reevaluation of relations between Europe and Israel. Due to profound differences among member states, the report will never be made public. The Italian and German governments, as well as the high representative for the Common Foreign and Security Policy, Javier Solana of Spain, believe that the report is not balanced, and that Europe's influence on Israel would be compromised if it were published. Several European Union governments, in fact, refuse to assume the political consequences of open opposition to Israel.

Three years later, in December 2008, another report by the European Union diplomatic community confirmed the statements and conclusions of the first report, and again it was suppressed for political reasons.

The Bush administration, however, always a close friend of Israel, had little enthusiasm for the E-1 project. Since the Clinton days, the State Department had been reticent about the plan for territorial continuity between Ma'ale Adumim and Jerusalem advanced by successive Israeli prime ministers. While it was assumed in Washington that international laws and agreements put into effect since 1997 made E-1 untenable, Israel continued with the project. Six years after the Clinton administration insisted that Binyamin Netanyahu put a halt to E-1, Secretary of State Condoleezza Rice visited the area and was furious to find construction well under way. At the time, Rice was strongly opposed to this project.[3] For several months after Rice's visit, the objections of the Bush administration delayed both construction of the barrier around Ma'ale Adumim and work on E-1, but did not succeed in stopping it completely.

One year earlier, at the beginning of 2005, the settlement town council had announced its intention to build a residential community and a police headquarters in E-1, assuming that these lands were under its authority. In August, the project was presented to the residents of Ma'ale Adumim for their approval. They were invited to give their opinions to the municipal council in writing or by speaking at a council meeting—all of which was really a matter of legal procedure before the project could be officially approved. At the same time, the Israeli army confiscated more than 390 acres of land belonging to the towns of El-Azariyeh, Abu Dis, and Sawahira a-Sharqiya, in order to build the southern part of the barrier around Ma'ale Adumim. Judging by the army's maps, and the location of the land seized from Palestinians in the area, the barrier surrounds not only the settlement, but additional land for its extension, including E-1. The route and general design of the section of the barrier were given the green light by Attorney General Menachem Mazuz.[4]

Would Ariel Sharon, who was not known for his patience or flexibility, find a way to implement the E-1 project without provoking the United States? In a word, yes. The former soldier seemed deaf to voices in his own government who advised him not to anger Washington. He listened instead to Binyamin Netanyahu, the settlers, and to his base on the Right, in order to regain the helm of the Likud Party. As early as spring 2005, Sharon set in place a plan to disassociate the construction of the new West Bank police headquarters—an essential security policy—from that of the residential buildings. That September, while Israel was evacuating settlers from the Gaza Strip, Ehud Olmert, who was deputy prime minister at the time, confirmed in an interview with the *Jerusalem Post* that, in accordance with a request from the U.S. government, Israel would "not build between Jerusalem and Ma'ale Adumim" and that "the contested project—including E-1—was indefinitely on hold." But, he added, "it is clear that at a certain point in the future, Israel will create continuity between Jerusalem and Ma'ale Adumim, and in the end, we will have to build the project."[5] Olmert did not, however, delay construction of the new police headquarters, a sign that the E-1 project was in fact progressing. Olmert stated that the headquarters would "help to combat illegal Palestinian construction in the vicinity, construction which could prevent the future realization of the plan."

Just as Sharon had imagined, Washington looked the other way as the new police headquarters of the West Bank broke ground. It would have been difficult for anyone to contest its construction—advertised as vital to Israel's security—when, at the same time, Israel was retreating from the Gaza Strip under a wave of international approval.

On January 5, 2006, Sharon had his second stroke and was replaced in the interim by Ehud Olmert, who went on to become prime minister in the March 2006 elections. He continued on Sharon's path, correctly assuming that the Bush administration, preoccupied by chaos in Iraq and the Iranian nuclear threat, would not forcefully oppose a police station.

In spring 2006, a hundred or so local Palestinian workers from the Hebron region were recruited, and they began setting the foundation for the four-story building. Given the unstable political circumstances, time was short. Divided into three teams, the Palestinians worked around the clock, in eight-hour shifts. It had to be finished by spring 2007. By August of that year, not only was the building completed, but so was its parking lot and many of the access roads between the station and the Israel road network.

Construction of the barrier around Ma'ale Adumim had slowed down through 2006 at the request of the government's legal counsel, who hoped to avoid challenges in the Supreme Court, but it was now back on track.

When the Jerusalem Envelope is completed, how will a Palestinian from Bethlehem travel to Ramallah or Nablus? The traditional route between the north and south of the West Bank is through Jerusalem. Or so it used to be. Since 2001, the Holy City has been off-limits to Palestinians from the West Bank and Gaza who do not have a permit. To get around it, travelers must take a long and dangerous path along narrow mountain passes. This path is controlled by a checkpoint, which has been accessible to authorized travelers only since 2002. This same path passes between East Jerusalem and Ma'ale Adumim, straight across E-1—and who knows whether it will still be there in the years to come.

"Of course we have thought of that," says Netzah Mashiah, director of the Seam Line Administration, which is in charge of the barrier at the Ministry of Defense. "We are going to build a north–south road to the east of Abu Dis. It will cross under the Jerusalem–Ma'ale Adumim Highway via a tunnel. Yes, we are going to invest two billion shekels[6] in this project. It will give the Palestinians a road network that is much better than the one in the Jerusalem region today. We're crazy, aren't we? But we believe the economy in the Palestinian territories should be developed, and better ties among the different regions will help to make that happen."[7] As construction of the barrier around Ma'ale Adumim continues to make steady progress, this ambitious road project has, for the moment, stalled. According to a map of areas under Palestinian control drafted in April 2007 by the Israeli army,[8] the proposed route around Ma'ale Adumim to the east, linking the north and south of the West Bank, is still being studied. The map does show, however, a future highway just over nine miles long running parallel to the barrier around Ma'ale Adumim that connects conveniently to the Jerusalem–Jericho Highway. The same map shows a 10.5-mile road connecting the Jordan Valley to the Ramallah region, and another one linking Bethlehem to Zayem, east of Jerusalem. But there are no roads planned for north of E-1.

GUSH ETZION IS A SETTLEMENT OF THIRTY THOUSAND PEOPLE JUST SOUTH of Jerusalem. Many Israelis believe that it should be annexed to the State of Israel, like Ariel, Alfei Menashe, Modi'in, and Ma'ale Adumim. The barrier's path goes around this block of settlements to the east and south, thus blocking all development in this direction from Bethlehem. Gush Etzion makes up the southern leaf of the clover-shaped Jerusalem Envelope. Already enlarged by 18.6 square miles of

Palestinian land with the annexation of Givat Ze'ev, and 37 square miles by that of Ma'ale Adumim and E-1, Jerusalem would grow another 45 square miles with the addition of Gush Etzion.

Current maps of the barrier running between the Holy City and Gush Etzion do not lie. Much like the section of the barrier that runs close to the Green Line between the villages of Al-Walaja and Wadi Fukin, this section also promises to facilitate easy travel for Israeli citizens between Gush Etzion and Jerusalem on Route 60. The Palestinians, however, do not have access to this highway, which is lined with a bulletproof wall running along the border of the annexed enclave.

"We live in the countryside, but it feels like a suburb of Jerusalem," says Gershon Barak, who runs a garage in Kfar Etzion, a religious kibbutz fifteen kilometers south of the Holy City. Kfar Etzion was destroyed by the Arab League in 1948 and reconstructed after 1967 as the first settlement of the West Bank. "My wife loves classical music," Barak says. "We're fifteen minutes from the concert halls of Jerusalem and an hour and a half from the Tel Aviv Opera." He admits to having "never believed" in Oslo, and is against the barrier, but not out of sympathy for his Palestinian neighbors—"if they had the chance," he says, "they'd come back and massacre us like in 1948"—but rather because the barrier is expensive and complicates land use. The kibbutz is home to a factory that produces high-tech armored plating, used by the U.S. Army in Iraq and Afghanistan. They also cultivate cherries, pears, nectarines, flowers, wheat, and cotton, and raise turkeys, on land that it possesses outside of its boundaries—this, in fact, makes up much of its economy.

The Etzion Bloc includes not only a dozen Israeli settlements, but seven Palestinian villages as well, where an estimated twenty thousand people live. Barak's Arab neighbors share his opposition to the barrier, but for different reasons. Their agricultural land is partly on one side of the barrier and partly on the other, and soon several villagers living east of the Etzion Bloc will have to cross the barrier in order to get to work, receive medical care, or to do their shopping in Bethlehem. The future does not look bright for Palestinians living in this region.

Still, the problems that villagers face using the barrier's agricultural gates are nothing compared to those of West Bank residents trying to cross into the new "Fort Jerusalem." In principle, when the Jerusalem Envelope is finished, between eleven and thirteen passage points will allow travelers holding a permit to enter or leave Jerusalem around the clock. This is what Dany Tirza is promising. These passage points will no longer be checkpoints guarded by soldiers, but rather will resemble airport terminals, he says, with military personnel completely tucked out of sight.

In spring 2006, four of these terminals were either operational or under construction. From the outside, they resemble airplane hangars or garages rather than airports. Inside, the walls are, yes, painted in bright colors—yellow, blue, orange—and waiting rooms with vending machines are planned, but an airport, even a basic one, is not the first comparison that comes to mind. All efforts have been made to prevent contact between travelers and terminal agents, but this has less to do with safeguarding the dignity of the former than protecting the safety of the latter. From behind bulletproof glass, the personnel—today, soldiers and police officers; tomorrow, apparently, security company employees—inspect the identity papers of travelers and look them up in computer databases. Loudspeakers are used to communicate with travelers, who are tracked with cameras from the moment they set foot in the terminal.

Airplane terminals usually do not require passengers to queue up in narrow steel-grilled corridors with remote-control turnstiles that allow only one traveler to pass through at a time. Security measures are in place to contain anyone who appears suspicious or who may be carrying an explosive—should someone detonate a bomb, there would be minimal damage—to the terminal. Checkpoint relations between the Israeli military and the Palestinians remain much the same as they were before, but with more modern security measures, and an arbitrary tone of politeness. "Welcome to Hazeitim Checkpoint," reads a sign in Arabic, Hebrew, and English, at this passage point into East Jerusalem. "You are entering a military zone. To facilitate your passage and to avoid a useless waste of time, read and follow these instructions. Please prepare your identity papers for inspection and proceed to the first available inspection window. Follow the instructions of the inspectors. Proceed one by one. Please keep this terminal clean. Have a good day."

For security reasons, Palestinian vehicles are no longer allowed to enter Israel, except for humanitarian purposes.[9] It is now impossible for a resident of Bethlehem, for example, to drive to Jerusalem, fill her car up with goods, and drive back. Drivers from the West Bank must leave their cars in the terminal parking lot, cross the terminal by foot— if they have a permit—and, on the other side, take one of the new buses from there into the city. The ticket costs 1.5 shekels. The bus drivers, carefully chosen and trained by Israeli security services, are responsible for verifying that their passengers have the required permits, and will lose their license should they make any error.

When I asked Netzahe Mashiah if he found all of this oppressive, he seemed shocked. "I don't see the problem. After they cross the terminal, the Palestinians find quick, cheap buses that will bring them anywhere they want in town. Everyone complains about not being able to find parking in Jerusalem. They no longer have to worry about it."

A checkpoint at the Qalqilya Gate. *Courtesy of Gary Fields*

CHAPTER 12

THE GOOD SIDE OF THE BARRIER

Do you want me to tell you why Ariel is on the good side of the barrier?" asks Ron Nachman, founder of the Ariel settlement, and its mayor since 1985. "Because when I created this community with forty pioneer families back in 1977, I had that barrier in mind."[1]

Ron Nachman, who is not exactly a mirthful man, squinted and almost smiled, as though he did not expect me to believe what he was saying. Once a member of the Likud Party under Sharon as its leader, Nachman was a fierce defender of the settlements, and to this day remains a staunch advocate for connecting large blocks of settlements to Israel. Negotiating with the Palestinians? He does not believe in it, and never has. As he has said for more than thirty years: "It's a waste of time. We're not going to give them land they never had."

He is not afraid to fight for his cause on politically hostile terrain. In his opinion, even calling the territories that have been occupied since 1967 the "West Bank" is too much of a concession; he never does, and rarely even says the word "Palestinian." The residents of Salfit and the villages surrounding Ariel are "Arabs." Nachman never says, "I disagree," but rather, "You are mistaken," and when he approves of what he hears, he responds with a "correct"—all in a tone that leaves little room for debate.

The six-line biography provided by his office states that he has diplomas in political science, law, and labor organization from the University of Tel Aviv; that he worked for thirteen years in the Israeli

Military Industries, a large national organization where he was assistant director-general of research and development; and that from 1983 to 1985, he was vice-president of the Israel Broadcasting Authority, the body that controls public radio and television. Regarding his military service—standard information on any Israeli résumé—there is not a word. According to the Knesset's website, Nachman left the army as a sergeant—a rather modest career, in a country where political leaders are often plucked from the military elite.

Nachman may lack military stripes and medals, but his heritage is highly patriotic. Originally from Odessa, his relatives arrived in the region in 1883, fourteen years before the First Zionist Congress in Bale, and were among the founding residents of Nes Ziona, a city southwest of Tel Aviv. Nachman's father became deputy mayor of Nes Ziona, where the Israeli army also chose to build its research center for bacterial and chemical weapons.

"Yes, I am a fourth-generation Sabra,"[2] proclaims this sturdy man with a large and expressive Coppertone face, as he looks out of his office window at the line of hills separating Ariel from the Palestinian city of Salfit. "How many sixty-four-year-old men in this country can say 'I built a city of eighteen thousand. I transformed arid earth into a prosperous and dynamic community. I gave Samaria a capital that George Bush himself recognizes?'"

Three framed pictures hang on the wall behind his desk. The smallest is the official portrait of the head of state, Moshe Katsav; the largest, an old photo of Ariel Sharon; and between them is an image of the menorah, symbol of the State of Israel. A large Israeli flag, along with several other pictures, fills the wall space. On a bookcase are more framed diplomas, commemorative certificates, snapshots of Ariel at different phases of its development, and several photos of Nachman with Sharon, and one of him with Ehud Barak wearing the red beret of a paratrooper. They tell the life story of a notable Israeli man, a righteous settler, a politician.

"In 1973, I was with the first core of Ariel pioneers in Tel Aviv," Nachman says, removing his telephone headset so he can recount to me the saga of his city without being disturbed. "At that time, it wasn't the Right that encouraged young people to create communities in the territories that were conquered in 1967; it was the Labor Party. Golda Meir was in power, and there must have been, maximum, around fifteen settlements with between two and three thousand Israelis concentrated in the Jordan Valley. The Right thought that this wasn't enough, that the Labor government was driving us to disaster and that we needed Jewish settlements on every hill in Judea-Samaria. This is what Sharon believed, and so did I. I dreamed of being part of this adventure. Like my grandfather and my great-grandfather, I wanted to found a city. Not a handful of houses on top of a hill, but a real city of one hundred thousand in the heart of Samaria."

Nachman does not make much of it, but in 1973 his group of "pioneers" presented the idea of building such a city to Moshe Dayan, minister of defense under Golda Meir. Dayan responded favorably, but the Cabinet rejected the proposal because it did not conform with the Allon Plan, which had been adopted, though never formally approved, by the Labor Party government in July 1967. This plan, created by General Yigal Allon, proposed building a string of settlement communities in the Jordan Valley and on the western bank of its river. These settlements would ensure a "Jewish presence" and, in the end, lead to the annexation of the Jordan Valley and the Judea Desert to Israel. For Allon, control of this eastern strip was one of the keys to the country's security.

Why was Nachman so persistent in his desire to build a city stretching seven and a half miles at the summit of a line of hills in the middle of the West Bank? "Because this was the site assigned to us by Ariel Sharon," Nachman tells me. Local archives reveal that these high, windbeaten hills attained symbolic significance on May 9, 1977. The army had put up two tents and had named their camp "Haris Outpost," taking the name from a nearby Arab village. No one had given much thought to the future of this isolated outpost when, a week after its installation, the Labor Party, who had been in power for twenty-nine years, lost the legislative elections. As the leader of Likud, Menachem Begin appointed Sharon president of the ministerial Settlement Committee. This gave Sharon the power to realize the strategy he had been advocating for years: to increase Jewish settlements in Judea-Samaria in order to "prevent the transfer [of the region] to Palestinian terrorists."[3]

"When I showed him my project," recounts Ron Nachman, "I explained that I had plans for a city of one hundred thousand inhabitants, but that, initially, our target was the creation of a core of six thousand. It seemed a modest number, but in my eyes, it was the critical mass we needed to ensure the durability of the settlement, and it greatly increased the number of settlers already there. Sharon listened. I had chosen this row of hills specifically with him in mind; it was a strategic position. Look at the map. We are exactly halfway between Tel Aviv and Jordan. A significant and sustainable Israeli presence here would ensure Tel Aviv's security and protect the city from invasions from the east. He gave the go-ahead, promising we would have all the support we needed. Near the end of 1977, the first forty families—including mine—moved there, close to the Haris Outpost. The following year we named the site Ariel."

In honor of Ariel Sharon? No. The name refers to a biblical passage in the Book of Isaiah, in which "Ariel" is the synonym for Jerusalem and the Temple Mount.

Ron Nachman's memory is a bit foggy on some of the details of Ariel's creation. It was in October 1977—three months after Begin took office—that the ministerial Settlement Committee approved the creation of a settlement on the site of the Haris Outpost, and gave Nachman and his group of forty pioneers the authorization to settle there. But they did not arrive on site until August 17, 1978. Defined as a military base by Ariel Sharon, the site was already equipped with a hundred or so barracks. The first settlers lived in this temporary housing for a few months as they waited for the Rural Building Administration to deliver their permanent homes. Three years later, the Haris Outpost, now Ariel, was established as a municipality, and its first mayor, Yaacov Feitelson, was appointed by the interim authority. Research by B'Tselem in 2002 shows that while most of the municipality's land was uncultivated rocky terrain where the villagers grazed their goats, some had been agricultural land belonging to the neigh-

boring Palestinian villages and had been expropriated by the army.
This land was where the barrier would be built.

"At the time, two diverging ways of thinking about settlements were
common among the Right," recalls Ron Nachman. "Sharon wanted to
create the largest number of settlements possible and to link them up
by roads. And the defense minister, Ezer Weizman, thought that we
needed to build a small number of large cities. My project had the advantage of bringing these two approaches together. As quickly as the
following year, events proved me right; after the Camp David Accords
in September 1978, Begin ordered the evacuation of the Sinai settlements. Do you think that Sinai would have been evacuated then if Israel had constructed two or three cities of fifteen thousand inhabitants?
Or that, in 2005, Sharon would have evacuated Gaza if, instead of
twenty or so settlements with eight thousand people, there had been
a city of eighty thousand? From the beginning, I was certain that we
had to build a critical mass of population large enough to prevent the
government—whether controlled by the Right or Left—from chasing
us out. In 1979, I even wrote a long letter to Begin making this point.
Yes, 1979."

The letter is fifteen pages long, in Hebrew, typed on Ariel's Local
Council letterhead and signed "Ron Nachman, Head of the Ariel
settlement." First, the letter reminds the prime minister that "the settlement in Samaria is a national objective."[4] Then Nachman goes into
a long explanation of his thesis, and provides technical and administrative propositions designed to implement it. "Action must be taken
at the ministerial level to give priority to the massive implantation of
thousands of Jewish families," he insists. "If not, the destiny of these
colonies will be the same as that of the Jewish communities in Sinai. I
have examined the quality of the land there. Clearly it is not suitable
for agricultural activity. I have concluded that we must build cities and
not agricultural settlements. These cities must reach a population of
fifteen thousand families within a limited space. It is intended that
they become regional centers of Samaria."

"My theory had a corollary," explains Nachman as he sets down
the photocopied letter on his desk, "that we could not be a religious

settlement. At that time, Gush Emunim [Bloc of the Faithful] and its idea of a multitude of small Jewish communities spread throughout Judea-Samaria had many supporters. It was a respectable option, originally adopted to prevent the Left from stretching settlements throughout all of Judea-Samaria. But it was in total contradiction to my idea: that with a religious foundation you would be able to build up a community of only a hundred or so people—not a city. Compare our situation to that of our neighbors in Tapuah. It is a religious community built at the same time as Ariel, but it has hardly more than five hundred inhabitants, while today we have close to twenty thousand. Forty-five percent are from the former Soviet Union, and would not have come had we been a religious settlement. As a result, we are on the good side of the barrier and Tapuah, like Eli or Ofra, are not."

NEARLY THIRTY YEARS AFTER ITS CREATION, ARIEL HAS NOT QUITE RE-alized the ambitions of its old city planners. It has a disorderly air about it. Some of its citizens still follow small settlement traditions, and can be seen picking up their morning newspapers in shorts, flip-flops, and pajama tops, their assault rifles slung over their shoulders. However, Nachman has succeeded in making Ariel more than simply a settlement. Everything needed for day-to-day life is available on the city's commercial strip: there are bakeries and book-stores, a post office, several falafel stands, two or three supermarkets, clothing boutiques, an optician, a pharmacy, a mobile phone shop, a few pet grooming salons, and several banks. There is also a rabbinical tribunal and a Holocaust museum. A brightly colored visitor's leaflet produced by the municipality mentions that Ariel also has four high schools, thirteen synagogues, three health clinics, a university with seven thousand registered students, a hotel, and a cultural center. To the west, about one hundred companies are located in the industrial zone. To the east, near the University of Judea-Samaria, there is a tech-nology park, which hosts thirty or so research projects in biotechnol-ogy, medicine, electronics, and biochemistry. But Nachman says that what makes him most proud is that, in 1995, during the city's third municipal mandate, it became Israel's first "smart city."

"This is an enormous project," he explains, suddenly smiling. "We began the whole initiative by installing a thousand computers with high-speed Internet access in our schools. Later we created a portal that gave all citizens and businesses direct access to all municipal services—available entirely online. You think I'm going to hand all of that over to the Arabs?

"This might surprise you, but I am against the barrier," Ron Nachman says, almost solemnly. "At a time when the whole world is opening up to us thanks to computer technology, finding myself behind a barrier is like being back in the ghetto. I would point out, by the way, that the first people to discuss building a barrier were actually on the left. In their minds, it was about protecting the State of Israel from suicide terrorists, and leaving people like me, my family, and all of us living in Judea-Samaria without protection. The Labor Party and their friends undoubtedly told themselves that the protection of some was worth the sacrifice of others. When I saw that the Left, the pacifists, had proposed building the barrier along the Green Line, I understood immediately that this barrier would become the future border of Israel, and I voiced my objections. I just couldn't grasp why, all of a sudden, I was to live on the other side of the border, outside of Israel. So, try to understand, I studied the Israeli reaction to suicide attacks, and I came to a simple conclusion: Israelis wanted separation. They didn't want to be mixed with the Arabs. They didn't even want to see them. This may be seen as racist, but that's how it is. So I realized that maybe the barrier was inevitable, but that it cannot be built on the Green Line, and that the time had come to do everything in our power to keep that from happening."

"When Sharon came to power, in March 2001, he was as much against the barrier as I was, and for the same reasons. Then, as you know, under the influence of Fouad [i.e., Ben-Eliezer], Dayan, and Dichter, he ended up changing his position. So I went to see him, and I asked him what was planned for us, what type of barrier we'd have and where it would be. He told me that his maps of the area showed that it was impossible to build a real barrier around Ariel, only a 'special security zone.' A 'special security zone?' That's what we left behind in Lebanon. I was furious. I reminded him that his maps were not sacred, that even those drafted at Oslo and Wye River Plantation had been corrected, and that I wanted to propose a new map of the barrier. He became sick with anger. He said, 'Make a map if you want, but get the hell out of here.' He fired me—even though we were very close and, in fact, are related. Look around you at all these photos of me and Arik.[5] Without the two of us, this city would not exist. We didn't speak to each other for almost three years. I understood then that Likud—yes, my party; not Labor—was going to build the barrier, and that's when I began my fight so that Ariel and the neighboring Israeli communities would be on the good side."

ALTHOUGH THE "SECURITY ZONE" SOLUTION SEEMED LESS EFFECTIVE than a real barrier—and, for Ron Nachman, too temporary—it did include Ariel in one of the enclaves annexed to Israel. In fact, in the earliest sketches of the barrier by Dany Tirza's team, it was clear that Ariel, like the other settlement blocks—Ma'ale Adumim, Gush Etzion, Givat Ze'ev, Alfei Menashe, and Modi'in Illit—would be on the "good" side of the wall. The idea, after all, was to annex the maximum number of settlements and the minimum number of Palestinians—and this enclave, with its total population of 140,000 people, contains approximately one third of the Israeli population in the West Bank. Palestinian protests and the critical observations of the international community made no difference. What were not agreed upon were the size and shape of the enclosure, the amount of land needed for expansion projects, the number of small satellite settlements planned, and the number of Palestinian villages that would end up contained within it.

The military did not take to Ron Nachman's initial design for the barrier's path. The enclave that he drew around Ariel, which extended deep into the West Bank, would create a gigantic pocket that stretched east to the small isolated settlements of Eli and Tapuah, nearly nine-

teen miles from the Green Line; to the north, it included all the settlements of the Immanuel and Kedumim blocs (about fifteen miles from
the Green Line); to the south, it went all the way to the Peduel settlement, which, as the crow flies, is some 15.5 miles from Kedumim and
6 kilometers east of the Green Line. About twenty settlements with
forty thousand inhabitants—as well as several Palestinian villages
and their land—are annexed by this wide, meandering of the barrier.
"When I showed my map to the military," recalls Nachman, "I was
told that my proposal would never be approved, because too many
Arab villages were in my enclave, and that I should prepare another
plan. I took all the maps and aerial photos available of the region and
I started by outlining what we called the 'Ariel bloc.' Actually, it is not
exactly a bloc, but several long finger-like loops. There was the Ariel
finger, the Kedumim and Ma'ale Shomron fingers, and the Peduel and
Ofarim finger. I wanted the Ariel finger to extend to Tapuah, but the
army refused. For protection, I wanted the fingers to be as thick as
possible—in fact, I wanted a fist, not fingers—but they refused again.
The military had its orders: avoid including too much land in the enclaves, because the Arabs won't hesitate to abuse Israeli democracy
and petition the Supreme Court, which can delay construction for
months."

According to a map approved by the Israeli government on February 20, 2005, the Ariel-Immanuel enclave annexes 76.4 square miles of
the West Bank to Israel. The enclave contains 14 settlements with
38,500 people, and four Palestinian hamlets with about a hundred.
The Ariel finger, bitterly negotiated by Nachman, extends almost seventeen miles east of the Green Line. Like Ma'ale Adumim, to the
south, this bloc of settlements sitting right in the center of the West
Bank violates international law and existing agreements between Israelis and Palestinians. Saeb Erekat, the principal Palestinian negotiator, calls it "territorial robbery, pure and simple, a clear rejection of
the idea of a two-state solution."[6] According to the United Nations,
this Israeli enclave is an obstacle to "territorial continuity and north–
south communications in the West Bank."[7] As for the "special security zone" planned by Sharon, it creates a no-man's land some 600 to

750 feet wide on each side of Route 5. This implies that hundreds of acres of agricultural land around each settlement will be seized, and that once the barrier is constructed around this land, it will become a real estate reserve protected by the military. If the villagers obtain a special permit, they will be able to cross the barrier to their farmland, but there is no guarantee that access will be granted during the crucial sowing and harvesting seasons.

By the time the electoral campaign started in the spring of 2006, Nachman's negotiations with the military architects of the barrier for a single Ariel-Immanuel settlement bloc were progressing. On March 14, 2006, he demonstrated his political clout by persuading the interim prime minister, Ehud Olmert, and three of his ministers, Tzipi Livni, Shaul Mofaz, and Roni Bar-On, to visit Ariel. After announcing to the media that the barrier in the region would be completed "at the end of the year," Sharon's successor turned to Nachman, who was standing next to him on a terrace overlooking the sunny hills of the West Bank, and said, "Ariel is in Israel. And we will make sure that security arrangements allow Ariel to prosper as an integral part of Israel."[8]

In Israel, as elsewhere, one should remain suspicious of campaign promises. On April 30, 2006, an unpleasant surprise was waiting for Nachman at the conclusion of the weekly ministerial meeting. The military had decided to modify the path of the barrier around the Ariel-Immanuel bloc. Not only did the Olmert government reject his petition to enlarge the fingers of the settlement bloc, but the military planners accepted the arguments presented by representatives of a half-dozen Palestinians sandwiched between the Ariel-Immanuel area and the Green Line. The path of the barrier that the government had approved cut Nachman's proposed enclave in half—the fist had once again become a finger. The enclave in the north, containing Immanuel and its satellites, would be linked to Israel by a large corridor ending in the Alfei Menashe pocket. The enclave in the south, containing Ariel, its industrial park, its land reserves, and satellites, would be attached to Israel by the protected Highway 5, via Elkana and Kafr Kasem. A strip of land a half-mile wide and almost two miles long reestablishes a semblance of territorial continuity between the Nablus region and the Palestinian villages to the south of Alfei Menashe. A 2.5-mile road, linking the villages of Deir Istiya to the east and Bani Hassan to the west, was under consideration by the Israeli army to further establish this territorial continuity, but as of July 2007, it still had not broken ground.

The same day that the route of the barrier was announced, B'Tselem replied with a statement, saying that "even as modified, the barrier in the region of Ariel-Kedumim, which would now allow for the annexation of fifteen Jewish settlements and lands earmarked for their extensions, would greatly reduce the rights of the Palestinians who live in the area. A barrier path that penetrates the West Bank as far as 13.6 miles from the Green Line is not dictated by security considerations. . . . This is a politically designed path that in no way responds to promises of security and violations of human rights."[9]

"The Ariel barrier cuts us off from seventy percent of our agricultural lands," says Mahafez Mansour, who for ten years was mayor of Deir Istiya, a Palestinian city of four thousand residents three miles northwest of Ariel.[10] "Also, it separates us, as well as six other villages, from Salfit, the main Palestinian city in the region and home to our county seat." A road spanning 1.5 miles between the Palestinian villages of Sarta, to the north, and Brukin, to the south, is planned to cross the Ariel finger—undoubtedly by tunnel—in order to reestablish communication with Salfit. But, here again, construction dates are unknown. As a disenchanted Fatah supporter, Mahafez Mansour chose not to run in the last municipal elections, and opted instead to work at his dental practice. But he continues to follow the commune's disputes with the Israeli military closely, especially since the new municipal council, run by an "independent of the Left," also consists of five Fatah supporters and three members of Hamas, one of whom is his own brother, Bilal.

The barrier, and the multiple rules and travel restrictions imposed on the Palestinians, have exasperated Mahafez Mansour. "My office is in Biddya, a sizeable village of ten thousand residents, nearly five miles from here. Before the barrier, the commute took me ten minutes," he explains. "Today, I never know how long it will take. It depends on the mood of the soldiers. It could be fifteen minutes or an hour. Or I might have to simply turn around and go home because the barrier is closed due to a 'terrorist risk.' Nablus used to take half an hour. Today, with the inspections, you need to allow two to three hours."

Until just a few years ago, the people of Deir Istiya lived off revenue from olive and citrus fruit cultivation—and many lived rather well, by the look of some of the houses. "I'm afraid that's all over, and not only because of the barrier," says Mahafez Mansour. "Come with me, I'll show you why."

Mansour takes me in a municipal truck a few miles north of the village. As we drive, the newly paved road grows more and more pocked with potholes. The inclines of the narrow valley that opens before us are crissscrossed by small stone walls supporting the terraced land, which is covered with olive, lemon, and orange trees. Wild crocuses grow by the roadside, alongside a stream, which, judging by its wide banks, must once have been a flowing river. From afar, the land seems to emanate peace and a serene coexistence of civilization and nature. "It is here that I learned to swim," says Mansour with a smile, showing me a large stone basin fed by the stream. "When I was a child, our families came here to picnic underneath the trees, to swim and to nap." In the middle of the orchards, a number of dilapidated sheds are spread out over the valley. "They shelter the pumps that used to bring the water to the terraces," Mansour explains. "But today we cannot use the water." Indeed, it is clear that the strong current from long ago has become a trickle of foamy, dark iridescent water polluted with chemical residue and garbage—an open-air sewer in this biblical valley.

"The people responsible for this are up there," says Mahafez Mansour, pointing to the cement walls and tiled roofs of the hillside settlements that overlook the valley. "Immanuel, Yaqir, Nofim, Qarne Shomron, Ma'ale Shomron. And Nof Kana. The last is a wild settlement, but clearly this has not prevented its inhabitants from receiving electricity. You can see the electrical poles from here. Don't think for a moment, though, that the people from the settlements are pouring their trash into our stream because they don't have sewers. They have plumbing, but it's easier to dump everything on us, including the chemical waste from the treatment of metal products in their workshops. We tested the stream water and the fruit we grow here. The water is not suitable for irrigation, and a portion of the fruits are not fit for consumption. I suppose they hope to push us out, that we'll simply abandon our land, which will eventually be on their side of the barrier once it is built. Maybe they hope to turn this valley into a garden for their settlements."

In spring 2007, the Israeli Ministry of the Environment, after being petitioned by the Yesh Din's Volunteers for Human Rights, finally turned its attention to the Palestinian village of Jinsafut, to the north of the Immanuel settlement. In the last three years, the villagers estimate that dozens of olive trees have been sterilized by the Immanuel factory and its runoff, which pollutes the ground and the subsoil of the orchards. After visiting and inspecting the pollution site, the Ministry of the Environment ordered the municipal council of the Immanuel settlement to "find an immediate solution to their drainage and runoff problem regarding the olive orchards."

"During the conversation I had on June 25, 2007, with the leadership of the Council of Immanuel," said a highly placed Israeli civil official in a letter released by Yesh Din, "the Council committed itself to putting an immediate end to this dangerous practice. If it does not, we have the authority to force it to do so."

But the letter makes no mention of a time frame by which Immanuel must make good on this commitment, nor does it make clear whether this applies to the other settlements of the Immanuel pocket. In other words, once again, time will tell.

The first inhabitants of the Shilo settlement, 1978. *Courtesy of Micha Bar-Am/ MAGNUM PHOTOS*

CHAPTER 13

SETTLING

Between the Six-Day War, in June 1967, and May 2006, when Ehud Olmert took office, Israel built more than 160 settlements in the West Bank, East Jerusalem, and the Gaza Strip. The twenty-one Gaza settlements, where eight thousand people lived, as well as four isolated settlements in the areas surrounding Jenin and Nablus, which are home to some six hundred settlers, were evacuated in August and September 2005. But in July 2007, the total number of settlers in the West Bank was nearing 450,000 including 190,000 Israelis living in the ten "urban" settlements of East Jerusalem.[1] In other words, one out of every six residents in the West Bank is a settler, and one Israeli out of every thirteen lives in a settlement. Given these numbers, it is clear that the fate of the settlements weighs heavily on the political choices of Israeli leadership.

For the last forty years, all governments, whether of the Right or the Left, and regardless of their various ambitions, strategies, and fortunes, have participated without exception in the settlement enterprise. The idea of a security barrier has enjoyed similarly enduring popularity throughout Israel's modern history. A brief detour into the settlement history of Israel provides insight into how the final decision to build the wall was made.

On June 14, 1967, only two days after IDF chief of staff Yitzhak Rabin was celebrating the victory of his "sons of light" over those who wanted to "cover the country with darkness," General Allon took over the Ministry of Labor and proposed to the Labor government a plan for settlements in the Old City and the Arab neighborhoods of Jerusalem.[2] On July 26, he submitted his project for dividing the West Bank to the Council of Ministers. According to this plan, Israel would claim a strip of territory six to seven miles wide for security purposes along the West Bank of the Jordan, and cover it with settlements and military bases. The rest of the West Bank, apart from a few strategic zones, would be handed back to Jordan. The Allon Plan would never be officially adopted by the Israeli Cabinet or even integrated into the Labor Party's platform. Nonetheless, successors to Ben-Gurion and Golda Meir used it for years as a guiding principle in their approach to the Palestinian question.

Indifferent to the strategic imperatives defined by Allon, the extreme religious Right, under the Israeli political movement Gush Emunim, with their spiritual guide Rabbi Zvi Yehuda Kook, had a completely different vision. Convinced that the Israeli victory was "the beginning of the redemption" and the first step toward reconquering Greater Jerusalem, their aim was to petition the Labor government for more settlements and to have these settlements dispersed as widely as possible over the whole of the "Land of Israel."

"Our control of a region is a function not only of the size of the population resident there," Gush Emunim puts forth in their literature, "but also of the size of the area in which this population exercises its impression and influence."[3]

The Jordan Valley, the Gush Etzion region to the southwest of Jerusalem, and the hills around Hebron had been defined as settlement priority zones by the Labor Party, so the leaders of Gush Emunim decided to concentrate their efforts on the mountainous ridge running north to south down the center of the West Bank—in other words, where the majority of Palestinians lived.

In December 1975, after seven attempts to establish camps on the hills surrounding Nablus without official authorization, the disciples of Rabbi Kook finally secured an agreement with the minister of defense, Shimon Peres, that allowed for a settlement on a military base almost five miles west from the large Palestinian city of Qadum. Two years later, it became the Qadumim settlement, where today a little more than three thousand Israelis live. In other areas, where their requests were denied, the messianic Gush Emunim pioneers turned to deception: the "work camp" that they were authorized to build to the north of Jerusalem thus became the Ofra settlement (2,200 inhabitants in 2004); and their "archeological digs" undertaken to the west of Salfit were transformed, in 1979, into the Shilo settlement (2,000 inhabitants in 2005).

By the time Menachem Begin assumed control in 1977, Israel had managed, over a ten-year period, to build thirty-six settlements that became home to forty-four hundred pioneers. By 1977, Gush Emunim had many friends in the new government, including agriculture minister Ariel Sharon. But despite the change of government, official doctrine remained the same: settlements could be created only where Israel planed to fully annex the land in future negotiations. As the boundaries of these zones remained unclear, the conflicts between Gush Emunim and the Israeli government continued for two more years.

But the Bloc of the Faithful had reasons to be hopeful. The new government's two-part settlement policy could have been written by the disciples of Rabbi Kook. The first part, presented by Mattiyahu Drobless, who was then the representative of the World Zionist Organization's Land Settlement Department, made a case for the rapid creation of settlements over all of the West Bank territory. "The civilian presence of Jewish communities is vital for the security of the State of Israel," he wrote. "Our intention to preserve Judea-Samaria must not leave any room for doubt. The best and most efficient way to eliminate any last trace of doubt is a rapid development of settlements in the region."[4]

The second part of the settlement policy consisted of a map prepared by Ariel Sharon showing the areas he deemed vital to Israel's security and that should thus be annexed. According to this map, only a few heavily populated Palestinian enclaves escape annexation. The area around the Green Line bordering the Israeli coastal plains, the periphery of Jerusalem, and the hills at the center of the West Bank between Ramallah and Nablus were, for Sharon, a priority. "Settlements are not an end unto themselves, but a means of attaining our objectives," he declared before a gathering of farmers in 2006. "As in the past, these settlements will have an influence on the fate of the country. We need to proceed in a way that will increase the Jewish population in the [occupied] territories, and that is why we intend to develop these settlement plans."[5]

From then on, public and private funds flowed to settlement organizations. Financial incentives and low interest rates were offered to settlement candidates in "the Territories." Special budgetary allocations were made available to local associations engaged in settlement activity. There was no shortage of land, either. The Israeli army handed over hundreds of thousands of acres of confiscated Palestinian land to the settlers—land taken by military requisition, or expropriated for public use, or seized through legal technicalities relating to "absentee properties." The hills and mountain ridges of the West Bank were suddenly home to new villages. The uniform houses, perched high like chateaus, seem to watch over and to control the Palestinian localities tucked in the valleys near water and vegetation.

Drobless and Sharon's goal to bring one hundred thousand settlers to the West Bank by 1986 would not be realized until 1992, the year the Labor Party returned to power under the leadership of Yitzhak Rabin. Likud and its political allies could take comfort in the fact that during the previous fifteen years, the number of settlements—by that time 120—had tripled, and the number of settlers had increased 23-fold. The Likud had also succeeded in paving the West Bank with a massive network of new roads and freeways that linked the Israeli settlements, annexing land from any Palestinian village in their path, while, at the same time, remaining completely inaccessible to Palestinians.

Less than a year after their return to power, the Labor Party was engaged in secret negotiations with the leadership of the PLO and, from September 1993, in a public "peace process." Would the Labor Party "change national priorities" as they had promised during the campaign and substantially reallocate funds from the settlements to help poor Palestinian villages, and combat the social inequalities that had worsened with each passing day? Hope, for those who had believed these promises, was short-lived. Even after the Oslo Accords II were signed on September 28, 1995, it was clear that the Rabin government would do nothing to halt settlement development, even though, according to Article XXXI (7) of the Oslo Accords II, "Neither side shall initiate or take any step that will change the status of the West Bank and the Gaza Strip pending the outcome of the permanent status negotiations."

To reassure the Clinton administration, which had grown concerned by delays in the peace process, the Rabin government agreed not to create any new settlements, and to limit the expansion of those that already existed. There would be no new construction, Israel promised, except that to accommodate the "natural development" of the population. And what does this mean? In Israel, between 1994 and 2004, the average demographic growth stagnated between 1.8 and 3 percent per year, but in the settlements it had swelled to 8.9 percent[6]— due largely to a flood of immigrants from the former Soviet Union, North America, and Europe who had come to live specifically in the "Judea-Samaria localities."

For Rabin and his successors, absorbing said "natural development" clearly means to quietly pursue settlement, not by creating new ones[7]— which would be difficult to hide from the international community— but by building new neighborhoods in existing settlements in the West Bank. Greater Jerusalem and the Jordan Valley seem to be completely exempt from these fictive restrictions on settlement. A survey of the Labor Party's prime ministers reveals a spectacular increase in the Jewish population in the Occupied Territories. Between the Oslo Accords in September 1993 and the failure of the negotiations in Taba in January 2001, 81,000 settlers moved to the West Bank—their number now totals 191,000. At the same time, 30,000 people had moved into the "urban settlements" of East Jerusalem, which had 177,000 inhabitants when Sharon succeeded Barak as prime minister on March 2001. Three years later, these same urban settlements had a population of 190,000.

Today, many Israelis find it hard to admit that Israel's pursuit of settlement development during the time of the peace process greatly undermined Palestinian confidence in the Oslo Accords. At the heart of Palestinian society, it fed the belief, particularly among radical Islamic groups, that Yasser Arafat had fallen into a trap set by the Israelis and had chosen peace while securing nothing in exchange.

Are the settlements an obstacle to peace? Should they be more closely examined? These questions are rarely taken under full consideration. Yasser Arafat, Mahmoud Abbas, the Palestinian Authority, and Hamas have each in their turn stalled the peace process, but is it right for Israeli political and military leaders to use this as an excuse to dodge the question of the settlements with an endless game of tit for tat? In 2002, when members of the Israeli Association of United Architects (IAUA) proposed a presentation for the Twenty-first World Architecture Congress in Berlin demonstrating "the strategic use of territory in the exercise of State power" through settlement, the ensuing scandal ultimately caused the IAUA to abruptly cancel the exhibit.[8]

Having come to power in a difficult political climate—the Al-Aqsa Intifada, the failure of the peace process, and a surge in terrorist attacks that killed 173 Israeli civilians over 16 months—Sharon was aware of the need to keep Washington happy, but more convinced than ever that the settlements were indispensable. Needless to say, he did not reverse Labor Party policy. He was satisfied simply to accelerate construction, and asked authorities to look the other way as wild settlements multiplied throughout the West Bank. The number of these "outposts," many of which sprouted up in areas with a dense Palestinian population, doubled under Sharon, reaching a record 102 outposts by January of 2006, when Sharon was hospitalized after his second stroke. Some of these camps are made up of little more than crude barracks and trailers, but they are indeed connected to the national electric grid, and in at least a third of the camps, permanent houses are under construction.

In 2002, Ariel Sharon found new reasons to push for fast settlement growth. After a long period of hesitation, he finally accepted the idea of a physical barrier between Israelis and Palestinians. Highly knowledgeable about Palestinian geography, he was familiar with the meanderings of the proposed barrier, some of which he had drafted himself. Under his leadership, more than 365,000 Israelis living in 69 settlements would find themselves to the west of the barrier in the enclaves annexed by Israel, leaving between 60,000 and 80,000 people dispersed among 80 settlements on the "bad side." Close to 45 percent of the settlements and more than 85 percent of the settlers will be annexed by Israel. Some of these settlers, who had moved to the West Bank for affordable housing and better quality of life, were prepared to leave once they were assured an indemnity and new housing. But other, more ideological settlers refused to abandon "the country of the Jews" to Arabs, and were determined to stay. Some, like Pinhas Wallerstein, press secretary for the regional council of Matte Binyamin, who was sentenced to three months of community service in 1988 for having killed a young Palestinian stone thrower, demanded a referendum on the evacuation of the settlements. Others threatened violent resistance.

In order to reassure the less ideologically driven settlers, and give something back to his traditional electorate, Sharon ordered the Ministry of Housing and Construction to "make an effort" in Judea-Samaria. In the first half of 2005, the number of apartments under construction in the Occupied Territories surpassed 4,200, as compared to 3,900 in the preceding year.[9] Most were funded by the State. Many are now in religious settlements.

In the end, 12,000 Israelis moved into West Bank settlements in 2005, one of the most active of the last five years. The following year, in 2006, 14,400 made the same choice and moved to the West Bank.

IN OCTOBER OF THAT YEAR, *HAARETZ* REVEALED THE CONTENTS OF A REPORT on the settlements issued by the Special Advisor to the Minister of Defense, General Baruch Spiegel. In this document, General Spiegel confirmed that a significant number of construction projects had begun without permits in several dozen settlements, and often on land belonging to Palestinians. Relying both on statistics gathered by the Civil Administration and on aerial photographs taken by the army using civilian aircraft, General Spiegel's investigation constitutes a priceless database on settlement expansion. It confirms that information had been deliberately and repeatedly hidden so that the settlers could extend their control over the West Bank. The Minister of Defense, whose entourage feared the potential impact that these revelations could have on relations between Israel and some of its allies, called the Spiegel report "explosive" and attempted to suppress it. General Mike Herzog, head of the Minister of Defense's cabinet, and Ehud Barak, opposed the publication of the report before the supreme court, arguing that it would be a detriment to national security and international relations.

As officials argued over whether to release the report, bulldozers and cranes went to work, and settlement activity continued to thrive. In the first half of 2008, construction on apartment buildings increased by 42 percent, compared to the same period in 2007. The number of Israeli settlers in the West Bank—not including East Jerusalem—went from 276,100 to 289,600 between December 2007 and 2008.[10] In July 2009, according to an Israel Defence Forces Civil Administration report, covering the first half of 2009, there were 300,000 Jewish settlers in the West Bank.[11] Apparently, the settlement enterprise is immune to both the fear of terrorism and the promise of reviving the peace process.

A demonstration held against Route 443, a road on which only Israeli citizens are permitted to drive. *Courtesy of Oren Ziv/Activestills.org*

CHAPTER 14

TWO ROADS FOR TWO PEOPLES

In March 2006, after five months as interim leader, and a highly contentious election, Ehud Olmert officially took over Sharon's seat as prime minister. The settlement map he inherited surpassed the dreams of Rabbi Kook, who had put "the holiness of the land of Israel and the duty to settle it" above all.[1] The number of settlers in the West Bank doubled between 1996 and 2006, with the urban settlements of East Jerusalem increasing by 20 percent. The network of roads constructed to accommodate and connect the settlements not only to one another but to major Israeli arteries was equally impressive. Paved with asphalt, lit by floodlights, and well marked with signage in both English and Hebrew, the roads conveniently avoided nearby Palestinian towns and villages. During 1995, more than sixty miles of road were paved by the Rabin government. Over the following years, the pace of construction slowed, although not in terms of the number of new construction sites. In July 2007, a United Nations report[2] stated that the network of roads linking Israel to its settlements, and to its industrial and military zones, in the West Bank measured 1,032 miles. What is surprising about these roads is that none of them intersects with the more crudely paved roads of the Palestinian villages. At intersections where the roads do meet, barriers have been erected to prevent traffic between them. Elsewhere, they are separated by bridges and tunnels. One may travel the thirty-seven miles between Jerusalem and Nablus, or the almost twenty-two miles between Jerusalem and Hebron, without seeing more than a handful of Palestinian vehicles, identifiable by their white or green license plates. Palestinian drivers are required to take routes that can double or triple their travel time. Yehezkel Lein, a researcher with B'Tselem, writes in a 2004 report, "contrary to the customary purpose of roads, as a means to connect people with places, the roads that Israel builds in the West Bank are at times intended to achieve the opposite purpose." The report says, "some of the new roads in the West Bank were planned as a physical barrier to stifle Palestinian urban development. These roads prevent both the natural joining of enclaves, and the creation of contiguous Palestinian communities in areas in which Israel wants to maintain control, either for military reasons or for settlement purposes."[3]

The West Bank is not a particularly large territory. It is 81 miles long from north to south and approximately 37 miles from east to west. Within this territory, which is not much larger than the state of Delaware, 17 roads covering 74.5 miles were officially off-limits to Palestinian drivers in 2004. Nearly 155 miles of "restricted use" paths were accessible only to those who had obtained special permits issued by the army. Another 224 miles of "partially prohibited" roads, with both fixed and mobile checkpoints, discourage Palestinian travelers, as each crossing may involve scrupulous vehicle inspections by the police, and a long wait. A faulty blinker or an unfastened seat belt can incur fines for the driver.

Three years later, in August 2007, B'Tselem conducted an investigation that found that 21 roads throughout the West Bank, spanning some 193 miles, were partially or completely off-limits to Palestinians.[4] The report identified nine different types of permits (varying depending upon place of issue, type of vehicle, and the specific reasons for travel), and concluded that "the Israeli authorities view the movement permit as an exception, a kind of privilege, which they grant if they are convinced that the applicant is not a security threat and has a 'justifiable reason' for wanting to go from one place to another inside the West Bank." Palestinians have nothing good to say about the permit system, and the B'Tselem report underlines many of their complaints. For example, the application process for obtaining a permit is "unclear and lacks transparency." Permit applicants are expected to meet two basic criteria: they must submit considerable documentation to the Civil Administration, and they must have a completely clean record with the Israeli police, at no time having been flagged as a security threat in the past. The B'Tselem report continues, "apart from these two criteria, the public is not informed of the Civil Administration's procedures . . . Ultimately, permits are granted at the discretion of DCO officials. The reason for denial, if provided, is brief—the word 'security' sufficing."

Out of the twenty-seven thousand requests filed in 2006 for permits to travel in the area between the separation barrier and the Green Line, more than 20 percent were rejected. It is also worth noting that possessing a permit does not necessarily solve all of one's travel problems. Palestinian movement in the West Bank is subject to a range of unwritten rules, enforced by checkpoint soldiers. At any time they may close a checkpoint, change itineraries, or restrict which vehicles are allowed to cross (e.g., soldiers may authorize buses and group taxis, but not individually owned vehicles).

"What do the Israelis want? A system of apartheid?" storms Saeb Erekat, a Fatah deputy in Jericho and a Palestinian negotiator. "That is what they are putting into place by building roads on which Palestinians can't drive. Do you know a single place in the world where, on the same land, there are two systems of roads, for two peoples?"[5]

These prohibitions, which apply to all major arteries of the road system, are part of the army's response to the Second Intifada. Aimed at strictly controlling the number of Palestinians authorized to travel, and reducing that number to a minimum, the army has erected a multitude of obstacles—dirt mounds, concrete blocks, trenches, iron gates, checkpoints—restricting access to most localities in the West Bank and protecting roads that are reserved for Israeli vehicles.

Route 443 is a modern four-lane highway, and a first-rate shortcut through the Occupied Territories between Jerusalem and Tel Aviv; but it is hard not to notice, as one drives down it, that all of the nearby roads leading to Palestinian villages are closed, barricaded by heavy metallic barriers or cement blocks. Until 2002, Route 443 was an important

artery for the nearly thirty-seven thousand Palestinians living in the
seven villages in this region, allowing them to drive to the nearest city,
Ramallah, in less than fifteen minutes. Today, the road is strictly off-
limits to vehicles with Palestinian license plates. Palestinians are even
prohibited from crossing the road on foot or walking along its shoulder. At the end of the 1980s, Israeli authorities wanted to reduce traffic
on Highway 1 between Tel Aviv and Jerusalem, and to create a quicker
route to the suburb of Modi'in, so they decided to expropriate a considerable amount of Palestinian land in order to widen Road 443 and
transform it into the semi-highway it is today. At the time the Supreme Court approved seizing the land, it stated that the new road
would be accessible to both Israelis and Palestinians in the region.
Since the explosion of the Second Intifada in 2002, however, in order to
reach Ramallah, the Palestinians living in the seven villages have had to
rely on three sinuous, narrow substitute roads built on their land by the
Israeli army. A journey of only fifteen minutes on Route 443 now takes
an hour to an hour and a half on these single-lane roads. Naturally,
the local economy has suffered because of this. A hundred or so small
Palestinian-owned boutiques along the 443—florists, furniture and tile
stores, restaurants—have disappeared. Ali Al Ori's tile factory on 443
used to sell most of its product in Israel and employ forty people; it
now has only six employees.

According to a United Nations report, there were 605 roadblocks
in the West Bank in April 2005, including approximately fifty guarded
checkpoints. By August of 2005, the number had declined to 376, but
then steadily increased through the following year to 518 in June 2006.
A map published by the United Nations in April 2007 shows 546 diverse
obstacles, including about 60 checkpoints. One year later, there were
611 obstacles; and in September 2008, 630.

Today, it is easier and faster for an Israeli to drive the 106 miles between Tel Aviv and Jericho than for a Palestinian to drive from Nablus
to Jenin, a distance of only about 19 miles. According to a United Nations document published in May 2006, "no Jenin resident has been
authorized to travel to the south of Nablus since December 2005."[6] In
other words, the residents of villages located just north of Nablus

cannot drive into town; instead they must take one of the seven authorized taxis. This system, which raises costs and puts merchandise
at risk, is also a daily source of frustration and anger. Sometimes only
one soldier is posted at a checkpoint to inspect Palestinian vehicles,
which causes a half-mile backup and hours of waiting, while, in the
neighboring lane, vehicles with Israeli drivers pass through without
even having to stop.

Over time, the construction of the barrier and the installation of
various security zones throughout the West Bank, combined with the
range of travel restrictions, have effectively divided the region into
three distinct zones. The first zone lies between the northernmost
point of the West Bank and Nablus, the second extends from the Ariel
settlement to Jerusalem, and the third encompasses the south of the
West Bank, with enclaves in Hebron and Karmel.

The proliferation of obstacles and local regulations has divided
these three zones into even smaller territories, between which the movement of Palestinians is strictly controlled. In a report published in
August 2007,[7] B'Tselem outlines six "sub-zones." The first, to the north,
covers most of Jenin, Tulkarem, Qalqiliya, Tubas, and Nablus, and extends to the hilltops overlooking the Jordan Valley. The second, at the
center, includes Salfit, Ramallah, and the city of Jericho, and is also
bordered to the east by the foothills of the Jordan Valley. The third is
made up of a half-dozen small Palestinian enclaves along the length
of the Green Line, which have been carved out by the swerving of
the separation barrier from just north of Tulkarem to Qalqiliya. The
fourth is a strip of land between one and five miles wide that covers
the whole of the Jordan Valley. The fifth is the enclave around East
Jerusalem created by the barrier. The sixth encompasses the entire
region from Bethlehem to the southernmost area of the Green Line.
According to B'Tselem, these divisions and subdivisions, "sometimes
completely detached from one another, seriously affect all aspects of
the Palestinians' lives." It is difficult to measure the adverse affect that
this fragmentation of essential Palestinian space has had on health,
education, economic growth, agriculture, social and family life, and
access to administrative services, but one can surmise that it weighs

heavily on the future of this people. Add to this the deeply divided and dysfunctional Palestinian Authority, and it is easy to understand the rise and success of Hamas.

Officially presented as a program to ease the daily travel problems of Palestinians, the Civil Administration has pledged to construct twenty-three liaison roads—called "fabric of life roads" by the military—between the multiple Palestinian "enclaves" of the West Bank. This promised development may turn out to be diplomatic rather than humanitarian, as the U.S. government, along with other institutions and individuals, has openly questioned whether the segmentation of the West Bank is intended to break up a future Palestinian State. A military map dated April 13, 2007, shows, however, that the proposed program would create ninety-four miles of new roadways and establish a semblance of "territorial continuity" between Palestinian population zones, although they would still be separated by settlement enclaves or protected roads reserved for Israelis. In the northwest of the West Bank, in the regions of Tulkarem, Qalqiliya, and Salfit, no fewer than nine new connecting roadways, from half a mile to nine miles long, are under construction. Seven others are planned for the Ramallah and Jerusalem region, four to the east of Jerusalem and three to the south of Bethlehem, around the settlement bloc of Gush Etzion.

Shay Karmona, who is in charge of this project for the Civil Administration, politely but firmly denies that the roads were planned to appease foreign interests. "My work," he explains, "consists of contributing to the fight against terrorist groups by installing a separation between Israel and the zones under control of the Palestinian Authority.[8] At the same time, I realize that a large majority of Palestinians only want to live in peace and are not at all linked to the terrorists. It is for them, so that they can have a daily life that is as normal as possible, that we are going to build nearly fifty miles of roads and tunnels between some Palestinian zones separated by the security barrier."

In a tall office building neighboring the Ministry of Defense, Major Karmona's office is buried in construction site maps and photos, and on his wall is a single picture, a photo of a group of Israeli soldiers in Auschwitz. Hunched over a large map on his desk, he traces the path of the barrier with his finger, and shows me a series of mauve lines, numbered from one to twenty-three. "You see," he says, "these are the Fabric of Life roads that we have already opened, or plan on opening, in order to facilitate Palestinian lives. This project is extremely costly, but we are going to do it."

Major Karmona's maps notably include three specific routes conceived by the Israeli army to allow Palestinians free travel between Bethlehem and Ramallah, and that connect the north and south of the West Bank. The shortest, most direct path is the 14.6-mile Route 60, which crosses Jerusalem from north to south. Since construction of the barrier, though, it has been closed to Palestinians. The first replacement road proposed by the military, the 23-mile Option B-1, goes through the towns of Abu Dis and El-Azariyeh, then follows the wall to the east of Jerusalem. Sections of this freeway are under construction or in partial service; it consists of two lanes—one for Palestinians, and one for Israelis—separated by a wall. Only the latter will have access to a crossway toward Jerusalem. The second, Option B-2, runs along the western side of the Ma'ale Adumim settlement and links back to Option B-1, north of the village of Anata. It is 26 miles long and varies in altitude more than 4,265 feet. Finally, the third, Option C, runs around Ma'ale Adumim and its satellites to the east, crosses Jericho, then climbs the steep inclines that overlook the Jordan Valley. This route, which varies in altitude more than 6,562 feet, forms a loop of 48 miles.[9] In terms of repairing the Palestinians' "fabric of life," these roads are undoubtedly useful, but nonetheless arduous and difficult to traverse.

With or without liaison roads, it perhaps should not come as a surprise that the fragmentation of the West Bank corresponds almost exactly to an Israeli delegation proposal presented at Camp David in July 2000 to mold the Palestinian State into three segments. And this is not the only revelation offered by the maps, which can be more revealing than the actual people making the decisions.

Here's an interesting experiment: Place a map of the barrier over a map showing the settlements and the distribution of natural resources in the West Bank, and you will have a vivid illustration of Israeli policy from Allon to Sharon.

First observation: the barrier, from one end of its sinuous 435-mile path to the other,[10] encircles 60 isolated or "bloc" settlements, their satellites, and land set aside for their development. After having studied twelve sections of the separation barrier, researchers at B'Tselem and Bimkom (Planners for Planning Rights) showed that the barrier always goes around the settlements, as well as their landholdings for expansion, regardless of whether this will improve security.[11]

Second observation: as it exists today, the barrier has de facto annexed 12.8 percent of the West Bank to Israel, notably in the hills bordering the Israeli coastal plain. This has had a dramatic effect on farmers in the region, because the subsoil along the Green Line holds precious water reserves. Clemens Messerschmid, a young hydrologist, who is currently a researcher with the German Cooperation Agency in Ramallah, has studied the impact of the barrier on the use of water reserves. According to Messerschmid, "the Palestinians in the northwest of the West Bank complain that they have lost a hundred or so water wells that are no longer accessible because of the barrier. But they are going to lose something even more important. The real problem," he says, "is that the strip of land annexed by Israel, between the barrier and the Green Line coincides almost exactly with the most promising future drilling zones. In fact, in recent years, because of the barrier, the Palestinians have lost three quarters of the available water production and the quasi-totality of production potential of the aquiferous layer. It is even more troubling and damaging since the exploitation of water reserves contained in the subsoil of the West Bank is already unequal, with the Israelis using 80 percent, and the Palestinians 20 percent."[12]

From this perspective, the barrier appears to be the next logical step in the settlement enterprise that began almost forty years ago. True, it does not successfully attach all of the settlements throughout the West Bank to Israel, but it does manage to envelop three fourths of the settlers in its meandering path. By including these water reserves on the Israeli side of the wall, Dany Tirza has come close to realizing the annexation dreams of the original settlers, from Allon to Sharon, with one significant strategic difference: Allon and Sharon had deemed control of the Jordan Valley vital to the security of Israel.

At the moment, no barrier is planned for this region. Why have Tirza and his superiors compromised their once-fervent belief that a security zone in this region is essential?

An answer to this question can be found along the Allon Road. Named in honor of the Labor Party settlement strategist, this bumpy road, which snakes along the eastern foothills of the West Bank, offers an unobstructed view of the network of settlements established in the Jordan Valley since 1967. A string of a dozen or so settlements sit on the ridges between the Jerusalem–Jericho Road and the Beit She'an region. Scattered among the settlements are at least half a dozen army bases where trucks, tanks, and artillery are stored under canvas tents and in hangars. From the belvederes installed alongside the Allon Road, one can see a second string of twenty-seven settlements nineteen hundred to twenty-three hundred feet below, surrounded by greenhouses and acres of verdant plains that run along the Jordan River to the north of Jericho. Nearly ninety-three hundred settlers and soldier-settlers live in these two lines of settlements. In addition to these well-established settlements, there are a dozen wild settlements, established since 2001 with the approval of the army in October 2008, where about a hundred families live.

Also scattered among these slopes, in the valley along Route 90, is the small city of Jericho and a group of villages, agricultural communities that are home to nearly fifty-three thousand Palestinians. Yet, apart from a few taxis and a handful of cars and trucks, only vehicles with yellow license plates—Israelis—or army Humvees seem to travel freely through the region, which covers a quarter of the West Bank. Why? "Only those Palestinians who live here, according to their identity cards, may enter the Jordan Valley," explains a young lieutenant posted at the Route 57 checkpoint, near the village of Hamra, twenty-five miles northwest of Jericho. Here, as elsewhere in the West Bank, severe restrictions on Palestinian movement were imposed by the Israeli army after the explosion of the Second Intifada in September 2000. Most of the villages and cities of the region, including Jericho, were accessible only by a single road, and a permit was required. These restrictions, imposed by the army, were made even more stringent in

2005. The first serious crackdowns took place in March of that year, when responsibility for security in Jericho, which had been under the control of the Israeli army since "Operation Rampart" in 2002, was handed back over to the Palestinian Authority. But the military left its cement blocks and obstacles in place, closing off all access points to Jericho except one. Then the travel restrictions previously in play became pure and simple prohibitions, and all movement between the Jordan Valley and the rest of the West Bank was cut off. "These are security measures," the army explained at the time. "They have no political intent."[13]

. Overnight, more than two million Palestinians were completely barred from the Jordan Valley, which cut many people off from their families. Thousands of permits, renewable every three months, were then issued to farmers, teachers, health care professionals, taxi drivers, and business owners. About five thousand permits were given to Palestinian field laborers working in the settlements of the Valley. Four permanent checkpoints—at Tayasir, Hamra, Ma'ale Efraim, and Yitav—were installed on access roads in order to filter traffic coming from the center of the West Bank. It was not until April 2007 that restrictions on travel were somewhat loosened, and Palestinians could enter the Jordan Valley via the Tayasir and Hamra checkpoints without a permit, but only on foot. Local taxis with special authorization from the Israeli army were also permitted to travel between the checkpoints and the Valley. The permit system is even more suffocating in this region, where, due to its treacherous terrain, there are only a handful of roads, all easy to control. As for the mountainous paths used by shepherds and Bedouin clans, they are guarded by the army and the settlers.

Today, Jericho is accessible via a single road to the south. Residents are still forbidden to leave the city and to move freely about the Jordan Valley. PLO chief negotiator Saeb Erekat, who still lives in his childhood house in Jericho, believes that the Israelis are simply using different means to achieve the same effect as the wall and barrier have done elsewhere, that is to "cut us off from the rest of the West Bank, as they wait for a favorable moment to annex us."[14]

Following the Olso Accords of 1993, when all of the Jordan Valley, with the exception of the Jericho enclave, was under Israeli civic and military control, the Israeli military had considered building an "eastern barrier" in the Jordan Valley. Retired general Uzi Dayan, who was president of the National Security Council when the "separation line" project was under examination, favored a "disengagement" that would have annexed all the territory between Jordan and the Allon Road, as well as the western bank of the Dead Sea. When he later founded his small movement, Tafnit, General Dayan revived the idea. On a map of the "disengagement line," pinned to the wall at Tafnit headquarters in Ramat Gan, the Jordan Valley is among the annexed zones.

This option was set aside for two principal reasons: First, Washington let it be known that the construction of a barrier along the Allon Road would be considered an unacceptable attempt to annex the Jordan Valley; then, on June 30, 2004, the Israeli Supreme Court demanded that the designers of the barrier take into account "humanitarian considerations" advanced by the Palestinians. An examination of the actual topography and population movement convinced the IDF that a "virtual wall" along the Allon Road would be diplomatically less awkward and, in terms of keeping the Palestinian population in check, as efficient as an electrical fence. But to what end? Even if a hypothetical Palestinian State built on 92 percent of the West Bank was discussed in the summer of 2007 and Ehud Olmert never uttered the taboo word "annexation," the prime minister made it publicly clear, several times, that "in all future accords with the Palestinians, the Jordan Valley will remain under Israeli control."

According to the NGO Peace Now, Olmert was simply expressing a conviction shared by many Israelis, that "the Jordan Valley must remain eternally Israeli, a vital buffer zone between Israel and the Arab lands to the east."[15] Was Yigal Allon saying anything different when, almost forty years ago, he sent pioneers to create Jewish communities around Jericho?

A message form the Israel Ministry of Tourism draped over the Gilo terminal.
Courtesy of Gary Fields

CHAPTER 15

FORCE IS THE PROBLEM

Until the summer of 2006, few people had heard of a kibbutz called
Kerem Shalom. Wedged between the Gaza Strip and the Egyptian border, it was founded in 1966 by a group of agrarian leftists known as
Hashomer Hatzair, or The Youth Guard. Their palm tree utopia went
bankrupt in 1996, but was then reestablished in 2001 under the direction of Avraham Hochman, an incurable optimist determined to live
on good terms with his Palestinian neighbors. But on June 25, 2006,
this small community nestled in the serenely rustic Negev Desert, became a bloody battleground.

Shortly before dawn, eight Palestinian militants broke into the kibbutz through a secret underground tunnel and attacked Israeli soldiers.
As one group of militants fired rocket-propelled grenades at a pair of
Israeli armored vehicles, another group tried in vain to scale a surveillance tower, but was pushed back by Israeli fire. Before reinforcements
could arrive, two Palestinian militants and two Israeli soldiers had been
killed, five more soldiers had been wounded, and nineteen-year-old corporal Gilad Shalit was kidnapped and taken back to Gaza.

According to army intelligence, the tunnel, which ran under the
Gaza barrier, was nearly 2,625 feet long and, at some points, 29.5 feet
deep. The army speculated that it had taken several months for the
militants to dig it. A few days after the attack, Avraham Hochman
would note that had the tunnel turned just slightly in a different direction, it would have broken through the kibbutz's cafeteria. "The

Islamists would not have gotten out of here alive, but at what a price,"[1] he said, implying that Israeli casualties could have been much higher.

Confronted with the reality that an armed group of terrorists had effectively breached a security barrier much like the one under construction in the West Bank—a barrier that was costing Israel €2 million per kilometer to build—Prime Minister Ehud Olmert and his minister of defense, Amir Peretz, had no response. The IDF chief of staff himself began to wonder whether Olmert, who had fulfilled his military service on the army's newspaper, and Peretz, who never rose above the rank of captain, were in fact the most competent people to lead a country under perpetual terrorist threat. As the government hesitated, the army moved ahead, feeding stories to like-minded journalists without necessarily causing public outcry. Three days after the attack, the government and the leaders of the Israel Defense Forces finally came to an agreement: punish Gaza; make an example of it. Presumably they thought that the people of Gaza would then pressure the Palestinian Authority, controlled by Hamas, to apprehend the Kerem Shalom attackers and return Corporal Gilad Shalit.

Gaza soon found itself under siege, as the Israeli army began a mission to destroy arms and munitions warehouses, all tunnels under construction, and to put a stop to Qassam rocket attacks that were being launched into neighboring Israeli towns. But after two and a half months of "targeted" remote-controlled drone attacks, helicopter and F-16 raids, and 155 cannon shellings, the army still had not secured the return of Shalit.

The 1.4 million residents of Gaza paid a high price. On September 5, Agence France-Presse reported that 214 Palestinians, mostly civilians, had been killed. The only power plant in the territory, which provided electricity to more than half of the region, was destroyed, as were three main bridges. Administrative and university buildings, workshops, and stores were blown apart by bombs and missiles. Entire neighborhoods where it was suspected that Qassam rockets had been launched were cleared by shell fire. More than sixty elected Hamas officials, including eight ministers and twenty-nine deputies, were taken into custody by the Israeli army. There were severe food shortages and, despite the outcry of humanitarian organizations around the world, the destruction continued. Gaza was in survival mode, cut off from the world. "The Palestinians of Gaza are living in miserable and dangerous conditions,"[2] stated John Ging, director of the United Nations Relief and Works Agency for Palestine Refugees in the Near East (UNRWA), at the beginning of September. Even Mario Vargas Llosa, a Jerusalem Prize laureate and old friend of the Jewish state, denounced the "arrogant" attitude of Israel.

Did the successful attack on Kerem Shalom inspire the Israeli government to question the strategic relevance of the barrier under construction in the West Bank?[3] "Not at all," says Avi Dichter, who had become minister of public security after five years of directing Shin Bet, Israel's domestic security and intelligence agency. I met Dichter on a bright weekend afternoon in July 2006 at his ministry's office in Tel Aviv, an old, faded building surrounded by barbed wire. The ministry was empty except for Dichter's bodyguards, and his young Cabinet head, who had arrived in a big armored Volvo. On the surface, it did not seem as though this tanned fifty-year-old former reconnaissance officer with IDF Special Forces, who still lives in his hometown of Ashkelon on the edge of the Gaza Strip, was bothered by the Kerem Shalom operation, nor by its potentially far-reaching consequences.

"It's clear that there was a problem with our objective," he admitted, referring to the Gaza barrier. "It failed. We were incapable of detecting a number of tunnels between the Gaza Strip and Egypt, and we weren't able to see this coming. But that doesn't mean we are wrong to build the [West Bank] barrier. First of all, the terrorists could not have found more favorable conditions for their underground tunnel than at Kerem Shalom. But, over time, we would have also found a way to detect the tunnels. That being said, the current operation not only aims to destroy the tunnels and the arms warehouses, but also to put an end to the Qassam attacks on southern Israel. Not that the Qassam are especially deadly: it took a thousand rockets for the terrorists to kill just eight Israelis; a single suicide attack in Tel Aviv, some weeks ago, killed eleven. Nevertheless, it's a threat to daily life in the region that we cannot tolerate. To be clear, though, we will not stop the Qassam attacks by reoccupying Gaza, but rather by establishing a more forceful relationship with the armed groups responsible for them. You must never forget that here, in the Middle East, the only reliable course is to discourage your enemies. Look at what's happening on our northern border with Hezbollah: from time to time, they send a Katyoucha into Galilee, but we then respond with an artillery shelling or aerial attack. As a result, they understand very well how far they can go."

Five days later, Hezbollah, whose members apparently had a different view of regional power dynamics from Dichter's, kidnapped two Israeli soldiers on the Lebanese border and dragged Israel into a new war. According to the IDF, the kidnapping took place on Israeli territory, although this is contested by Lebanon.

In other words, Hezbollah militants managed to cross the security zone at the border, infiltrate Israel, mount an ambush, take prisoners, and return to their base, demonstrating once again the vulnerability of fences wired with security sensors. This time there was no hesitation, and the IDF chief of staff Dan Halutz, Ehud Olmert, and Amir Peretz moved swiftly to punish Lebanon and set an example. Thirty-four days later, when the war was over, twelve hundred Lebanese had been killed and four thousand wounded, the majority of whom were civilians. Nearly a million Lebanese—a quarter of the population—fled their bombed-out villages or neighborhoods, and at least eight hundred thousand left the country. Several airports, including the one in Beirut, were destroyed or seriously damaged, along with ports, water sanitation stations, water reservoirs, and power plants. Also bombarded were 391.4 miles of roads, 32 gas stations, 145 bridges and highway overpasses, 900 factories, and countless stores and workshops. Between the Litani River and the Israeli border, countless fields, forests, and orchards were polluted by hundreds of thousands of unexploded cluster bombs. According to the Council for Development and Reconstruction, damages amounted to $3.6 billion. The United Nations Development Programme (UNDP) estimated the overall destruction in Lebanon at $15 billion.

In Israel, the damages were not as extensive, but were by no means negligible. Throughout the incursion, Katyoucha rockets and ground-to-ground missiles rained down on northern cities, killing about forty civilians—yet another reminder that barriers, however sophisticated, are useless against certain kinds of attack.

The Israeli government was most surprised, though, by Hezbollah's formidable resistance to the incursion. The army suffered unexpected losses: nearly 120 soldiers were killed in combat and approximately 50 out of the 400 deployed Merkava tanks were destroyed by Hezbollah's Russian-, U.S.-, and Iranian-manufactured missiles. This was especially disconcerting since the IDF chief of staff had always promoted its "Made in Israel" tanks as the best in the world.

The political backlash in Israel was powerful. Sixty-three percent of Israelis called for Ehud Olmert's resignation, and blame for the failures of the war was liberally diffused. Dan Halutz, the first aviator to hold his position, was accused by his military colleagues of relying too heavily on air offensives; the military intelligence and Mossad were criticized for providing insufficient information to the army; soldiers complained about the poor quality of their equipment; and some in the IDF acknowledged that the army had at times been outmaneuvered by the highly organized Hezbollah resistance, which had ensnared tanks and infantry units in deadly surprise attacks. It seemed that the Israeli army was not what it used to be, and for Olmert, who had been in office only four months, this came as a devastating blow.

The war had also thrown many of Olmert's settlement and security plans into disarray. His election campaign had included the creation of a new eastern border using the barrier. This initiative, called the Convergence Plan, had also called for the dismantling of many isolated settlements throughout the West Bank, and for their seventy thousand residents to be transferred to annexed territory. The goal was to enclose West Bank Palestinians between the barrier to the west and the virtual wall of settlements along Allon Road to the east, with the Israeli army omnipresent throughout. This plan, however, would quickly become another casualty of Israel's new war with Lebanon. "At this time, the Convergence Plan is no longer on our list of priorities," Olmert admitted on September 4, 2006, before announcing that he "intends to have a conversation" with the Palestinian president Mahmoud Abbas.

A conversation? After avoiding him for months? And on what basis would they begin talks: the "Roadmap" proposed by President Bush back in April 2003?

Indeed, this is what Shimon Peres had proposed. But the terms of the Roadmap, which had called upon the Palestinians to "halt all acts of violence and terrorism" and for the Israelis to "dismantle the settlements built since 2001" and to "freeze all settlement activity," had clearly been ignored. Although the Israeli Cabinet had officially approved the Roadmap in May 2003, at that time the vote included fourteen reservations, which had rendered the plan almost impossible to implement. And while the United Nations Security Council officially approved the plan on November 19, 2003, it specified no concrete measures to enforce implementation. Sharon had candidly told his ministers at the time that he thought the Roadmap was too constraining and out-of-date. So, in order to give Israel the leverage it would later need to renegotiate it, he created a smoke screen of historic proportions by evacuating all of the Gaza settlers. Ten months before this grand gesture, designed to show the world that Israel could make concessions, the head of Sharon's cabinet, Dov Weisglass, had told *Haaretz* in an interview that the withdrawal from Gaza was necessary "so that there will not be a political process with the Palestinians."[4]

With the peace process abandoned, the Roadmap in tatters, and the Convergence Plan permanently on hold, would the barrier now finally come under scrutiny? Had the time come to admit that this "fait accompli" put the whole negotiating process at risk? Would the government at least suspend work on this monument to unilateralism?

No. The barrier, like the settlements, seemed to have become untouchable, as though in this time of crisis and doubt it was one of the last bastions of certainty for Israeli leaders, a solution on the horizon.

But that was not the opinion of Shaul Arieli, a young retired colonel who once served as commander of the Gaza Strip. He was one of Ehud Barak's closest advisors during the informal negotiations with Palestinians that preceded the Geneva Accords. A member of the Council for Peace and Security, an organization of former military, police, and Shin Bet officers and Mossad agents, he is considered an expert on the barrier.

"I am not opposed to the existence of a material obstacle between us and the Palestinians in principle," he explains. "For security, economic, and/or demographic reasons, a barrier can be justified, but only under two conditions: it must be built with the agreement of the Palestinians, and it must be built on the Green Line. Until something else comes along, the Armistice Line, even if it can be renegotiated with our neighbors, is the only border between Israel and the Palestinian territories that is recognized by international law. The problem with the barrier as it exists today is its route. I know its original designer very well; ten years ago, Dany Tirza was my assistant during the negotiations of the interim peace accord. And I know full well that the decisive factor for the path was not security, but the settlements—you'd have to be blind not to see it. For example, look at any part of the barrier both before and after a modification ordered by the Supreme Court, and you'll see that the new path is always closer to the Green Line, but that it still includes exactly the same number of Israelis. And I don't believe that the barrier's original route would have ensured better security, either. Quite the contrary, it inflames the frustration of the Palestinians, and in the long run it contributes to the development of a terrorist infrastructure. I know that, in general, the Israelis approve of the barrier, but unfortunately they don't appreciate the implications of choosing one route over another."[5]

Israel's attorney general, Menachem Mazuz, criticized Dany Tirza in July 2006 for using the security justifications of the barrier as a cover for expanding the settlements. In a letter to the minister of defense, Amir Peretz, Mazuz complained that "the official responsible for the barrier's design had obfuscated the fact that its route had been determined by unauthorized settlement expansion plans, and not by security considerations." Standing before the court responsible for hearing Palestinian petitions to the barrier, and visibly irritated by "the official responsible for the barrier's design," Mazuz added that because of this "error," a "judicial decision based on incomplete evidence had been rendered," and he requested that the minister order an investigation. Tirza had already been brought to court several times to respond to Palestinian petitions against the barrier, and judges had repeatedly reprimanded him for having provided incomplete or erroneous information to the courts, information that would then be repudiated by military experts—mainly members of the Council for Peace and Security—who had been invited by the courts to give their expert opinion. Accused by the attorney general of being "intolerably lacking" as a citizen and an official, Dany Tirza finally left his post at the end of 2006 when his contract was up. Shortly thereafter, he became a Cabinet member and was placed in charge of bridge, tunnel, and road construction connecting Palestinian districts in the West Bank.

Ever since the first section of the barrier broke ground in 2002, nearly one hundred petitions challenging its route have been submitted to Israeli courts. In spring 2006, fifty-five were heard before the Supreme Court, and about fifty others had been resolved. In several cases, the courts found in favor of the Palestinians—most notably in the cases of the Alfei Menashe enclave, Biddu, Jayous, Sheikh Sa'ad, and, in September 2007, Bili'n. The judges based their decisions solely on whether the barrier fulfilled its goal as defined by the Council of Ministers, namely "to reduce the influx of terrorists coming from Judea and Samaria with the intention of committing attacks in Israel." There are no official documents generated by the Israeli government stating that the barrier must serve as protection for the settlements.

THE ATTACKS ON KEREM SHALOM AND THE LEBANESE BORDER SHOW that the security zones built by the Israeli army are not impenetrable. Has the barrier in the West Bank, whatever its form—electronic fence or wall—proven to be as effective as promised? "Indisputably," confirms Dany Tirza. "Along the first section of the barrier, near Route 65 between the Israeli cities of Afula and Pardes Hanna-Karkur, the number of Israeli victims of terrorist attacks dropped from fifty-eight in 2002 to zero in 2004 and 2005. For me, this speaks volumes."

Avi Dichter adds: "In 2003, nearly fifty-five percent of those responsible for attacks against Israelis came from Samaria. In 2006, they were no more than twelve to fifteen percent. The wall complicates the lives of terrorists: it forces them to take long detours in order to find a point of entry into Israel, and it heightens the risk of getting caught during an inspection at a checkpoint. At the beginning of July 2006, we arrested a member of the Al-Aqsa Brigade of Jenin who was going to bomb Nazareth Illit. Because of the barrier, he had to make an enormous detour to Ramallah and Jerusalem, and he was stopped near Ramallah."

Neither Tirza nor Dichter, however, can provide statistics that differentiate among the many possible reasons for the reduction in terrorist attacks. Is the barrier the cause of this reduction, or should we credit the successive truces negotiated since 2004?

As soon as its sinuous route had been revealed to them, the Palestinians tried to make it known that the barrier was a breach of international law, and sometimes they even had the assistance of Israeli human rights organizations. In February 2004, at the behest of the Association for Civil Rights in Israel, an organization of British lawyers called OXPIL (Oxford Public Interest Lawyers) published a very well argued report of approximately 50 pages that clearly establishes, in 311 points, the illegality of the barrier. "In its current form," wrote the editors of the document, "Israel's construction of the separation barrier in the Occupied Territories violates both international humanitarian law and international human rights law. Israel has not presented any compelling justification on security grounds for the barrier as it is currently being constructed, and the barrier imposes unnecessary and disproportionate restrictions on the human rights of the Palestinians."[6]

Five months later, the International Commission of Jurists, a nongovernmental organization based in Geneva, published an equally well organized sixty-page document that arrived at the same conclusion.

And finally, on July 9 of that same year, the International Court of Justice at The Hague, which the United Nations General Assembly had petitioned since December 2003, rendered its advisory opinion on the "Legal Consequences of the Construction of a Wall in the Occupied Palestinian Territory." After a decidedly indifferent reaction to the NGOs, the Israeli government was more attentive when confronted with the advisory opinion of the International Court of Justice, which is the principal judicial instrument of the United Nations.

First, Israel contested the competence of the Court, asserting that the UN has historically been biased against it; then it argued that the judges did not have the necessary security intelligence to hear the case; then it refused to recognize the Court's right to override decisions made by Israel's judges. It even argued in vain that the intervention of the Court could "hinder a negotiated political solution to the Israeli-Palestinian conflict under the Roadmap." And at no point did the Israeli government send an official to The Hague, only written explanations of their arguments.

In July 2004, seven months after having been petitioned by the General Assembly, the International Court of The Hague rendered a crushing sixty-four-page advisory opinion against Israel. Each of the court's five conclusions was individually approved by a margin of at least thirteen out of fifteen possible votes. For example, Point A, approved by fourteen votes to one, states that "the construction of the wall being built by Israel, the occupying Power, in the Occupied Palestinian Territories including in and around East Jerusalem, and its associated régime, are contrary to international law . . ." Point B, also approved by fourteen to one, requires Israel to "dismantle forthwith the structure therein situated, and to repeal or render ineffective forthwith all legislative and regulatory acts relating thereto." Point C, approved by fourteen to one: "Israel is under an obligation to make reparations for all damages caused by the construction of the wall." Point D, approved by thirteen to two: "all States are under an obligation not to recognize the illegal situation resulting from the construction of the wall and not to render aid or assistance in maintaining the situation created by such construction." Finally, Point E, approved by fourteen to one, states that "the United Nations, and especially the General Assembly and the Security Council, should consider what further action is required to bring to an end the illegal situation resulting from the construction of the wall and the associated regime, taking due account of the present Advisory Opinion."

Eleven days later, on July 20, during its tenth emergency session, the UN General Assembly adopted Resolution ES-10/15, by a vote of 150 in favor, 6 against, and 12 abstentions.[7] The resolution demands that Israel, "the occupying Power," and "all States Members of the UN," comply with their "legal obligations as mentioned in the advisory opinion," and requests that the secretary-general "establish a register of damage caused to all natural or legal persons concerned." Would the Security Council, in turn, adopt a binding resolution, or at least threaten sanctions against a State that has clearly violated international law? No. Two years later, on the first anniversary of The Hague's advisory opinion, no punitive decision had been made. It was not until December 15, 2006, that a new General Assembly resolution, ES-10/7, established a "United Nations Register of Damage Caused by the Construction of the Wall in the Occupied Palestinian Territory." Meanwhile, the wall had advanced more than 225 miles. In July 2008, in a report published on the fourth anniversary of the advisory opinion, the United Nations Office for the Coordination of Humanitarian Affairs (OCHA)[8] issued a report stating that "the construction of the barrier continues, that 57 percent of the project is completed, 9 percent under construction, and that the majority of its trajectory—approximately 87 percent—is inside the West Bank and not along the Green Line." What better way to remind the Palestinians, and the rest of the world, that as far as the settlements and the barrier are concerned, Israel can ignore international law with impunity.

This begs the question: What if today's security threat to Israel came not only from the surrounding region, but also from the misguided decisions of its own leaders? Does Israel imperil its chances at peace and security by showing indifference to Palestinian human rights; by refusing to acknowledge or at least entertain the possibility that Palestinian anger springs from a legitimate desire for liberty; by assuming that all Palestinians are complicit with international terrorism; and by repeatedly casting irresponsible accusations of anti-Semitism at anyone who attempts to criticize Israeli policies and decisions? And doesn't the generally accepted mode of solving political dilemmas with military action carry significant risks as well? "Have we not learned yet that in the relationship between us and our neighbors," wrote Akiva Eldar, an editorialist with *Haaretz*, during the Gaza crisis of summer 2006, "force is the problem. Not the solution."[9]

CHAPTER 16

A New Border

By the end of 2008, contrary to the hopes of Israeli politicians and military leaders, the West Bank barrier had still not been completed. Officials have been careful not to release definitive plans for the rest of the barrier, but maps created by both the military and the UN suggest that 256.6 miles of the barrier were operational in June 2009. Back in February 2005, 130 miles of the barrier were declared operational; 225 miles were operational by July 2006; and 254 miles by September 2007. But in September 2008, the wall measured only 257.8 miles—in other words, after having initially progressed at a pace of 5.3 miles per month until the summer of 2006, construction of the barrier had slowed down significantly. At the end of 2007, it was advancing at only 1.24 miles per month, and by the end of 2008, construction was virtually at a standstill. Only 57 percent of the 450 miles[1] of fencing and cement planned by the military had seen the light of day. Why was the project suffering from so many delays?

A partial explanation came in October 2007, when Deputy Prime Minister Haim Ramon, the man in charge of supervising the barrier project, told *Haaretz*[2] that a recently approved sixty-two-mile section of the barrier was being held up because companies contracted to build it had not been paid. According to *Haaretz*, Ramon had been unnerved to find that the 2008 Defense Ministry budget did not include a line of credit for the barrier. Over the course of the following weeks, however, Ramon did not make any follow-up statements to the media—it seemed that the requested funds had been found and released. Yet almost a year later, the issue of how the Defense Ministry would fund the wall was still on the table. In September 2008, as construction remained at a standstill, a contentious debate over the barrier's budget had pitted IDF chief of staff Gabi Ashkenazi against several members of the government, including Prime Minister Olmert. According to Ashkenazi, the barrier serves both political and national security goals, and therefore the Ministry of Defense should not be the only department footing the bill.

There may be another explanation: more Palestinians than ever had begun to challenge the route of the barrier in court. Michael Sfard estimated that by the end of 2007, at least eight petitions had been filed against the route of the barrier, often with the support of Israeli human rights associations. One year later, more than a hundred cases had been filed. But many of the courts held that the barrier did not violate the fundamental rights of the Palestinians, when weighed against the security benefits to the State of Israel.

In a few cases, though, the court held in favor of the villagers and ordered the army to revise its plans. In September 2007, in the case of a village just west of Ramallah called Bili'in, the army was actually ordered to move a barrier already in place, based on a ruling that the security rationale invoked by the military to justify the barrier's path was invalid. The army was told to dismantle 1,700 meters of the barrier and to return 494 acres of expropriated land to the villagers. In July 2008, the military proposed a new path that would allow for the restitution of only 4.9 acres. The villagers refused the offer, and Michael Sfard brought the case before the Supreme Court. "Until then," Sfard said in July 2008, "the Supreme Court had rejected four sections of the barrier that had already been built. But the government refused to implement these four decisions."[3]

In another case, in June 2006 the Court had reprimanded the State for falsely claiming that the barrier section at the edge of Qalqiliya was a necessary security measure; in fact, the barrier route in this area was designed solely to allow for the northward extension of the Tzufin settlement, home to 1,000 Israelis.

In August 2008, the Supreme Court ordered the prime minister and the minister of defense to return to the villages of Abu Dis and Sawahira a-Sharqiya half of the 1,977 acres expropriated around the Ma'ale Adumim settlement for the barrier, and for the settlement's expansion.

And after five years of litigation, the army agreed to dismantle a 1.49-mile-long section of the barrier to the north of Qalqiliya, which had deprived Palestinian villagers of 642.4 acres of farmland.

In many cases, the courts attempted to negotiate an agreement that would satisfy both parties, as with the five Palestinian villages enclosed within the Alfei Menashe settlement enclave. When proceedings began in August 2004, the courts had accepted the arguments filed by three of the villages, but had temporarily set aside the petitions of the other two—for the moment, those two villages would have to remain inside the enclave. The army then completely disregarded the court's ruling and refused to move a single meter of the barrier, enclosing the five villages on the "Israeli" side of the separation line. Arie Zissman, who was responsible for the security of Alfei Menashe, confirmed this: "A new route for the separation line was proposed to the army, but they counterargued with security imperatives, and nothing for the time being has been truly halted."[4]

It takes time for petitions to be reviewed by the Israeli courts and the minister of defense. Meanwhile, the military ignored all Supreme Court orders to dismantle sections of the barrier, opting to wait out the appeals process. This explains in part why the barrier, which should have been completed by the end of 2005, was still under construction at the end of 2008. All along the separation line, a number of construction sites remain dormant. In November 2007, construction was suspended between the settlements of Beit Arieh and Ofarim, near Ramallah, for "technical reasons," according to the minister of defense. Construction was also halted near the Green Line between the Palestinian villages of Al-Midya and Bili'n, pending court decisions. To the south of Ma'ale Adumim, where several Bedouin families had taken legal action against the wall, there is a 1.86-mile-long construction site that has been inactive since March 2006. In spring 2008 near Bethlehem, where cement blocks twenty-six to thirty-nine feet high were installed along Highway

60, construction was at a standstill—again, held up by court hearings and petitions.

There is a third, perhaps less obvious explanation for the delay of the barrier. In February 2007, General Dan Halutz was forced to resign after multiple errors in judgment during the war in southern Lebanon, and General Gabi Ashkenazi took over as IDF chief of staff. Formerly a member of the infantry brigade of Golani, he had served in Sinai and Beirut, and took part in Operation Entebbe in 1976. From 2002 to 2005 he served as IDF deputy chief of staff, and in that role had supervised the construction of the separation barrier. On December 23, 2003, testifying before the Knesset Foreign Affairs and Defense Committee, he stated that the barrier would be "the largest construction site in the country," costing nearly 10 billion shekels ($2.3 billion). At that time, he had envisioned mobilizing 15,000 Israelis and Palestinians to build a 206-mile section between the southwest of Jerusalem and the region south of Hebron, with about forty companies bidding on the contract. Ashkenazi was intimately familiar with the separation barrier when he took over as commander of the IDF,[5] and the press reported that he was enraged when, at the beginning of 2007, he had heard the Supreme Court's June 15, 2006, decision regarding the path of the barrier to the north of Qalqiliya. The Court had reprimanded the army for falsely representing the wide circle of the barrier around the Zufin settlement, which had been justified as a security measure to protect two neighboring Israeli villages—in fact, the Palestinian land north and east of the settlement had simply been earmarked for the settlement's expansion. In response to the Court's reprimand, General Ashkenazi told Minister of Defense Amir Peretz that he would no longer allow officials of the IDF to defend the route of the barrier in court. "The path is a political question," he explained at the time, "it should thus be the responsibility of the government." According to a July 2008 report in *Haaretz*, "the army was much less involved in determining the barrier's route" after the Court's reprimand.[6] Political leaders in turn found it more difficult to back up their security argument for the barrier without the support of the military, and were forced to take a step back and to wait out petition proceedings filed by the Palestinian villagers before embarking upon any new construction sites.

These court proceedings and delays have also occasionally served the special interests of Israelis, as in the case of a small settlement called Eshkolot. This minuscule community, with a population of about three hundred, sits on the summit of a rocky plateau at the far southwest point of the West Bank, about a mile from the Green Line. From the border of Eshkolot, the electronic barrier, with its barbed-wire-lined patrol routes, can be seen running precisely along the Armistice Line. Interestingly, the barrier terminates less than a mile to the north and to the south of Eshkolot. Military and UN maps show that the army had originally intended for the barrier to form a mushroom-shaped loop around the settlement and part of its land, creating an enclave open to the west, toward Israel. A settler who spoke to me on condition of anonymity said, "the barrier should have made a detour not only around the houses, but also around the municipal lands that extend to the north of us. The army has been telling us for years that the question of Eshkolot is still under discussion. But we know what is really happening. They don't want to build a three-mile loop for a hundred or so people. In their minds, Eshkolot has already been sacrificed. The day when an agreement is reached with the Palestinians, we will be forcibly evacuated, like the settlements in Gaza, and they will close up the barrier with a straight line."[7]

Meanwhile, the Eshkolot gap has become an unofficial passage point for the Palestinian workforce employed, often illegally, in Israel. Literally hundreds of Palestinians converge at the intersection of Highways 358 and 3255 on any given work day, right near Eshkolot, where they are transported by minibuses in and out of Israel. "The people that you see here come from the south of the West Bank," explains the Ehkolot settler. "Some of these buses go all the way to Hebron. The Israeli entrepreneurs have profited from this situation; they have been able to keep some of their Palestinian workers at a reduced price. For us," he adds, "a job in Israel, even temporary and illegal, is a great opportunity."

Given Israel's emphatic security concerns, it is a little surprising to find so many Palestinians traveling freely around the Eshkolot settlement. At dusk, I watched a procession of Palestinian workers step off of the Israeli minibuses and disperse into the rocky West Bank terrain after a day of labor, as a blue-and-white police car and two army Humvees passed by without stopping. Despite the existence of a military base a few miles away, the risk of terrorist infiltration that had been invoked by the barrier's architects does not seem to trouble the security services.

In March 2009, *The Humanitarian Monitor,* a monthly report on conditions in the Occupied Territories, issued by the UN Office for the Coordination of Humanitarian Affairs (OCHA), stated that "land leveling started around the Eshkolot settlement. Once constructed, this section [of the barrier] will isolate approximately 4000 dunums of land, encompassing the settlement built up area and grazing area used by Palestinian herders." Some three hundred agricultural water cisterns and the seasonal dwellings of four Palestinian families will be isolated as well.

Thirty-one miles east of Eshkolot is another huge gap, running between the barrier and the shores of the Dead Sea. UN and military maps show no dotted lines or any hint of a planned barrier in the area. Why has the army decided not to build a barrier in these inhospitable hills? Major Shay Karmona, from the Command Headquarters of the Civil Administration in the West Bank, says that it is because "this region links the Negev Desert to the Judean Desert, and forms a zone of passage for a multitude of wild and protected animals. Environmental associations and animal protection activists were able to secure from the IDF something that the Palestinians could never get: a promise of no physical obstacle in the region. Nothing will interfere with the lives of the desert fauna.

"That does not mean, however, that the area will not be guarded. We are assembling a special mobile unit equipped with portable detection systems to patrol the region day and night. I can assure you that it will be just as efficient as the electronic fence."[8]

The "security barrier" is often credited with the dramatic, and very real, decline in terrorism in the region,[9] and appears to have fulfilled its stated purpose as such. However, Israeli leaders are lately finding it more and more difficult to deny either the barrier's value as a bargaining chip in future peace negotiations, or that Israel had always intended the barrier to be the future border of a Palestinian state. These assumptions are clearly illustrated by the distribution of settlements along the wall. According to a UN report made public in July 2007,[10] 365,744 out of 421,660 settlers surveyed in the West Bank or East Jerusalem (86.7 percent) lived west of the wall. One year later, in July 2008, Peace Now estimated the number of settlers living west of the wall to be 388,800 out of 454,200,[11] based on statistics from the Israeli Central Bureau of Statistics. More important, the five most heavily populated settlements of the West Bank (Ma'ale Adumim, Ariel, Alfei Menashe, Gush Etzion, and Modi'in Illit) and the twelve settlements of East Jerusalem[12] were on the western side of the barrier, sitting right on the very fringe of the West Bank.

These are not merely the paranoid delusions of Israel's enemies. During a debate broadcast live by France Inter in August 2007, former Israeli ambassador to France Nissim Zvili called the Green Line "the former border" between Israel and the future State of Palestine.[13] Without going quite that far, numerous Israeli officials have said for years that the Green Line is not sacred, and that in the context of negotiations on final status, they were open to exchanges of territory with the Palestinians. Obsessed with reducing the non-Jewish population in Israel, some politicians have even suggested exchanging regions of Israel with an Arab-Israeli population for some border enclaves where principal settlements are located.

In a thirty-five-page study published in September 2008,[14] General Giora Eiland, who presided over Israel's National Security Council from 2004 to 2006 after having served thirty-three years in the army, states that he is in favor of a future border that runs primarily along the "security barrier." This new border would annex most of the settlements west of the existing barrier. As compensation, Eiland suggests a range of possible territory exchanges, including a triangular barter among Israel, Palestine, and Egypt. He also believes that hostilities between Israelis and Palestinians are now so strong that all future negotiations must include the existence of a "security barrier." Since the collapse of Oslo, the Second Intifada, and the rise to power of Hamas, Israeli public opinion, according to Eiland, is less and less in favor of "land for peace," which had always been an underlying assumption of all formal negotiations. According to a study conducted by the Institute for National Strategic Studies (INSS), in Tel Aviv, 56 percent of the Jewish population in Israel favored a Land for Peace program in 1977. By 2007, that number had fallen to 28 percent.[15] And in a booklet issued by the Jerusalem Center for Public Affairs in 2007,[16] three former ambassadors, a general, and the director of the National Defense Institute, stated that the barrier/border was insufficient. They suggested a line of separation much farther east, in which Israel assumes control of the Jordan Valley and widens the Tel Aviv–Jerusalem corridor in order to create a zone of defense for Jerusalem.

These ideas do not take into account the reluctance or outright resistance of the Palestinians. Israeli military leaders seem convinced that whatever is good for Israel's security is permissible, and they have ignored international law, UN resolutions, and even their own commitments with almost complete impunity. In 2004, a close collaborator of the state prosecutor, Talia Sasson, was commissioned by Ariel Sharon to create a report on the wild settlements in the West Bank. Her research found that many of these "outposts" had received direct funding from the ministries of Housing, Energy, Education, and Defense, in violation of Israeli law. Submitted to the government in March 2005, Sasson's report was relegated to a drawer, where it still lies. Sasson promptly resigned. "We have built a magnificent country, of which I am proud," she confided in April 2008, on the eve of Israel's sixtieth anniversary, "but our democracy is in danger. The military thinks they can do as they please, we are almost incapable of appreciating the distress of others, and since Rabin's assassination, all of our leaders have lacked courage."[17]

For some time now, the Palestinians have generally accepted limited exchanges of territory, as long as the barter was equal—one square mile for one square mile—and the land in question was of comparable quality. But it would be rash to assume that Mahmoud Abbas or his successors would simply hand over some 12 percent of West Bank territory sitting between the Green Line and the barrier, even for an equal exchange of land elsewhere. After Hamas assumed power in Gaza in June 2007, and the armed confrontation with Fatah, Israeli leadership may have begun to dramatically miscalculate the balance of power in the region.

The gulf between both sides was never clearer than at the meetings leading up to the Annapolis Conference, on November 27, 2007. Palestinian negotiators wanted to return to the terms of reference from the Oslo Accords in 1993, which had served as the basis for all subsequent negotiations. They also drew terms of reference from UN resolutions 194, 242, and 338,[18] from the conclusions of Camp David (2000) and Taba (2001), from the Arab Peace Initiative proposed at the Beirut Summit (2002), and from President Bush's Roadmap (2003), which had been endorsed by the United Nations, the European Union, the United States, and Russia. One month before Annapolis, President Mahmoud Abbas stated in a televised interview[19] that the future State of Palestine should be established over the whole of the Gaza Strip and West Bank—that is, 3,856 square miles. And on the eve of Annapolis, the Palestinian leadership was encouraged to find that two of their most important reference texts—UN resolutions 242 and 338—were mentioned in the letter of invitation addressed to Mahmoud Abbas by George Bush.

On the Israeli side, the basis for negotiation was very different, which is why the discussions that preceded Annapolis were so difficult. The two parties, lacking any better option, had to be content with a generous but vague "common declaration" at the opening of the conference, and an equally vague set of commitments at the conclusion. "Today, it is no longer a question of Camp David, of Taba or the Clinton parameters," a high-ranking Israeli diplomat who requested not to be named explained a week before the opening of Annapolis; "the circumstances are completely different. We are beginning at almost zero."[20] Rather, the Israeli delegation placed major importance on a letter from President Bush dated April 14, 2004, and addressed to the prime minister at the time, Ariel Sharon. In this document, solemnly approved by the U.S. Senate (95 votes to 3) and by the House of Representatives

(407 votes to 9), Bush states that Israel must have secure borders as set forth in UN Security Council resolutions 242 and 338. But, he adds, "In light of new realities on the ground, including already existing major Israeli population centers, it is unrealistic that the outcome of final status negotiations will be a full and complete return to the armistice lines of 1949, and all previous efforts to negotiate a two-state solution have reached the same conclusion." In other words, the most populated settlements in the West Bank are now completely off the table. Under the Bush administration, all negotiations were based, therefore, on the path of a border unilaterally drawn by Israel. The peace process, already dying during this exchange of letters between Bush and Sharon, did not survive Israeli unilateralism or bloody confrontations among the Palestinians, and was rendered diplomatically invisible to the United States.

Can Barack Obama reopen the road to peace? Perhaps. Even before his election, he had said the he planned for the United States to play a major role in the resolution of the Middle East conflict. In his opinion, the most pressing international issues—Iraq, Iran, Afghanistan, terrorism, the Israeli-Palestinian conflict—were linked. To neglect one link would break the whole chain, and it is clearly with this conviction that he entered the White House. His first acts as president have demonstrated a will to change the course of U.S. diplomacy in the Middle East. Mahmoud Abbas was the first foreign leader whom he called after stepping onto the world stage. And his commitment to resolving the conflict was further confirmed when he named former Democratic senator George Mitchell, an expert on the region who had moderated an international commission on the Israeli-Palestinian conflict in 2000, U.S. special envoy to the Middle East at the end of January 2009.

The Palestinians have responded positively to these gestures while the Israelis have not hidden their vexation, especially following the election of Netanyahu and establishment of the most right-leaning government in Israeli history. Obama's speech to the Muslim world at the University of Cairo on June 4, 2009, would further irritate them.

After clarifying that "America is not and never will be at war with

Islam," he stated that "America's strong bonds with Israel are well known" and that "this bond is unbreakable." But he added that the Palestinians "endure the daily humiliations—large and small—that come with occupation," and that there circumstances are "intolerable." He concluded by stating that in order to resolve this conflict it was necessary to create "two states, where Israelis and Palestinians each live in peace and security." Then he uttered the sentence that sparked perhaps the most ire: "The United States does not accept the legitimacy of continued Israeli settlements."

Ten days later, Netanyahu tried to reassure his electorate by declaring his opposition to freezing settlement activity, and by enumerating a set of unacceptable conditions under which he would accept the creation of a Palestinian State. It is clear that Obama's words also sent a shock wave through both the Palestinian community and the Arab world. "The United States did not change alliances. Israel remains their privileged partner," notes the Palestinian journalist Akram Haniyeh, advisor and confidant of President Abbas. "But we now have the assurance of a more equitable attitude and of a less simplistic vision of the Middle East situation."[21]

As for the "new beginning" that Obama proposed to the people of the Middle East in his Cairo speech, can it be anything but a chimera as long as half a million Israelis live in the settlements of the occupied West Bank? And as long as a ribbon of iron and cement snakes its way through the Holy Land?

CHRONOLOGY

(Dates directly pertaining to the wall are noted with a •)

FEBRUARY 1896   Theodor Herzl publishes *The Jewish State: Proposal of a Modern Solution for the Jewish Question*, an important text of early Zionism.

OCTOBER 1910   The first kibbutz in Palestine, Degania Alef, is founded on the banks of the Sea of Galilee.

MAY 16, 1916   After the fall of the Ottoman Empire during World War I, the secret Sykes-Picot Agreement is signed, dividing the Middle East between France and the United Kingdom.

NOVEMBER 2, 1917   The British foreign minister Lord Arthur Balfour writes a letter to Lord Rothschild, the representative of British Jews, announcing that "His Majesty's Government view[s] with favor the establishment in Palestine of a national home for the Jewish people." The letter is later known as the Balfour Declaration.

DECEMBER 9, 1917   At the Battle for Jerusalem, the Holy City is taken by British troops.

APRIL–MAY 1920   Tension between Jewish immigrants and the indigenous Arab population sparks riots throughout Jerusalem. Five Jews and four Arabs are killed. The British temporarily hault Jewish immigration to Palestine. Haganah, a Jewish paramilitary organization, is founded, and will later become the Israel Defense Forces.

JULY 24, 1922 The League of Nations transfers power over Palestine to the United Kingdom, in what would be called the British Mandate.

AUGUST 23–29, 1929 Riots flare up again in Jerusalem, spurred by a dispute over access to the Western Wall, leading to the deaths of 116 Arabs and 133 Jews. Arab demonstrations take place throughout Palestine.

APRIL 21, 1936 A general Palestinian strike marks the beginning of an uprising in protest of Jewish immigration, later known as the Great Arab Revolt. The revolt will continue until 1939.

MAY 17, 1939 The British government issues the White Paper of 1939, or the MacDonald White Paper, which proposes the creation of a unified state in Palestine where Jews and Arabs would share power. Jewish immigration and land acquisition by Zionists would be limited.

MAY 12, 1942 In response to the White Paper of 1939, the World Zionist Organization adopts the Biltmore Program, which calls for "Palestine [to] be established as a Jewish Commonwealth" with no limits on immigration.

FEBRUARY 14, 1947 The British government addresses the problem of the future of Palestine before the United Nations.

NOVEMBER 29, 1947 The United Nations General Assembly adopts Resolution 181 by a two-thirds majority. This resolution calls for dividing Palestine into a Jewish state and an Arab state, with Jerusalem and Holy Places under "special international regime." According to the Resolution: "Free access to the Holy Places and religious buildings or sites and the free exercise of worship shall be secured in conformity with existing rights and subject to the requirements of public order and decorum."

MAY 14, 1948 Israel's first prime minister, David Ben-Gurion, announces the birth of the State of Israel. The Arab League declares war on the new state.

MAY 15, 1948 Egypt, Syria, Jordan, Lebanon, and Iraq invade, launching the 1948 Arab-Israeli War.

FEBRUARY 24–JULY 20, 1949 Armistice agreements are signed between Israel and its Arab neighbors.

APRIL 24, 1950 The West Bank is annexed by Jordan, and Egypt takes control of Gaza.

OCTOBER 29, 1956   Egypt nationalizes the Suez Canal. Israeli, British, and French forces invade the Sinai Peninsula to regain control of the canal in what is later known as the Suez Canal Crisis. Israel withdraws several months later under pressure from the United States and the Soviet Union.

MAY 29, 1964   In Jerusalem, the Palestine Liberation Organization (PLO) is created.

JUNE 5, 1967   The Six-Day War breaks out, and Israel occupies the Sinai, the Golan Heights, the Gaza Strip, the West Bank, and East Jerusalem.

AUGUST 29, 1967   The 1967 Arab League Summit adopts the Khartoum Resolution, also known the "Three Nos": no to peace with Israel, no to recognition of Israel, no to negotiations with Israel.

NOVEMBER 22, 1967   The United Nations Security Council unanimously adopts Resolution 242, which recognizes the right of Israel to exist, as well as the right of "every State in the area . . . to live in peace within secure and recognized boundaries." The resolution also calls for the withdrawal of Israeli forces from the Occupied Territories as a condition for sustainable peace—essentially, the idea of "land for peace."

FEBRUARY 1–4, 1969   At the Fifth Palestinian National Council, Yasser Arafat becomes president of the PLO.

OCTOBER 6–24, 1973   Egypt and Syria, with a coalition of Arab forces, invade Israel on Yom Kippur, sparking the the Yom Kippur (or October) War.

OCTOBER 22, 1973   The United Nations Security Council adopts Resolution 338, calling for the immediate implementation of Resolution 242 and the start of negotiations.

NOVEMBER 26–28, 1973   At the Arab Summit in Algiers, the PLO is recognized as the "sole representative of the Palestinian nation." The Hashemite Kingdom of Jordan expresses reservations.

MARCH 12–20, 1977   During the thirteenth session of the Palestinian National Council in Cairo, leaders of the PLO accept the idea of an independent Palestinian State in part of Palestine.

JULY 30, 1980   The Knesset issues the Basic Law, proclaiming the "complete and united" Jerusalem the capital of Israel.

JUNE 6, 1982 After a terrorist attack in London against the Israeli ambassador Shlomo Argov, who is seriously wounded, Israel invades Lebanon.

SEPTEMBER 16–18, 1982 Israeli troops enter West Beirut. Christian militiamen massacre Palestinians in the camps of Sabra and Shatila; Israeli troops do nothing to stop it. According to the Commission of Inquiry into the Events at the Refugee Camps in Beirut, conducted by Judge Yitzhak Kahane, eight hundred Palestinians were killed. The PLO estimates the number of dead at fifteen hundred.

DECEMBER 9, 1987 The First Intifada erupts in the Gaza Strip and, over the next five years, will rage throughout the Palestinian territories.

NOVEMBER 12–15, 1988 At its nineteenth session, the PNC proclaims the creation of the State of Palestine, recognizes UN resolutions 181, 242, and 338, and once again condemns acts of terrorism.

OCTOBER 30, 1991 President George H. W. Bush and Mikhail Gorbachev co-sponsor the Madrid Peace Conference.

NOVEMBER 3, 1991 Bilateral negotiations between Israel and the Syrian, Lebanese, and Jordanian-Palestinian delegations begin.

JANUARY 20, 1993 Secret Oslo negotiations are initiated between a Palestinian delegation led by Ahmed Qurei (Abu Ala) and an Israeli team led by academics Yair Hirschfeld and Ron Pundak.

AUGUST 19, 1993 In Oslo, the Israeli envoy Uri Savir and the Palestinian negotiator Abu Ala sign the "Declaration of Principles" on Interim Self-Government Arrangements" for Palestinians.

SEPTEMBER 9, 1993 The State of Israel, represented by Prime Minister Yitzhak Rabin, and the PLO, represented by President Yasser Arafat, exchange letters of mutual recognition.

SEPTEMBER 13, 1993 In the presence of Yitzhak Rabin and Yasser Arafat, Shimon Peres and Mahmoud Abbas (Abu Mazen) sign the Oslo Accords (formally known as the "Declaration of Principles) before Bill Clinton at the White House. Witnesses include the U.S. secretary of state, Warren Christopher, and the Russian minister of foreign affairs, Andrei Kozyrev.

FEBRUARY 25, 1994 Baruch Goldstein, an Israeli settler, opens fire on Muslim worshippers at the Cave of the Patriarchs, in Hebron, killing twenty-nine people.

MAY 4, 1994   Yitzhak Rabin and Yasser Arafat sign the Cairo Agreement, which details implementation of the Oslo Accords. A five-year period of self-government begins.

JULY 1, 1994   Yasser Arafat returns to Gaza.

DECEMBER 10, 1994   Yasser Arafat, Yitzhak Rabin, and Shimon Peres receive the Nobel Peace Prize.

• END OF JANUARY 1995   Twenty Israeli soldiers and two civilians are killed by a terrorist attack at a highway intersection near Natanya, about twenty miles north of Tel Aviv. Prime Minister Yitzhak Rabin creates a study group under the authority of the minister of security, Moshe Shachal, to examine the construction of a continuous barrier between Israel and the Palestinians.

SEPTEMBER 28, 1995   Yasser Arafat and Yitzhak Rabin sign the Oslo II Accords in Washington, extending self-government in the West Bank.

NOVEMBER 4, 1995   Yitzhak Rabin is assassinated in Tel Aviv by Yigal Amir, a religious nationalist extremist. Shimon Peres takes over as prime minister.

JANUARY 20, 1996   General elections are held in the West Bank, Gaza, and in East Jerusalem. Yasser Arafat is elected president of the Palestinian Authority. His supporters carry two thirds of the seats in the Legislative Council.

FEBRUARY–MARCH 1996   Israeli secret services assassinate Yahya (Yihyeh) Ayyash, an explosives expert with Hamas. Hamas retaliates with a campaign of terrorist attacks, which results in more than one hundred deaths in several Israeli villages, destabilizing the Peres government.

APRIL 24, 1996   The Palestinian National Council (PNC) gathers in Gaza, for the first time on Palestinian soil, to eliminate from its charter all articles challenging the State of Israel's right to exist.

MAY 29, 1996   Binyamin Netanyahu is elected prime minister of Israel, heading a coalition that unites the Right, the extreme Right, and religious parties.

SEPTEMBER 27–29, 1996   The municipality of Jerusalem opens a tunnel below the Esplanade of the Mosques, sparking widespread violence. Nearly eighty Palestinians and fifteen Israeli soldiers are killed.

JANUARY 17, 1997   The Israeli army withdraws from part of Hebron.

• **JULY 1997**   Yitzḥak Mordechai decides to put an end to considerations of a wall, begun two years earlier.

OCTOBER 1, 1997   Sheikh Ahmad Yassin, founder of Hamas, returns to Gaza after nine years in an Israeli prison.

OCTOBER 23, 1998   Binyamin Netanyahu and Yasser Arafat sign the Wye River Memorandum. Israel promises to relinquish 13 percent of the West Bank within three months, in exchange for a commitment from the Palestinian Authority to take greater measures to prevent acts of terrorism.

DECEMBER 14, 1998   The Palestinian National Council and the Palestinian Legislative Council meet in Gaza with President Bill Clinton to confirm an amendment to the PLO Charter, removing articles that call for the destruction of the State of Israel.

MAY 17, 1999   Legislative elections are held in Israel. Labor Party candidate Ehud Barak wins by a large margin. His term of office begins July 7.

SEPTEMBER 4, 1999   The Sharm el-Sheikh Memorandum is signed by Yasser Arafat and Ehud Barak. Its purpose is to establish the implementation of the Wye River Memorandum.

SEPTEMBER 10, 1999   Israel transfers administrative control of 7 percent of the West Bank to the Palestinian Authority.

JULY 11–25, 2000   Yasser Arafat and Ehud Barak enter negotiations at Camp David, under the leadership of President Bill Clinton. The negotiations end in failure, notably because of a major disagreement on Jerusalem.

SEPTEMBER 28, 2000   Ariel Sharon, who succeeded Netanyahu as Likud leader, visits the Esplanade of the Mosques, in Jerusalem, causing violent confrontations between Israelis and Palestinians to flare up throughout the West Bank and the Gaza Strip. This marks the beginning of the Second Intifada.

OCTOBER 22, 2000   In less than one month, 127 Palestinians and 8 Israelis have been killed by violence throughout Israel and the West Bank. Prime Minister Ehud Barak officially suspends the peace process.

NOVEMBER 2000   Ehud Barak approves the construction of a barrier along the Green Line in some northern and central regions of the West Bank, in order to prevent the passage of vehicles.

JANUARY 18–28, 2001   Israeli-Palestinian negotiations in Taba end without an agreement.

FEBRUARY 6, 2001   Ariel Sharon is elected prime minister of Israel with 62.5 percent of the vote.

• **MAY 2001**   The Labor Party deputy Haim Ramon calls for the creation of a movement for "unilateral separation" with the Palestinians.

JUNE 1, 2001   A suicide attack at the Tel Aviv nightclub Dolphinarium kills nineteen young Israelis. Over the next several months, the Israeli military will conduct several strikes on Palestinian territory, killing dozens.

• **JUNE 2001**   Prime Minister Ariel Sharon creates a steering committee, under the director of the National Security Council, Uzi Dayan, to form a plan to prevent Palestinian terrorists from infiltrating Israel. The first recommendations of the group are to be put into place as an extension of the plan studied under Barak.

• **JULY 2001**   The route of the barrier conceived by the National Security Council is presented to the Ministerial Committee on National Security and, in principle, is approved.

• **DECEMBER 2001**   The Ministerial Committee on National Security approves most of the wall project plans around the region of Jerusalem, also known as the "Jerusalem Envelope."

• **MARCH 2002**   The "Jerusalem Envelope" is approved in its entirety by the Ministerial Committee on National Security.

MARCH 27, 2002   In a hotel in Netanya, to the north of Tel Aviv, twenty-nine Israelis are killed in a suicide attack during a Passover celebration. Hamas claims responsibility.

MARCH 28, 2002   In Beirut, the Arab Summit proposes an "end to the Israeli-Arab conflict" and an "agreement with Israel" " in exchange for withdrawal from the territories occupied since 1967.

MARCH 29, 2002   Israel launches "Operation Rempart" in the West Bank. All of the larger towns and cities—Hebron, Jericho, Nablus, Jenin, Qalqiliya, Ramallah, and Tulkarem—are reoccupied. In Ramallah, Palestinian Authority headquarters are under siege by Israeli tanks. Suicide attacks continue in Israel.

APRIL 9, 2002 Fifty-three Palestinians and fifteen Israelis are killed during an Israeli army incursion into a refugee camp in Jenin.

• **APRIL 14, 2002** Sharon places the Ministry of Defense in charge of the construction of a separation barrier, officially designed to protect Israel from Palestinian terrorists. An administrative body for the "separation zone," under the authority of the director-general of the Ministry of Defense, is created. The army begins to requisition land for the construction of the barrier.

JUNE 6, 2002 After seventeen Israelis are killed in a suicide attack in Galilee, Israeli military helicopters destroy many Palestinian targets. In Ramallah, Israeli tanks and bulldozers destroy a part of the Palestinian Authority headquarters.

• **JUNE 14, 2002** Near the Givat Oz kibbutz, to the north of Jenin, the minister of defense, Binyamin Ben-Eliezer, attends the groundbreaking of the first section of the barrier. He informs the journalists present that the entire barrier will measure approximately 217 miles when completed.

• **JUNE 23, 2002** With Decision 2077, the Israeli government formally approves the route of the first phase of the barrier, between Salem and Elkana, in the northern region of the West Bank. The section will be between seventy-six and eighty-seven miles long. In the same document, the government also approves the construction of nearly twelve miles of barrier or wall in the Jerusalem region. "The sole purpose of the Security Fence" as stated in the decision, is "security [and] Israel's response to suicide bombers who enter into Israel."

JUNE 24, 2002 In a speech from the White House, President George W. Bush states that the Israeli-Palestinian conflict will not be resolved without a two-state solution. He requests the departure of Yasser Arafat.

• **AUGUST 14, 2002** The first section of the wall is granted final governmental approval. It is to be completed by July 2003.

SEPTEMBER 6, 2002 As "Operation Rempart" continues, Ariel Sharon announces that the Oslo Accords no longer exist.

SEPTEMBER 30, 2002 Two years after the start of the Second Intifada, 1,599 Palestinians and 577 Israelis have been killed.

• **DECEMBER 2002** The Israeli government approves the route of the second section of the barrier, between Salem and Beit She'an. Thirty miles long, it is expected to be finished some time between late 2003 and mid-2004.

JANUARY 28, 2003   Legislative elections are held in Israel. The Likud Party of Ariel Sharon and the extreme Right win an absolute majority.

MARCH 19, 2003   Yasser Arafat appoints Mahmoud Abbas prime minister of the Palestinian Authority. Abbas succeeds Ahmed Qurei.

APRIL 30, 2003   The United States, the European Union, the United Nations, and Russia announce the Roadmap for Peace. This new plan calls on Palestinians to renounce terrorist attacks against Israel, and for Israel to recognize Palestine as an independent state.

JUNE 4, 2003   Bush, Sharon, and Abbas meet for a summit in Aqaba, Jordan.

• JULY 31, 2003   The first section of the barrier, between Elkana and Salem, is completed, as well as eleven miles of barrier in the Jerusalem region.

• AUGUST 2003   The Israeli government gives the green light to the construction of a forty-two-mile barrier around Jerusalem.

SEPTEMBER 6, 2003   Mahmoud Abbas resigns.

• OCTOBER 1, 2003   For the first time, the Israeli government releases a map showing the entire path of the barrier.

• OCTOBER 3, 2003   The Israeli government approves the decision to build 267 miles of barrier between Elkana and Karmel (to the south of Hebron).

• OCTOBER 2, 2003   General Moshe Kaplinsky issues order number 378-5730-1970, in which all areas between the barrier and the Green Line in the regions of Jenin and Tulkarem are classified as "closed military zones."

• OCTOBER 7, 2003   The Civil Administration announces that the five thousand Palestinians residing in the "closed military zones" of the Jenin, Tulkarem, and Qalqiliya regions must apply for special permits if they wish to continue living on their land.

• NOVEMBER 2003   Construction begins on Phase 3 of the barrier, between Elkana and Camp Ofer, to the north of Jerusalem.

DECEMBER 1, 2003   The Geneva Initiative is presented and signed by Israelis and Palestinians seeking peace.

DECEMBER 8, 2003   The United Nations General Assembly requests that the International Court of Justice at The Hague (ICJ) review the legality of the barrier.

• **FEBRUARY 2004**   Palestinian villagers and the Council for Peace and Security file petitions with the Israeli Supreme Court, temporarily delaying construction of the barrier.

MARCH 22, 2004   The founder of Hamas, Sheikh Ahmed Yassin, is assassinated by the Israeli army.

• **JUNE 30, 2004**   The government releases a new map of the barrier, with many changes from the one originally released in October 2003—the route had been effectively redrawn to accommodate requests (and anticipated requests and challenges) from the Supreme Court. On the same day, the Supreme Court rules that the army must redraw nineteen miles of the barrier for a better balance between Israeli security and Palestinian humanitarian concerns.

• **JULY 9, 2004**   The International Court of Justice at The Hague finds the wall illegal under international law, and calls upon Israel to dismantle it.

• **JULY 20, 2004**   In resolution ES-10/15, the United Nations General Assembly requests that Israel fulfill its legal obligations as defined by the ICJ.

• **SEPTEMBER 2004**   Under military orders, a 164-to-218-yard-wide buffer zone to the east of the barrier, where all new construction is prohibited, is cleared.

• **END OF OCTOBER 2004**   The army announces that the 138 miles of Phase 2 are operational.

NOVEMBER 11, 2004   Yasser Arafat dies in a hospital near Paris.

JANUARY 9, 2005   Mahmoud Abbas, the Fatah candidate, is elected president of the Palestinian Authority.

• **FEBRUARY 20, 2005**   The Israeli government releases a revised barrier route. According to the new trajectory, ten thousand Palestinians (0.4 percent of the population) will find themselves west of the barrier when it is completed.

• **FEBRUARY 2005**   According to the United Nations, 130 miles of the wall/barrier have been built, 65 miles are under construction, and 114 more miles are planned. Total: 309 miles.

AUGUST 15, 2005   Israeli settlements begin evacuation from the Gaza Strip.

SEPTEMBER 12, 2005   Withdrawal of the Israeli army from the Gaza Strip ends.

• **SEPTEMBER 15, 2005**   The Israeli Supreme Court rules that the route of the barrier/wall is legal under international law, contradicting the July 9, 2004, ruling of the International Court of Justice. The Court commits to examining problems presented by specific sections of the barrier/wall in terms of the balance between security demands and humanitarian concerns. At the same time, it also rules on a petition bought before the Court back in August 2004 by Palestinian villages near the Alfei Menashe settlement, ordering that the State redraw the barrier with greater regard to Palestinian humanitarian concerns.

JANUARY 4, 2006   After suffering a stroke, Ariel Sharon falls into a coma. Ehud Olmert assumes power as interim prime minister.

JANUARY 25, 2006   Hamas carries the Palestinian legislative elections with 76 seats out of 132.

MARCH 28, 2006   The Kadima Party wins the Israeli legislative elections. Ehud Olmert is elected prime minister.

APRIL 7, 2006   The European Union suspends aid to the Palestinian government of Ismail Haniyeh, of Hamas.

• **APRIL 18, 2006**   The Israeli Supreme Court rejects the case of six villages in the Al-Ram region, to the north of Jerusalem, which had claimed that the wall obstructs freedom of movement there.

JUNE 25, 2006   Palestinian combatants attack a kibbutz south of the Gaza Strip, capturing Israeli soldier Gilad Shalit. Israel responds with a series of air raids and ground incursions in the Gaza Strip, destroying a sizeable amount of infrastructure.

JUNE 27, 2006   All Palestinian political movements—with the exception of the Islamic Jihad—sign a document implicitly recognizing Israel and its borders of pre–June 5, 1967.

JULY 12, 2006   Hezbollah kidnaps two Israeli soldiers on the Israeli-Lebanese border. War breaks out between Israel and Hezbollah until a cease-fire is called on August 14. A total of 1,300 Lebanese and 156 Israelis are killed. Israel's failed military strategy during the conflict plunges the country into a political crisis.

• JULY 2006   According to the United Nations, 225 miles of wall have been built, 55 miles are under construction, and 157 miles are in the planning stages. Total: 437 miles.

NOVEMBER 26, 2006   A cease-fire in the Gaza Strip officially ends. Armed confrontations between Hamas and Fatah are on the rise.

JANUARY 29, 2007   Islamic Jihad and Al-Aqsa Martyrs' Brigade of Fatah claim responsibility for a suicide attack that kills three people in Eilat.

MARCH 15, 2007   The new Palestinian government begins carrying out its functions. Although Hamas and Fatah had signed an agreement the previous month to create a national unity government, tensions remain high in the Gaza Strip.

APRIL 25, 2007   • The Supreme Court rejects a petition from the residents of the Palestinian village of Dir Kadis, paving the way for the army to annex 415 acres of their agricultural land for the barrier.

• MAY 2007   According to the United Nations, 247 miles of wall have been built, 43 miles are under construction, and 146 miles are in the planning stages.

• MAY 16, 2007   The United Nations issues a report calling for the army to dismantle the barrier along Route 317, which the Israeli Supreme Court had originally ordered dismantled on December 14, 2006. Since the Supreme Court ruling, the military closed the gaps in the barrier that had previously allowed local Palestinians access to their farmland.

JUNE 2007   The Gaza Strip falls into chaos as Hamas seizes power. Mahmoud Abbas prohibits Ismail Haniyeh from carrying out his functions and creates an emergency government in Ramallah.

JULY 16, 2007   President George W. Bush announces a series of measures aimed at reinforcing the Abbas government, and proposes an international conference in Annapolis in the fall.

• AUGUST 2, 2007   The Supreme Court rejects a petition against the barrier from the residents of Umm Salamuna, a village south of Bethlehem.

• AUGUST 29, 2007   In the case of five Palestinian villages petitioning the barrier around the Alfei Menashe settlement, the Supreme Court rules that two of the villages will remain enclosed with the settlement, and that the barrier will be moved to exclude the other three.

• **SEPTEMBER 4, 2007**   The Supreme Court orders the minister of defense to dismantle a one-mile section of the barrier built on land belonging to residents of the Palestinian village of Bil'in. Over the months leading up to the decision, Bil'in had become a symbol of Palestinian resistance to the barrier.

• **SEPTEMBER 18, 2007**   The Israeli army issues an order to requisition seventy-seven acres of Palestinian land in the Bethlehem region for a section of the separation barrier.

OCTOBER 1, 2007   Israeli minister of internal security Avi Dichter announces that Israel will build its West Bank police headquarters in zone E-1. The annexation of this zone, between Jerusalem and the Ma'ale Adumim settlement, constitutes a major obstacle to the territorial continuity of a future Palestinian State.

OCTOBER 10, 2007   The president of the Palestinian Authority, Mahmoud Abbas, states that the future Palestinian State will cover an area of 3,856 square miles and will include most of the West Bank and East Jerusalem. Abbas adds that he is ready to accept territorial exchanges with Israel, which would involve 2 percent of the area of the West Bank.

OCTOBER 15, 2007   U.S. secretary of state Condoleezza Rice visits Jerusalem, and requests once again that the Israelis and the Palestinians come to an agreement on a "concrete" document, and determines that it is time to create a Palestinian State.

• **OCTOBER 24, 2007**   According to Deputy Prime Minister Haim Ramon, construction is interrupted on a sixty-two-mile section of the barrier due to lack of funds.

• **NOVEMBER 8, 2007**   The Israeli army requisitions three acres of land in Bethlehem and Beit Sahour in order to build the Mazmouria terminal.

NOVEMBER 12, 2007   A demonstration of about two hundred thousand people, organized by Fatah on the third anniversary of the death of Yasser Arafat, is violently dispersed by Hamas police. Seven people are killed and more than a hundred wounded.

NOVEMBER 27, 2007   In Annapolis, Maryland, Ehud Olmert and Mahmoud Abbas commit to new negotiations toward signing a peace agreement before the end of 2008, and toward the creation of a Palestinian State.

DECEMBER 12, 2007   As part of the Annapolis agreements, Israeli and Palestinian delegations meet in Jerusalem, but negotiations stall on the issue of Israeli settlements.

DECEMBER 15, 2007   Leaders of Hamas (Islamic Resistance Movement) threaten to launch a new intifada before a crowd of more than three hundred thousand people gathered in Gaza to celebrate the twentieth anniversary of Hamas.

• FEBRUARY 23, 2008   The Israeli army requisitions 189 acres from the towns of ad-Dhahiriya, Doura, and Al-Ramadin for the separation barrier.

FEBRUARY 27, 2008   The Israeli army launches "Operation Hot Winter" in response to a series of Qassam rocket attacks from Gaza on towns in the south of Israel. The operation ends March 3. There are 120 Palestinian casualties.

MARCH 6, 2008   Eight students are killed and nine wounded when a Palestinian gunman infiltrates the Merkaz Harav Talmudic school in Jerusalem and opens fire with an assault rifle. The gunman is killed by an Israeli soldier.

MARCH 18, 2008   The Israeli Supreme Court rules that Route 443, which runs on Palestinian land along the Green Line between Jerusalem and the Modi'im region, will be reserved for Israeli traffic only.

• MARCH 20, 2008   The IDF General Staff announces that they will reduce the budget for maintaining defense mechanisms in the settlements by 70 percent, in order to repair the electronic detectors, cameras, and sensors along the separation barrier.

MARCH 31, 2008   According to a report by Peace Now, the pace of construction in the Israeli settlements of the West Bank increased dramatically through February and March.

• APRIL 14, 2008   On Israeli television, a retired general says that along several hundred feet of the separation barrier near Ramallah, the barrier was pulled out, the electrical cords cut, and the fuse boxes destroyed.

• **APRIL 24, 2008**   *Haaretz* reports that eight months after a Supreme Court ruling to dismantle part of the separation barrier near the Palestinian village of Bili'n, that it is still completely intact.

• **MAY 2008**   According to a United Nations report, 254 miles of the barrier/ separation wall are complete, 41 miles are under construction, and 154 miles are in the planning stages.

MAY 5, 2008   On a visit to Jerusalem, U.S. secretary of state Condoleezza Rice says that "the United States continues to hold the view that settlement activity is contrary to Roadmap obligations." The opening celebration for the already operational police headquarters in zone E-1 is delayed because of Rice's visit.

• **JUNE 4, 2008**   The Supreme Court rejects a petition filed by the residents of the Palestinian village of Ni'lin. Construction of the separation barrier in that region resumes.

JUNE 15, 2008   Condoleezza Rice returns to Jerusalem and again states that the continued expansion of settlements in the West Bank is jeopardizing peace negotiations with the Palestinians.

• **JUNE 20, 2008**   The army requisitions 371 acres of land from the Palestinian village of Beit Hanina (Al-Balad) in order to build the separation barrier between the village and the Ramot settlement.

JULY 2, 2008   Three Israelis are killed and sixty-six wounded when a Palestinian driving a bulldozer rams into two cars and two buses in central Jerusalem. The driver is killed by police.

• **JULY 9, 2008**   Four years after the Supreme Court ordered the army to dismantle three sections of the barrier, the Israeli human rights organization B'Tselem publishes a report finding that the barrier in these regions remains completely intact.

JULY 22, 2008   Sixteen people are wounded when a Palestinian man rams a construction vehicle into a bus, and four other vehicles, in the center of Jerusalem. The man behind the wheel of the tractor is killed by police.

• **AUGUST 4, 2008**   The Supreme Court gives the state forty-five days to propose a new route for the section of the barrier built on land belonging to Bili'n, and admonishes State officials for ignoring the Court's earlier ruling on the matter.

AUGUST 25, 2008   Israel releases 198 Palestinian prisoners.

AUGUST 26, 2008   Condoleezza Rice returns to Jerusalem to encourage Israeli and Palestinian leaders to renew negotiations, while asserting that neither side has fulfilled its commitments outlined in the Roadmap, i.e., the Israelis continue settlement expansion and have not withdrawn wild settlements, and the Palestinians have not dismantled the terrorist infrastructure. Peace Now releases a report stating that the number of active construction sites between January and May 2008 was twice that of the same period in 2007.

SEPTEMBER 2008   The United Nations Office for the Coordination of Humanitarian Affairs (OHCA) releases its biannual report on road closures in the West Bank. The report finds that between April 30 and September 11 there were 630 obstacles—93 checkpoints and 537 roadblocks, an increase in 19 obstacles since the previous report.

SEPTEMBER 4, 2008   In an interview on Al Jazeera, Israeli defense minister Ehud Barak states that some Arab neighborhoods of East Jerusalem, along with neighboring villages, could become part of the Palestinian capital in a future peace agreement.

SEPTEMBER 16, 2008   Prime Minister Ehud Olmert states that he will reach an agreement with the Palestinians before the end of 2008.

SEPTEMBER 21, 2008   Ehud Olmert is implicated in several corruption scandals and announces his resignation. He remains at the head of a transition Cabinet until the formation of a new government by his minister of foreign affairs, Tzipi Livni, who succeeds him as leader of the Kadima Party.

• **SEPTEMBER 24, 2008**   Israel's domestic security agency, Shin Bet, publishes a statement finding that recent acts of violence in Jerusalem by Palestinians of East Jerusalem were likely inspired by mounting resentment over the separation barrier. The report makes clear that there is no connection between those responsible for these acts of terrorism and armed Palestinian groups.

SEPTEMBER 29, 2008   In an interview with the daily paper *Yedioth Ahronoth*, Ehud Olmert asserts that Israel must withdraw from almost all of the West Bank and East Jerusalem to achieve peace with the Palestinians.

OCTOBER 26, 2008   Kadima Party leader Tzipi Livni informs President Shimon Peres that she has failed to form a government.

OCTOBER 28, 2008   The press secretary of the Knesset announces legislative elections for February 10, 2009.

• **DECEMBER 14, 2008**   The Israeli army confiscates 4,000 dunums (about 988 acres) of Palestinian land from the village of Al-Ramadin for the construction of the separation barrier.

DECEMBER 15, 2008   *Le Nouvel Observateur* publishes a March 2009 report from the heads of European Union diplomatic missions in Jerusalem and Ramallah asserting that Israel "is actively pursuing the illegal annexation of East Jerusalem."

That same day, *Yedioth Ahronoth* reports that according to a study from the University of Ariel the population in the West Bank doubled over the previous twelve months, while, in the same period, the total Israeli population in the West Bank increased by only 29 percent.

DECEMBER 27, 2008   Hamas accuses Israel of violating the conditions of the June 2008 cease-fire. Shells and rockets from Gaza rain down on southern Israeli villages, and the Olmert government launches "Operation Cast Lead" against the Gaza Strip.

• **JANUARY 5, 2009**   The Israeli army designates parts of Bethlehem, Jerusalem, Ramallah, and Salfit located between the Green Line and the barrier to be "military zones." The Palestinians are required to show army-issued visitor permits to access land located in these areas.

JANUARY 17, 2009   "Operation Cast Lead" draws to an end, leaving 1,330 Palestinian dead—including 437 children, 110 women, and 123 elderly persons—as well as 5,450 injured. Thirteen Israelis were killed, ten of whom were military personnel.

JANUARY 22, 2009   As the last Israeli soldiers pull out of the Gaza Strip, Mahmoud Abbas, the president of the Palestinian Authority, is the first foreign leader called by the new U.S. president, Barack Obama, only hours after taking his oath of office.

FEBRUARY 10, 2009   Legislative elections are held in Israel. Tzipi Livni's Kadima Party wins 28 seats, Binyamin Netanyahu's Likud wins 27, Avigdor Lieberman's Yisrael Beiteinu wins 15, Barak's Labor Party wins 13, the ultra-orthodox Sephardic party, Shas, wins 11, and the ultra-orthodox Ashkenaze of the United Torah Judaism wins 5.

FEBRUARY 20, 2009   Binyamin Netanyahu, who seems the only person capable of creating a coalition, is enjoined by President Shimon Peres to form a government.

MARCH 2, 2009   According to a report from Peace Now, Israel plans on doubling the number of settlements in the West Bank, including the construction of 70,000 new housing units, of which 5,700 will be located in the annexed neighborhoods of East Jerusalem.

At an international conference held in Sharm el-Sheikh, Egypt, the international community pledges $4.5 billion in aid for the reconstruction of Gaza and to stimulate the Palestinian economy.

MARCH 3, 2009   On her first visit to Jerusalem, U.S. secretary of state Hillary Clinton affirms the Obama administration's committment to protecting Israeli security. Received the following day in Ramallah by the Palestinian president Mahmoud Abbas and prime minister Salam Fayyad, Clinton condemns the demolition of Palestinian houses in East Jerusalem. She repeats that the Israeli government "must accept the two-state solution" and stop settlement construction.

MARCH 5, 2009   The Israeli police recommend a third investigation of Prime Minister Ehud Olmert, already under investigation for fraud and breach of trust when he was mayor of Jerusalem between 1993 and 2003, and when he was trade and industry minister between 2003 and 2005.

MARCH 7, 2009   The *Guardian* uncovers a confidential European Union report, dated December 15, 2008, accusing Israel of "pursuing the illegal annexation" of East Jerusalem.

That same day, Palestinian prime minister Salam Fayyad resigns.

MARCH 8, 2009   Israel's attorney general charges the former Israeli president, Moshe Katsav, with rape and sexual harassment of several of his employees.

MARCH 10, 2009   In Cairo, negotiations begin between Hamas and Fatah toward forming a unity government.

MARCH 24, 2009   The Israeli Labor Party congress votes 608 to 507 to join the coalition government of incoming prime minister Binyamin Netanyahu.

MARCH 29, 2009   In an article published by *Haaretz*, Shaul Arieli, a member of the Council for Peace and Security states that of the 472 miles of the planned barrier, only 60 percent (about 283 miles) have been completed. The slow pace of construction can be explained, in his opinion, by budget constraints, legal challenges to the barrer, and strong disagreement between Israelis and Palestinians on the future of Ariel, Ma'ale Adumim, Gush Etzion, and the southern Judean desert.

MARCH 30, 2009   During the Arab Summit at Doha, Qatar, Palestinian president Mahmoud Abbas asks Arab leaders to take steps outlined by the Quartet to draw Israel back into the peace process.

In Ramallah, the Arafat Foundation creates a commission to investigate the death of Yasser Arafat.

MARCH 31, 2009   Prime Minister Binyamin Netanyahu's government is invested by the Knesset. Ehud Barak (Labor Party) is appointed vice prime minister and minister of defense. Avigdor Lieberman (Yisrael Beiteinu Party) is named foreign affairs minister and vice prime-minister. The government is made up of 30 members. It has the support of 70 out of 120 deputies.

In Cairo, Hamas and Fatah continue negotiations, which had been interrupted March 19, toward forming a unity government.

APRIL 1, 2009   Regarding the creation of a Palestinian State, Avigdor Lieberman states that Israel is only bound by its commitments to the Roadmap, and not to the negotiations at the 2007 conference in Annapolis. He contends that Ehud Olmert and Mahmoud Abbas have skipped important steps in the Roadmap in order to negotiate key issues (borders, the future of the settlements, Jerusalem).

APRIL 2, 2009   The discussions in Cairo are suspended for three weeks.

Avigdor Lieberman excludes all concessions on the Golan Heights and, in particular, the retreat of Israel.

APRIL 6, 2009   In a speech before the Turkish parliament, in Ankara, Turkey, President Obama declares: "The United States strongly supports the goal of two states, Israel and Palestine, living side by side in peace and security. That is a goal shared by Palestinians, Israelis, and people of goodwill around the world. That is a goal that the parties agreed to in the road map and at Annapolis. That is a goal that I will actively pursue as President of the United States."

APRIL 7, 2009   For the third time since his nomination, Avigdor Lieberman is questioned by the police on suspicion of receiving large sums of money from abroad to finance his electoral campaigns.

APRIL 16, 2009   U.S. special envoy to the Middle East George Mitchell meets in Jerusalem with Israeli Netanyahu. Netanyahu states that the Palestinians must recognize the State of Israel as the State of the Jewish people, and that the time had come for "new approaches and ideas."[1]

APRIL 17, 2009   Following a meeting with George Mitchell in Ramallah, Mahmoud Abbas asserts that the Obama administration has a crucial role to play in establishing peace in the Middle East. Saeb Erekat, advisor to Mahmoud Abbas and head of the Negotiations Affairs Department of the PLO, states that Netanyahu's April 16 statement implies resistance to the peace process. He notes that the PLO has already recognized the State of Israel while Netanyahu "refuses to even mention a Palestinian State."[2]

APRIL 18, 2009   In Cairo, George Mitchell states that "it has been the policy of the United States, for many years, under presidents of both political parties, that the solution to the Israeli-Palestinian conflict lies in a two-state solution."[3]

APRIL 20, 2009   The head of Israeli military intelligence, Amos Yadlin, states during a special meeting of the Cabinet that Barack Obama's position on the Middle East could put Israel at risk. He adds that Hamas, who had been deterred by "Operation Cast Lead," is now interested in establishing a peace agreement with Israel.[4]

APRIL 21, 2009   After receiving King Abdallah II of Jordan at the White House, President Obama calls for "gestures of good faith" from both the Israelis and Palestinians, demonstrating their will to revive the peace process.

Mairead Maguire, the 1976 Nobel Peace Laureate, accuses the Israeli authorities of conducting "ethnic purification" in East Jerusalem, where the municipality plans on demolishing dozens of Palestinian homes.

APRIL 22, 2009   According to a massive investigation published under the authorization of Israeli Army Chief of Staff General Gabi Ashkenazi, the IDF operated in accordance with international law during "Operation Cast Lead."

A group of Norwegian lawyers announce from Oslo their intention to file a complaint against top Israeli leaders, including former prime minister Ehud Olmert, for "war crimes" and "serious human rights violations" during the war in Gaza.

Omar Suleiman, head of Egyptian intelligence arrives in Israel.

Hillary Clinton states before the U.S. House Committee on Foreign Affairs that the United States will not hold discussions with or finance in any way a Palestinian government that includes Hamas, until Hamas agrees to renounce violence, recognize Israel, and abide by previous commitments of the Palestinian Authority.

APRIL 27, 2009 Negotiations for a reconciliation between Hamas and Fatah start up again. It is the fourth series of discussions since March 20. In Damas, a top leader of Hamas announces that Khaled Mechaal has been re-elected as head of the organization's political bureau.

According to figures published by the Israeli Central Bureau of Statistics on the sixty-first anniversary of Israel's statehood, the country's population totaled 7,411,000 (up from 7,282,000 in 2008), with a total Jewish population of 5,593,000, or 75 percent. The Arab population totaled 1,498,000, or 20.2 percent of the overall population of Israel.

Barack Obama asks the Congress to authorize an increase in aid to Palestinians, even if leaders close to Hamas participate in a Palestinian Authority government.

APRIL 28, 2009 The Hamas and Fatah delegations negotiating in Cairo interrupt their discussions to examine new Egyptian proposals. The principal negotiator for Hamas, Mahmoud Zahar, announces that the discussions will continue May 17 or 18.

APRIL 30, 2009 According to a survey released by the University of Maryland, 75 percent of Americans believe that Israel should not build settlements in the Occupied Palestinian Territories.

MAY 1, 2009 A document released by the United Nations Office for the Coordination of Humanitarian Affairs (OCHA) states that 60,000 Palestinians out of 225,000 living in East Jerusalem face the possibility of their houses being demolished by the Israeli authorities. According to this document, only 13 percent of annexed East Jerusalem will be reserved for new construction for the Palestinians, while 35 percent of East Jerusalem has been expropriated for the construction of settlements to accommodate 195,000 Israelis.

MAY 4, 2009 Israeli president Shimon Peres declares that the Arab Peace Initiative of 2002 must become the foundation for a final agreement between Israel and its neighbors. According to this plan, sponsored by Saudi Arabia, the participating Arab countries would offer Israel complete diplomatic recognition in exchange for its retreat to pre-June 4, 1967, borders, allowing for the creation of a Palestinian State.

In apparent contradiction to Israeli president Shimon Peres, Foreign Minister Avigdor Lieberman, while on official visit to Rome, does not cite the creation of a Palestinian State as a basis for future negotiations.

MAY 5, 2009 Foreign Minister Avigdor Lieberman declares that if international efforts to thwart the Iranian nuclear program through dialogue produce no results in the next three months, then more "practical measures" should be taken.

In an interview with the *New York Times*, the leader of Hamas, Khaled Mechaal, in exile in Damas, states that his movement is open to the creation of a Palestinian State with 1967 borders, at the conclusion of a lengthy truce. In exchange, he requests the dismantling of the Israeli settlements and the right of return for Palestinians. Asked about the length of the truce, he responds: 10 years.

Before a gathering of 350 donors of AIPAC (the American Israel Public Affairs Committee, a principal pro-Israel lobby), White House Chief of Staff Rahm Emanuel insists that "two States for two peoples" is the only solution to which the United States is committed.

MAY 13, 2009 On the sixth day of his visit to the Holy Land, Pope Benedict XVI states his support for the creation of a Palestinian State and, during a visit to the Aïda refugee camp near Bethlehem, calls the West Bank Barrier "tragic."

JUNE 4, 2009 During a speech to the Muslim world delivered at the University of Cairo, Barack Obama recalls "America's strong bonds with Israel" but rejects the "legitimacy of continued Israeli settlements" and stresses the necessity of a two-state solution.

JUNE 14, 2009 In a speech delivered at Bar Ilan University near Tel Aviv, Binyamin Netanyahu accepts the possibility of a Palestinian State, but then proproses conditions widely considered unacceptable to Palestinian negotiators. He rejects any freeze on settlement construction.

NOTES

PROLOGUE

1. Expression borrowed from the title of the book by Elias Sanbar: *Palestine, the Country to Come*, L'Olivier, 1996.

CHAPTER 1: EVEN THE COLOR OF THE LIGHT

1. Ma'ale Adumim, which sits between Jerusalem and Jericho, is the largest settlement in the West Bank, with twenty-five thousand residents.

2. Interview with the author, August 14, 2005, in Abu Dis.

3. Essentially a checkpoint that moves to a different location every day, made up of two or three jeeps parked across a road. Sometimes they are stationed in a location for only ten minutes; sometimes for hours.

4. Figures confirmed by United Nations publication *Humanitarian Update*, February 2006. "Access to Jerusalem: New Military Order Limits West Bank Palestinian Access."

CHAPTER 2: WE'RE HERE. THEY'RE THERE.

1. "Greater" Jerusalem is composed of East and West Jerusalem, and all of the adjacent neighborhoods within approximately one hundred square miles of the municipal boundaries of the city.

2. The intermediary agreements, included in the Oslo Accords (1993), covered a period of "self-government" planned until 1999.

3. Interview with author, August 29, 2005, in Jerusalem.

4. According to the database at B'Tselem, the Israeli Information Center for Human Rights in the Occupied Territories, and that of Israel Defense Forces, this June 11, 2003, suicide attack on Bus 14 killed eighteen people, of which one was younger than eighteen years old.

5. Figure from the B'Tselem website, www.btselem.org/english/statistics/casualties.asp.

6. Ze'ev Jabotinsky, "The Wall of Iron (The Arabs and Us)," pp. 537–42, in *Zionism's Fundamental Texts*, collected and presented by Denis Charbit, Albin Michel/Menorah, 1998. Paris.

7. Gush Emunim is a political movement founded in February 1974 by Rabbi Moshe Levinger and Rabbi Haim Druckmann, after a split in the National Religious Party. It is known for its religious fundamentalism and nationalist fanaticism.

8. Meron Rapoport, "A Wall in Their Heart," article in *Yedioth Ahronoth*, July 10, 2003.

9. That is, the Southern Command of the Israel Defense Forces (IDF), in charge of the southern part of Israel, comprising the Gaza Strip.

10. The buffer zone was entirely in Palestinian territory.

11. The towers are equipped with cameras with night vision and enhancing optics. They are connected on a network to a central control post. In the event of a serious security breach, a patrol of soldiers can be dispatched to the barrier in less than fifteen minutes, and helicopter gunships in less than thirty minutes.

12. "Lessons of the Gaza Security Fence for the West Bank," note from General (Reserves) Doron Almog in *Jerusalem Issue Brief*, published by the Institute for Contemporary Affairs 4, no. 12, December 23, 2004.

13. Other experts on security are less certain on this point. In an August 2005 interview, an officer noted that the barrier in Gaza did not prevent the Palestinians from smuggling in large amounts of arms via Egypt; nor did it stop Russian prostitutes from entering over the same border, or contraband marijuana from the Sinai.

14. www.btselem.org/English/Statistics/Casualties_Data.asp.

CHAPTER 3: THE EVE OF PESACH

1. Figures reported by Arnon Sofer in "We Have Outlined the Separation Fence," published by *Outre-Terre: française de géopolitique*, Paris: Eres, 2004.

2. "A Wall in the Heart," article by Meron Rapoport, in *Yedioth Ahronoth*, July 10, 2003.

3. Interview with author, November 29, 2005, in Ramat Gan.

4. The attack occurred on June 1, 2001.

5. This was the term originally used by the Shahal Commission, which Rabin had assembled to begin studying the wall.

6. During the legislative elections of March 28, 2006, Tafnit did not attain the minimum 2 percent votes required to secure a seat in the Knesset.

7. Interview with author, August 30, 2005, in Tel Aviv.

8. In September 1970, after three airliners were hijacked at a Jordan airport by Palestinian militants, Amman exploded into widespread violence between the armed Palestinians and the Jordanian army. After days of clashes in which more than five thousand Palestinians, both bystanders and fighters (they were not soldiers of a regular army, but rather members of various Palestinian movements), were killed, King Hussein's army crushed the Palestinians, who then fled to Lebanon. Black September was thereafter the name of a very active terrorist organization, which, among other attacks, killed eleven Israeli athletes during the Munich Olympics in 1972.

9. The First Intifada is sometimes referred to as the War of Stones because the young Palestinians who fought in it were largely armed with rocks.

10. Interview with author, July 7, 2006, in Tel Aviv.

11. Interview with the author, August 30, 2005, in Tel Aviv.

12. Interview with the author, August 31, 2005, in Tel Aviv.

CHAPTER 4: THE DAYAN CAMPAIGN

1. According to Dany Tirza, fifty-eight Israelis were killed in 2002 by terrorists entering from the northwest side of the West Bank. In 2003, after the construction of the first part of the barrier, the number of Israeli fatalities fell to three, then to zero in 2004 (interview with author, August 29, 2005). On April 17, 2006, a young Palestinian member of Islamic Jihad, from the village of Arqa, near Jenin, detonated explosives at the entrance of a restaurant in a middle-class neighborhood of Tel Aviv. The attack killed ten people, including the terrorist. The army did not disclose where or how he had crossed the barrier.

2. Figures from B'Tselem. During the same period, 1,754 Palestinians were killed.

3. Charles Enderlin, *Le rêve brisé* [The dashed dream], Paris: Fayard, 2002.

4. Clayton E. Swisher, *The Truth About Camp David*, New York: Nation Books, 2004.

5. Conversation with author, February 8, 2001, in Ramallah.

6. Interview with author, August 31, 2005, in Tel Aviv.

7. Interview with author, November 10, 2005, in Jerusalem.

8. Shlomo Ben-Ami, *What Future for Israel?*, Presses universitaires de France, Paris. 2001.

9. This crisis was analyzed with finesse and erudition by Sylvain Cypel in *Walled: Israeli Society at an Impasse*, The Other Press, 2006. New York (USA).

10. *Le Monde*, June 19, 2004.

11. Asher Arian, "Israeli Public Opinion on National Security 2003," Memorandum no. 67, October 2003, Jaffe Center for Strategic Studies, Tel Aviv University.

12. *The Israël Lobby and U.S. Foreign Policy*, Faculty Research Working Paper series, by John J. Mearsheimer and Stephen M. Walt, Cambridge, Mass.: Harvard University, John F. Kennedy School of Government. March 2006. Shortly after the publication of the study, Harvard University decided to remove its logo from the document and to distance itself from the conclusions of the report.

13. Interview with the author, July 9, 2003, in Ramallah.

CHAPTER 5: HOW MANY OLIVE TREES?

1. Sharon is alluding to the summit on June 4, 2003, in Aqaba which brought together President Bush, King Abdallah of Jordan, and the Israeli prime minister.

2. "The Humanitarian Impact of the West Bank Barrier on Palestinian Communities," report published in March 2005 by the United Nations Office for the Coordination of Humanitarian Affairs in the Occupied Palestinian Territories (OCHA/OPT) and the United Nations Relief and Works Agency for Palestinine Refugees in the Near East (UNRWA).

3. The Israeli government and army have sometimes gone that far. According to the anthropologist Jeff Halper, coordinator of the Israeli Committee against House Demolitions (ICAHD), twelve thousand houses have been demolished by Israel in the Occupied Territories since 1967. Since the beginning of the Second Intifada, in September 2000, between four thousand and five thousand houses have been demolished in the West Bank, and more than twenty-five hundred in Gaza, in the context of the "cleaning" operations to punish the occupants or because their owners were not in possession of the required permits. Jeff Halper, *Obstacles to Peace: A Reframing of the Palestinian-Israeli Conflict*, 3rd ed., Jerusalem: ICAHD, 2005.

4. "Behind the Barrier: Human Rights Violations as a Result of Israel's Separation Barrier," position paper, March 2003, B'Tselem.

5. In 1948, Palestine had approximately 1.4 million inhabitants. Today, there are 3.8 million in the West Bank and Gaza.

6. *Not All It Seems: Preventing Palestinians Access to Their Lands West of the Separation Barrier in the Tulkarem-Qalqiliya Area*, information sheet, June 2004. Published by B'Tselem, the Israeli Information Center for Human Rights in the Occupied Territories. Jerusalem.

7. "Humanitarian Impact of the West Bank Barrier. Special Focus: Crossing the Barrier: Palestinian Access to Agricultural Land," published in January 2006 by the United Nations Office for the Coordination of Humanitarian Affairs in the Occupied Palestinian Territories (OCHA/OPT) and the United Nations Relief and Works Agency for Palestine Refugees in the Near East (UNRWA).

8. In the spring of 2006, only 40 percent of farming families who had their land to the west of the barrier or wall had access to it. In the north of the West Bank, only twenty-six "agricultural gates" were open on a regular basis. "The Humanitarian Impact on Palestinians of Israeli Settlements and Other Infrastructures in the West Bank," United Nations Office for the Coordination of Humanitarian Affairs.

9. *The Wall in Palestine*, Jerusalem: Palestinian Environmental NGOs Network, 2003.

CHAPTER 6: THE KIBBUTZ MONTENEROS

1. Interview with the author, on August 19, 2005.
2. Interview with the author, September 3, 2005.
3. About 2,471 acres.
4. About fifty to seventy-five acres.
5. About fifteen acres.

CHAPTER 7: THE GREAT LIE

1. www.yesh-din.org.
2. UNRWA Emergency Appeal, "The West Bank Barrier." Profile: Alfei Menashe and Habla. Update August 2005. Published by UNRWA (United Nations Relief and Works Agency).
3. Interview with the author, August 21, 2005.
4. Machsom Watch is an organization founded in January 2001 by a group of Israeli women to report and prevent Israeli soldier abuse of Palestinians, online at http://online at www.machsomnwatch.org/en.
5. In the 1920s, these "revisionists" tried to reinvent the politics of Zionism—but not Zionism itself—by revisiting the original goals of Theodor

Herzl; their objective was to create a Jewish State by ensuring that the majority of inhabitants on both banks of the Jordan were Jewish. (*Cf.* Marius Schattner, *Histoire de la droite israelienne*, Brussels: Complexe, 1991.)

6. Ten acres.

7. Interview with the author, August 21, 2005.

8. "Under the Guise of Security: Routing the Separation Barrier to Enable the Expansion of Israeli Settlements in the West Bank," Bimkom and B'Tselem report, December 2005.

9. Interview with the author, August 25, 2005, in Alfei Menashe.

10. On June 21, 2005, Dany Tirza admitted before the Supreme Court that the path of the barrier around zone 115/8 was designed to include an extension of Alfei Menashe. He also stated he had placed the villages of a-Dab'a and Ras a-Tira inside the Alfei Menashe enclave in order to protect this extension.

11. "A Wall in the Heart," by Meron Rappaport, *Yedioth Ahronoth*, July 10, 2003.

12. Decision of the Cabinet no. 2077, from June 23, 2002, Section B-3.

CHAPTER 8: QALQILIYA IN THE NET

1. Interview with the author, July 10, 2003.

2. This explanation for the closure was given to the local authorities and is cited in a United Nations document, "The Humanitarian Impact of the West Bank Barrier on Palestinian Communities," March 2005. No August 2004 attack near Qalqiliya is registered in Israeli army records, accessible on the website of the Ministry of Foreign Affairs. B'Tselem also has no such record. www.mfa.gov.il/mfa/terrorism.

3. Interview with the author, November 16, 2005, in Tel Aviv.

4. The Center for the Defence of the Individual is described on their website as "an Israeli human rights organization whose main objective is to assist Palestinians of the Occupied Territories whose rights are violated due to Israel's policies."

5. HCJ 1348/05 and HCJ 3290/05.

CHAPTER 9: THE SIEGE OF SHEIKH SA'AD

1. In the Jewish faith, Gehenna is similar to the Christian concept of hell, a place for the wicked.

2. "Facing the Abyss: The Isolation of Sheikh Sa'ad Village—Before and After the Separation Barrier," report by B'Tselem, February 2004.

3. An elected notable, or sometimes a position handed down through a clan-line; in rural communities, the notable has an administrative function, between an unofficial mayor and justice of the peace.

CHAPTER 10: SPARTHEID

1. Interview with the author, August 27, 2005, in Jerusalem.
2. *Kol Ha'Ir*, September 23, 2005.
3. Interview with the author, November 11, 2005, in Jerusalem.
4. Interview with the author, August 31, 2005, in Tel Aviv.
5. "A Policy of Discrimination: Land Expropriation, Planning, and Building in East-Jerusalem," B'Tselem, May 1995.
6. In July 2009, one U.S. dollar was equal to about 3.8 shekels
7. Interview with the author, August 27, 2005, in Al-Ram.

CHAPTER 11: THE E-1 FILE

1. In 2006, the population of Ma'ale Adumim reached thirty-three thousand inhabitants. Approximately seven thousand more Israelis live in the satellite settlements such as Kedar and Kfar Adumim, its industrial park, and space set aside for development that extends almost to Jericho.
2. Interview with the author, January 30, 2006, in Ramallah.
3. Isabel Kershner, "Unilateral Thinking," *The Jerusalem Report*, April 17, 2006.
4. *Haaretz*, August 24, 2005.
5. *Jerusalem Post*, September 2, 2005.
6. About $492 million.
7. Interview with the author, August 31, 2005, in Tel Aviv.
8. Document provided to the author, July 23, 2007, in Tel Aviv.
9. Five merchandise transfer centers are operational or being put into place along the wall and barrier's path. They are located in the cities of Bethlehem, Tulkarem, and Jenin, and to the north of the Jordan Valley. The merchandise is transferred at these points from Palestinian to Israelis trucks, or vice-versa, so that no vehicle has to cross the separation line.

CHAPTER 12: THE GOOD SIDE OF THE BARRIER

1. Interview with the author, March 26, 2006, in Ariel.
2. Legend has it that Jews born in Israel were called Sabras because, much like the Sabra fruit, their destiny was both sweet and sour.
3. Sharon speech at the Knesset, July 31, 1974.
4. Document made available to the author by Ron Nachman.
5. Arik is Ariel Sharon's nickname.

6. Interview with the author, January 30, 2006, in Ramallah.

7. "The Humanitarian Impact of the West Bank Barrier on Palestinian Communities," Humanitarian Emergency Policy Group, March 2005.

8. *Haaretz*, March 15, 2006.

9. Statement from B'Tselem, April 30, 2006.

10. Interview with the author, November 18, 2005, in Deir Istiya.

CHAPTER 13: SETTLING

1. For the Israeli government, these ten residential areas (East Talpiot,
French Hill, Gilo, Givat Hamakos-Har Homa, Ma'alot Dafna, Neve
Ya'acov, Pisgat Ze'ev, Ramat Eshkol, Ramat Shlomo, and Ramot Allon)
built inside the boundaries of Greater Jerusalem and unilaterally established in 1967, are considered Holy City neighborhoods. According to international law, these neighborhoods, all located east of the Green Line,
are settlements.

2. In July 1968, Yigal Allon was named deputy prime minister and
Minister of Immigrant Absorption.

3. Gush Emunim, "Master Plan for Settlement in Judea and Samaria,"
translated from Hebrew and cited in the B'Tselem report "Land Grab: Israel's Settlement Policy in the West Bank," May 2002.

4. Mattiyahu Drobless, "The Settlement in Judea and Samaria,"
translated from Hebrew and cited in the B'Tselem report "Land Grab: Israel's Settlement Policy in the West Bank," *op. cit.*

5. Daniel Haïk, *Sharon: Un destin inachevé* [Sharon: An Unfulfilled
Destiny], Paris: l'Archipel, 2006.

6. Israeli Central Bureau of Statistics, 2006.

7. Since 1995, more than one hundred "wild" settlements, with almost two thousand total settlers, have been created in the West Bank. An
investigation conducted in 2005 by Judge Talia Sasson at the request of the
prime minister showed that a number of official government services have
actively supported these "wild" settlements by providing funds and land,
and by granting the settlements the right to water and to run electricity out
to these locations. The Ministry of Defense and its Israel Defense Forces, the
Ministry of Housing and Construction and Housing, and the Ministries of
the Interior and of Agriculture all have provided assistance to wild settlements.

8. *A Civil Occupation: The Politics of Israeli Architecture*, directed by
Eyal Weizman and Rafi Segal, Les Editions de l'Imprimeur, 2004.

9. Israeli Central Bureau of Statistics, 2006.

10. Israeli Central Bureau of Statistics (ICBS), Monthly Bulletin of Statistics, December 2008 (http://www.cbs.gov.il/population/new_2009/table1 .pdf).

11. *Haaretz*, July 27, 2009

CHAPTER 14: TWO ROADS FOR TWO PEOPLES

1. Marius Schattner, *Histoire de la droite israélienne de Jabotinsky à Shamir* [The History of the Israeli Right from Jabotinsky to Shamir], Paris: Complexe, 1991.

2. "The Humanitarian Impact of the West Bank Barrier on Palestinian Communities," Humanitarian Emergency Policy Group, March 2005.

3. "Forbidden Roads: Israel Discriminatory Road Regime in the West Bank." B'Tselem report, August 2004.

4. "Ground to a Halt: Denial of Palestinians' Freedom of Movement in the West Bank," B'Tselem report, August 2007.

5. Interview with the author, May 21, 2005, in Jericho.

6. "Territorial Fragmentation of the West Bank," United Nations Office for the Coordination of Humanitarian Affairs, May 2006.

7. "Ground to a Halt: Denial of Palestinians' Freedom of Movement in the West Bank," B'Tselem report, August 2007.

8. Interview with the author, July 23, 2007, in Tel Aviv.

9. The length of the roadways and the value of cumulative differences in altitude were calculated by the geographer Jan de Jong. See "Report on Israeli Settlement in the Occupied Territories," 17, no. 6, Foundation for Middle East Peace, November–December 2007.

10. The exact length of the barrier is difficult to estimate, as a number of its sections are in legal dispute, and its planned path may be modified. Dany Tirza says it will be 454 miles long. In January 2006, the United Nations estimated its length at 416.3 miles.

11. "Under the Guise of Security: Routing the Separation Barrier to Enable the Expansion of Israeli Settlements in the West Bank," Bimkom and B'Tselem report, December 2005.

12. Interview with the author, August 15, 2005, in Ramallah.

13. Article by Amira Hass, *Haaretz*, February 13, 2006.

14. Interview with the author, May 21, 2005, in Jericho.

15. "A New Jordan Valley Settlement:—Facts, Background, and Analysis," October 2008. Document available online at the site www.PeaceNow.org.

CHAPTER 15: FORCE IS THE PROBLEM

1. Interview with the author, July 2, 2006, in Kerem Shalom.
2. Declaration to Agence France-Presse, September 6, 2006.
3. Interview with the author, July 7, 2006, in Tel Aviv.
4. October 8, 2004.
5. Interview with the author, August 31, 2005, in Tel Aviv.
6. "Expert Legal Opinion on the Separation Barrier, Part 1 and 2," by Oxford Public Interest Lawyers (OXPIL), February 3, 2004.
7. Votes against: Australia: Israel, the Marshall Islands, Micronesia, Palau, and the United States; Abstentions: Cameroon, Canada, El Salvador, Nauru, Papua New Guinea, the Solomon Islands, Tonga, Uganda, Uruguay, and Vanuatu.
8. "The Humanitarian Impact of the Barrier: Four Years After the Advisory Opinion of the International Court of Justice on the Barrier," July 2008, OCHA/UNRWA.
9. *Haaretz*, June 28, 2006.

CHAPTER 16: A NEW BORDER

1. These numbers were established by the United Nations based on the route officially approved by the government in April 2006, and published on the website of the Israeli ministry of defense. Another path—about 485 miles long—was published on the same site in April 2007, then removed. In July 2008, the organization Peace Now rendered public a map showing that the total length of the separation barrier would be 490 miles—24.8 miles of wall and 466 miles of barrier. According to this document, 494.5 miles have already been built, 49 are under construction, and 147.2 are in the planning stages. ("West Bank and Jerusalem Map," Peace Now Settlement Watch Team, July 2008.)
2. *Haaretz*, October 24, 2007.
3. *Haaretz*, August 4, 2008.
4. Interview with the author, July 23, 2007, in Alfei Menashe.
5. It is worth noting that Ashkenazi had openly aspired to become chief of staff, and had even resigned in protest of Dan Halutz's appointment to the position in May 2005.
6. *Haaretz*, August 28, 2008.
7. Interview with the author, July 20, 2007, in Eshkolot.
8. Interview with the author, July 23, 2007, in Tel Aviv.
9. During a press briefing in which the author participated on October 9,

2007, in Paris, the Israeli internal security minister, Avi Dichter, admitted that three weeks earlier, during Yom Kippur, a Palestinian terrorist who had succeeded in getting over the wall had been intercepted in an Israeli city some moments before setting off his charge of explosives.

10. "The Humanitarian Impact on Palestinians of Israeli Settlements and Other Infrastructure in the West Bank," published in July 2007 by OCHA (United Nations Office for the Coordination of Humanitarian Affairs).

11. West Bank and Jerusalem Map, Peace Now Settlement Watch Team, July 2008.

12. B'Tselem counts 12 settlements (where 192,918 residents lived at the end of 2005) in East Jerusalem. In October 2007, the Foundation for Middle East Peace estimated that there were 13 settlements in East Jerusalem, where, in 2005, 184,057 Israelis lived.

13. *The Telephone Is Ringing*, live show, August 16, 2007, in which the author participated.

14. "Rethinking the Two-State Solution," Giora Eiland, *Policy Focus* 88 (September 2008), The Washington Institute for Near-East Policy.

15. Yehuda Ben-Meir and Dafna Shaked, "The People Speak: Israeli Public Opinion on National Security, 2005–2007," Memorandum no. 91, INSS, Tel Aviv, 2007.

16. Freddy Eytan, Dore Gold, General Yaakov Amidror (Reserves), Meir Rosenne, "Defensible Borders for a Lasting Peace," Jerusalem Center for Public Affairs, Jerusalem, 2007.

17. Interview with the author, April 27, 2008, in Moza Illit.

18. UN resolution 194 (December 11, 1948) affirms the right of Palestinian refugees who wish to return to their homes to do so, and their right to indemnities. Resolution 242 (November 22, 1967) requests the evacuation of the Occupied Territories. Resolution 338 (October 22, 1973) requests in particular the implementation of resolution 242 "in all of its parts."

19. Interview broadcast on October 10, 2007, by Palestinian television.

20. Interview with the author, November 20, 2007.

21. Interview with the author, June 9, 2009, in Ramallah.

CHRONOLOGY

1. Isabel Kershner, "Palestinians Urge Envoy to Press Israel on Statehood," *The New York Times*, April 18, 2009.

2. Ibid.

3. Mitchell's full statement is available at the website for the Embassy of the United States, Egypt, http://cairo.usembassy.gov/pa/trmitchellpm.htm.

4. Barak Ravid, "MI Chief: Obama Mideast Policy Threatens Israel," *Haaretz*, April 20, 2009.

BIBLIOGRAPHY

Ben-Ami, Shlomo. *Quel avenir pour Israël? Entretien avec Yves Charles Zarka, Jeffrey Andrew Barash, et Elhanan Yakira* [What Future for Israel? Interview with Yves Charles Zarka, Jeffrey Andrew Barash, and Elhanan Yakira]. Paris: Presses Universitaires de France, 2001.

Benvenisti, Meron. *Jerusalem: Une histoire politique.* [Jerusalem: A Political History.] Arles: Solin/Actes Sud, 1996.

Bishara, Azmi. *Checkpoint.* Arles: Actes Sud, 2004.

Blanc, Pierre, Jean-Paul Chagnollaud, Sid-Ahmed Souiah. *Palestine: La dépossession d'un territoire.* [Palestine: The Dispossession of a Territory.] Paris: L'Harmattan, 2007.

Cypel, Sylvain. *Les Emmurés: La société israélienne dans l'impasse.* [The Walled-In: Israeli Society at an Impasse.] Paris: La Découverte, 2005.

Dieckhoff, Alain. *Les Espaces d'Israël.* [The Spaces of Israel.] Paris: Presses de la Fondation Nationale des Sciences Politiques, 1989.

Enderlin, Charles. *Broken Dreams: The History of the Failure of the Middle East Peace Process, 1995–2002,* trans. Susan Fairfield. New York: Other Press, 2003.

———. *Paix ou guerres: Les secrets des négociations israélo-arabes, 1917–1995* (nouvelle édition). [Peace or War: The Secrets of the Israeli-Arab Negotiations, 1917–1995 (new edition).] Paris: Fayard, 2004.

———. *Par le feu et par le sang: Le combat clandestin pour l'indépendance d'Israël, 1936–1948.* [By Fire and by Blood: The Clandestine Combat for the Independence of Israel, 1936–1948.] Paris: Albin Michel, 2008.

Faure, Claude. *Shalom, Salam: Dictionnaire pour une meilleure approche du conflit israélo-palestinien.* [Shalom, Salam: Dictionary for a Better

Approach to the Israeli-Palestinian Conflict.] Paris: Fayard, 2002.

Gresh, Alain. *Israël, Palestine: Vérités sur un conflit.* [Israel, Palestine: Truths About a Conflict.] New updated edition. Paris: Fayard, 2007.

Gresh, Alain, and Dominique Vidal. *Palestine 1947: Un partage avorté.* [Palestine 1947: An Aborted Division.] Paris: André Versailles, 2008.

Haik, Daniel. *Sharon: Un destin inachevé.* [Sharon: An Unfulfilled Destiny.] Paris: l'Archipel, 2006.

Halper, Jeff. *Obstacles to Peace,* The Israeli Committee Against House Demolitions (ICHAD). Jerusalem, 2005.

Hass, Amira, *Correspondante à Ramallah, 1997–2003.* [Correspondent in Ramallah, 1997–2003.] Paris: La fabrique, 2004.

Khalidi, Rashid. *Palestine: Histoire d'un Etat introuvable.* [Palestine: History of a Lost State.] Arles: Actes Sud, 2007.

Miller, Aaron David. *The Too Much Promised Land: America's Elusive Search for Arab-Israeli Peace.* New York: Bantam, 2008.

Morris, Benny. *1948 and After.* Oxford, UK: Clarendon Press, 1994.

Novosseloff, Alexandra, and Franck Neisse. *Des murs entre les hommes.* [Walls Between Men.] Paris: La Documentation française, 2007.

Nusseibeh, Sari, *Il était un pays: Une vie en Palestine* [Once Upon a Country: A Palestinian Life.] Paris: JC Lattès, 2007.

Ristelhueber, Sophie. *WB.* Paris: Thames and Hudson, 2005.

Ross, Dennis. *The Missing Peace.* New York: Farrar, Straus and Giroux, 2004.

Sanbar, Elias. *Figures du Palestinien: Identité des origines, identité de devenir.* [Faces of the Palestinian: Identity of Origins, Identity of Becoming.] Paris: Gallimard, 2004.

Schattner, Marius. *Histoire de la droite israélienne: De Jabotinsky à Shamir.* [History of the Israeli Right: From Jabotinsky to Shamir.] Brussels: Complexe, 1991.

———. *Israël, l'autre conflit: Laïcs contre religieux.* [Israel, the Other Conflict: Secular versus Religious.] Paris: André Versailles, 2008.

Segev, Tom. *1967: Six jours qui ont changé le monde.* [1967: Six Days That Changed the World.] Paris: Denoël, 2007.

Shlaim, Avi. *Le mur de fer: Israël et le monde arabe.* [The Iron Wall: Israel and the Arab World.] Paris: Buchet Chastel, 2007.

Sternhell, Ze'ev. *Aux origines d'Israël.* [On the Origins of Israel.] Paris: Gallimard, Folio histoire, 2004.

Swisher, Clayton E. *The Truth About Camp David.* New York: Nation Books, 2004.

Vidal, Dominique, with Sébastien Boussois. *Comment Israël expulsa les*

Palestiniens (1947–1949). [How Israel Expelled the Palestinians (1947–1949).] Paris: Editions de l'Atelier, 2007.

Warschawski, Michel. *Sur la frontière*. [On the Border.] Paris: Stock, 2002.

Zertal, Idith, and Akiva Eldar. *Lords of the Land: The War over Israel's Settlements in the Occupied Territories, 1967–2007*. New York: Nation Books, 2007.

JOINT PUBLICATIONS

Applied Research Institute (ARIJ). *A Geopolitical Atlas of Palestine, The West Bank, and Gaza, October 2004*. Jerusalem, 2004.

B'Tselem, and Association for Civil Rights in Israel (ACRI). *Ghost Town: Israel's Separation Policy and Forced Eviction of Palestinians from the Center of Hebron*. Jerusalem, 2007.

B'Tselem. *Land Grab: Israel's Settlement Policy in the West Bank*. Jerusalem, 2002.

———. *Crossing the Line: Violation of the Rights of Palestinians in Israel Without a Permit*. Jerusalem, 2007.

———. *Ground to a Halt: Denial of Palestinians' Freedom of Movement in the West Bank*. Jerusalem, 2007.

———. *Human Rights in the Occupied Territories: Annual Report 2007*. Jerusalem, 2008.

Bimkom and B'Tselem. *Under the Guise of Security*. Jerusalem, 2005.

Center for International Cooperation. *The Wall of Annexation and Expansion: Its Impact on the Jerusalem Area*. Jerusalem, 2005.

Dieckhoff, Alain, ed. *L'Etat d'Israël*. [The State of Israel.] Paris: Fayard, 2008.

PENGON (The Palestinian Environmental NGOs Network). *Stop the Wall in Palestine: Facts, Testimonies, Analysis, and Call to Action*. Jerusalem, 2003.

Weizman, Eyal, and Rafi Segal, eds. *Une occupation civile: La politique de l'architecture israélienne*. [A Civil Occupation: The Politics of Israeli Architecture.] Besançon: Les Éditions de l'Imprimeur, 2004.

FILMS

Broken Dreams. Charles Enderlin. Produced by Dan Setton and Tor Ben-Mayor, 2002.

Metzer: Entre les murs. [Metzer: Between the Walls.] Directed by Anne Abitbol, L&A Films.

Mur. [Wall.] Directed by Simone Bitton, 2004.

ACKNOWLEDGMENTS

In approaching this complicated subject, my colleagues and friends Charles Enderlin, Patrice Claude, and Sammy Ketz opened their doors, and their address books, and shared their experiences with me. My friends Leila Shahid and Elias Sanbar didn't notice the time passing as they helped me to understand the structure and complex functioning of Palestinian society, nor when they facilitated meetings with some interview subjects. Rafael Barak, chargé d'affaires at the Israel embassy, Barnéa Hassid and Nina Ben Ami, embassy spokespersons, and Carole Amar of the press department persuaded a number of people from the military and the government involved in the design, construction, and daily management of the wall/barrier to meet with me and respond to my questions. In Jerusalem, Khalil Toufakji, cartographer of the Palestinian delegation during negotiations with Israel, gave me access to his scrupulous work on the settlements; and the researchers from B'Tselem provided me with documents and advice that furthered my research. Thank you to all, Israeli and Palestinian, who agreed to meet with me and respond to my questions. I also thank those cited anonymously who provided me with information and different perspectives. All of these voices and points of view have helped to fully realize this investigation.

My gratitude to my friend Laura Brimo-Evin; my agent, Tom; my translator, Ann Kaiser; my editor, David Rogers; and the team at Picador, who have given my book a second life, this time in the anglophone world—is immense. At *Le Nouvel Observateur*, Claude Perdriel and Jean Daniel and the Editorial Department, with whom I work in precious freedom, did all they could to facilitate my investigation. Henri Guirchoun took the helm of the Foreign Service Department during my absences and answered my questions on Israeli history, a subject he knows well. Mehdi Benyezzar put his talent in computer graphics to work transforming the complicated documents I brought him into legible maps.

Everyone deserves my thanks.

I will never be able to express all the thanks I owe my wife, Pascale. She supported this invasive project from the beginning. For two years, she spared me no advice, no criticism, no encouragement. Without her, this book would not exist.

René Backmann

INDEX

Abbas, Mahmoud, 55, 59, 172, 193, 209, 210
Abdu, Mohammad, 120–22, 124
Abu Dis, 8, 9, 10–13, 17–21, 118, 122, 145, 183, 203
Abu Ismael, 83–85
a-Dab'a, 87, 112, 115
Afula, 196
agriculture, Palestinian, difficulty and ruin imposed by the wall, 71–73, 83–85, 239n.8
Ahmed, Mourad Ahmed Muhammad, 110
Al-Aqsa Martyrs' Brigade, 45, 79, 197
al-Aqsa Mosque, restrictions on visits to, 139
Alfei Menashe settlement, 68, 87–88, 92–99, 101–2, 162, 196, 203, 207
    expansion plans of, 94–99, 112
    petition to move wall, 106–15
al-Karmi, Raed, 45
al-Khatib, Munir, 14
al-Khatib, Youssef, 14
Allenby Bridge, 13
Allon, Yigal, 28–29, 155, 167–68, 184, 187

Allon Plan, 155, 167–68
Allon Road, 29, 185, 187
Al-Midya, 203
Almog, Doron, 30–31
Al Ori, Ali, 180
Al-Ram, 118, 136–37
Amal, Sister, 16
Amir, Yigal, 32
Amman airport, 13
Anafeh, Adnan and Mona, 20–21
Anata, 19, 137, 183
Annapolis Conference (2007), 209
apartheid claim, 132, 179
Arab Abu Farda, 87, 113, 115
Arab a-Ramadin, 87, 113, 115
Arab Peace Initiative, 209
Arabs
    living in harmony with Israelis, 75–80
    percentage of population, 207
    separation from, 52, 159
    term for Palestinians, 153
Arab Studies Society, 129–30
Arad Valley, 63
Arafat, Yasser, 3, 24, 30, 37, 41, 45, 53–55, 57–58, 79, 141, 172
Argentina, immigrants from, 75

Arieli, Shaul, 55, 132, 194–95
Ariel settlement, 33, 61, 63, 111, 153–63, 207
Arikat, Mahmoud, 20
Armon, 125
army. *See* Israel Defense Forces
Arnona, 125
Ashkenazi, Gabi, 202, 204
Aslan, Mohammad, 136
Assad, Ahmad, 72
Association for Civil Rights in Israel (ACRI), 110, 197
Atalla, Assad, 102–3
Augusta Victoria hospital, 21
Avital, Dov, 76–80
Awaydat, Nuhaila, 102
Ayyad, Salah, 8, 12–13
Az Zayyem, 11
Azzun, 89
Azzun Atma, 68

Bani Hassan, 163
Baqa al-Gharbiya, 68, 80, 81
Baqa al-Sharqiya, 81
Barak, Aharon, 110, 114, 125
Barak, Ehud, 33, 43, 53, 54, 56, 59, 131, 142, 174
Barak, Gershon, 148
Bar-On, Roni, 162
Barta'a, 81
Barta'a Asha Sharqiya, 67, 68
Bedouins, 186, 203
Begin, Menachim, 29, 90, 91, 155, 157, 169
Beinisch, Dorit, 110
Beirut Summit (2002), 209
Beit Arieh, 203
Beit El settlement, 64
Beit Hanina Al-Balad, 135
Beit Jala, 23–25
Beit Lid Junction attack, 31–32
Beit Sahour, 124

Beit She'an, 185
Beit Surik, 125, 134
Ben-Ami, Shlomo, 131
Ben-Eliezer, Binyamin ("Fouad"), 39–43, 44, 45–46, 65, 97, 98, 159
Ben-Gurion Airport, 1
Ben-Zvi, Yitzhak, 133
Bethlehem, 14, 17, 23, 36, 45, 69, 144, 146, 147, 181, 182, 183, 203
Biddu, 196
Biddya, 163
Bili'n, 196, 202, 203
Bimkom (Planners for Planning Rights), 95, 111, 184
Bir Nabala, 50, 135, 137
Boim, Ze'ev, 63
Border Police, 12, 15, 38, 82
Boullata, Terry, 7–13
British Mandate, 68–69, 90, 118–19
Brukin, 163
B'Tselem (Israeli Information Center for Human Rights in the Occupied Territories), 68, 71, 95, 109, 121, 132, 163, 178–79, 181, 184
Burg, Avraham, 56
Bush, George W., 57, 63–64, 144–45, 194, 209–10

Camp David accords (1978), 157
Camp David negotiations (2000), 4, 53–55, 131, 209
cards
    blue, 10, 13, 121, 123
    orange, 12, 121, 124
cars, parking of, 120, 150
Center for Strategic Studies, 56
Central Bureau of Statistics (CBS), 15, 139
checkpoints
    number of, 180
    opening and closing of, 72

passing through, 81, *152*
  See also gates; passage points;
    terminals
Cheshin, Mishel, 110, 125
Chiyah, 7, 15
Christians in Palestine, 16, 24, 64
Civil Administration, 2–3, 10, 68–71,
    88, 122, 124, 182
Cliff Hotel (Jerusalem), 8–9, 15
Clinton, Bill, *54–55*, 144, 171
closed zones (by the wall), 70–71
  percentage of land taken by, 68
"colonists" (the term), 2
colonization policy
  and international law, 106
  morality concerns, 108–9
Community of the Daughters of
    Charity, 16
Convergence Plan, 193
Council for Peace and Security, 132

Daher al-Abed, 81
Dahiyat Al-Barid, 136–37
Dahiyat Al-Salam, 137
Damari, Tirza, murder of, 79
Davir, Yuval, 126
Dayan, Moshe, 56, 155
Dayan, Uzi, 32, 37–39, 45, 47,
    51–53, 63, 64–65, 101, 159,
    187
Decision 2077, 46
Deheishe refugee camp, 25
Deir Istiya, 163
Democratic Front for the Liberation
    of Palestine (DFLP), 8
demographics, 35–36, 133, 171
Detektor, 48
Dichter, Avraham (Avi), 31, 39,
    43–45, 159, 191, 196–97
Dolphinarium club, Tel Aviv, 37
Drobless, Mattiyahu, 169
Drori, Yitzhak, murder of, 79

East-1 (E-1) land, 141–47
East Jerusalem
  annexation, 8, 122, 129, 131–32
  cut off from surrounding
    Palestinians, 135, 144, 181
  Palestinian residents of, 10–11
  settlements in, 171, 177, 207
Economic Cooperation Foundation,
    132
Eiland, Giora, 207–8
Eitam, Effi, 142
Eiwisat, Hussein, 123, 125
El-Azariyeh, 7, 118, 124, 145, 183
Elbit (construction firm), 48
Eldar, Akiva, 199
Eli, 160
Elkana, 63, 162
El-Khatib, Imran, 20
Elon, Binyamin "Benny," 62, 64
Enderlin, Charles, 54
environmental activists, 206
Erekat, Saeb, 143, 161, 179, 186
Eretz Israel, 28
Eshkol, Levi, 28
Eshkolot, 205–6
Etzion Bloc, 148
Europe, immigrants from, 171
European Union, 143–44, 209
Eve of Pesach attack, 39
Eytan, Yitzhak, 45
Ezra, Gideon, 44

Fabric of Life roads, 182–83
Falamya, 67
Fares, Sister Laudy, 16
Fatah Party, 79, 103, 104–6, 209
Fedayeen, 40
Feitelson, Yaacov, 156
Feldman, Avigdor, 109
Felner, Eitan, 132–33
First Intifada, 82, 124, 237n.9
forest license, 34

gates
    agricultural, 72, 83, 105
    See also checkpoints
Gaza Strip
    fence around, 30–31, 39, 44
    Hamas in, 209
    Israeli attacks on, 58, 190–91
    Israeli withdrawal from, 30, 43, 95,
        110, 145–46, 167, 194
    tunneling incident, 189–91
Geneva Accords, 129, 131
German Cooperation Agency, 184
Germany, 144
Gilo, 23–25
Ging, John, 191
Givat Oz, 43
Givat Ze'ev, 133–35, 136, 137
Givon Hadasha, 134
Gladstein, David, 125–27
Gour, Batya, 56
Government House, 118
Greater Israel, 37
Greater Jerusalem, 23, 171, 235n4
    (ch. 2)
Green Line
    as future border, 23, 35, 159, 195,
        207
    and route of the wall, 37, 41, 62,
        75, 83, 96, 98
Grossman, David, 56
Guevara, Che, 75
Gulf War, 85
Gush Emunim (Bloc of the Faithful),
    29, 158, 168–69, 236n7
Gush Etzion, 33, 61, 147–48, 182, 207

Haaretz (newspaper), 53, 173, 199,
    201, 204
Habla, 68, 88, 91, 92, 93, 97
Hadasha, Ze'ev and Givon, 134
Hadera, 42

Halutz, Dan, 192–93, 204
Hamas party, 104–6, 172, 190, 209
Hamoked, 109
Hamra, 185, 186
Hanatziv, 125
Haniyeh, Akram, 211
Harashi, Taisir, 78, 80–85
Haris Outpost, 155–56
Harvard University, 238n.12
Hasdai, Eliezer, 95, 98
Hashomer Hatzair, 189
Hasson, Israel, 44
Hazeitim terminal, 122, 149
Hebron, 31, 36, 178, 204
Herzog, Mike, 174
Heshin, Amir, 126
Hever, Ze'ev, 45
Hezbollah, 192–93
Highway 1, 180
Highway 5, 87, 162
Highway 6, 66
Highway 45, 135
Highway 55, 96–97, 113
Highway 57, 185
Highway 60, 148, 183, 203–4
Highway 65, 42, 46, 196
Highway 90, 185
Highway 358, 205
Highway 437, 134, 135
Highway 443, 134, 179–80
Highway 3255, 205
Highway 5250, 113
Highways B-1, B-2, and C, 183
Hinnanit, 67
Hizma, 137
Hochman, Avraham, 189
Holy City, 23
Home of Our Lady of Suffering,
    16–17
hospitals and medical care, access to,
    71, 88, 89, 135

houses, demolitions of, 68, 238n.3
Humanitarian Monitor, 206
human rights violations, by Israeli
    army in the Occupied
    Territories, 87, 90–95, 108

Ibrahim, Muhammad Aiman
    Youssef, 80
Ikermawi, Hassan, 13–15
Ilanit (Qaniel), 94
Immanuel, 161, 162, 164
Institute for National Strategic
    Studies (INSS), 208
International Commission of Jurists,
    197
International Court of Justice of the
    United Nations (ICJ), 3, 111–12,
    197–98
Irgun, 90
Islamic Jihad (organization), 32
Islamic Resistance Movement. *See*
    Hamas
Israel, criticism of, 90
Israel Defense Forces (IDF), 2–3,
    38
    human rights violations by, 87,
        90–95, 108
    reprimanded by Court for wall
        routing decisions, 204
Israeli Association of United
    Architects (IAUA), 172
Israeli-Palestinian commercial
    exchanges, 103–4
Israeli-Palestinian conflict
    failure of negotiations, 58
    U.S. wish to resolve, 210–11
Israelis, vocabulary of, 2
Italy, 144
Izbat Salman, 89
Izhiman, Soufian, 18
Izhiman, Yahia, 17–19

Jabel Mukaber, 119, 121, 122–27
Jabotinsky, Vladimir (Ze'ev), 27–28,
    91
Jalud, 101
Jayous, 101, 196
Jenin, 31, 36, 45, 68, 70, 72, 73, 167,
    180, 181, 197
Jericho, 30, 36, 106, 180, 181, 183,
    185–87
Jerusalem
    eastern. *See* East Jerusalem
    expansion of, after Six-Day War,
        122–23, 130–34, 169
    importance of, to Jews and
        Palestinians, 133
    "Jewish neighborhoods" around,
        2, 23, 130–34, 167, 242n.1
    off-limits to most Palestinians in
        the West Bank, 121, 138–39,
        146–50
    Old City, 117
    territorial continuity with East-1,
        planned, 141–47
    wall around, 38, 63, 66–67, 69,
        117–27
Jerusalem Center for Public Affairs,
    208
Jerusalem Envelope, 101, *128,*
    129–39, 147–50
Jerusalem–Jericho Road, 14, 147,
    185
Jewish fundamentalists, 108
Jezreel Valley, 62
Jinsafut, 165
Jordan, 156, 168
    border with, 13
    Palestinians in, 237n.8
Jordan Valley, 29, 62, 147, 155, 171,
    181, 184–87, 208
    settlements in, 185
Judean Desert, 206

Judea-Samaria, 29, 41, 155–58, 169,
    173
    the term, 2

Kafar Adumim, 143
Kafr Aqab, 136
Kafr Kasem, 162
Kafr Thulth, 89
Kaplinsky, Moshe, 70, 110
Karmona, Shay, 182–83, 206
Karnei Shomron settlement, 89
Kedar, Alexander, 91
Kedar, Paul, 87, 90–91
Kedar, Ruth, 86, 87, 89–93, 106
Kedumim settlement, 89, 161
Kerum Shalom, 189–90
Kfar Adumim, 23
Kfar Etzion, 148
Kfar Qasem, 97
Kfar Saba, 97, 103
Khoury, Stephanie, 59
kibbutz living, 76–77
Kidmat Zion settlement, 15
Klein, Menachem, 55–56, 131
Kol Ha'Ir newspaper, 131
Konitzer, Helmut, 17
Kook, Rabbi Tzvi Yehuda, 168–69,
    177

Labadi, Eitaf, 19
Labor Party, 41, 62, 95, 159, 168,
    170–72
land
    agricultural, destroyed by the wall,
        72
    annexed to settlements, 101, 161
    confiscation and expropriation of,
        68–69, 84–85, 93, 104, 170
    exchanges of, with a future
        Palestinian State, 208–9
    pressure on Palestinians to leave,
        93, 165

    requisitioned to build the wall, 7,
        46, 69, 73, 145
Land for Peace program, 208
Lebanon
    border attack (2006), 192–93
    Christians of, 40
    fence with Israel ("the good
        border"), 40
Left, the, 41
Lein, Yehezkel, 121, 178
license plates, colors of, 1–2, 123, 178
Lieberman, Avigdor, 37, 57, 64
Likud Party, 27, 62, 145
Livni, Tzipi, 59, 162

Ma'ale Adumim settlement, 14, 18,
    33, 61, 122, 140, 141–47, 183,
    203, 207
Ma'ale Efraim, 186
Ma'ale Shomron, 97–98, 161, 164
Maariv (newspaper), 53
Machsom Watch, 90
Magal (construction firm), 48
Makassed Hospital, 21
Mansour, Bilal, 163
Mansour, Mahafez, 163–65
Mara'be, Zaharan Younis
    Muhammad, 110
Mashiah, Netzah, 47–49, 65, 69, 73,
    147, 150
Maslamawi, Assad, 137
Matan, 97, 101, 112, 113
Matte Binyamin, 173
Mazuz, Menachem, 145, 195
Mazza, Eliahu, 110, 125
Megiddo, 62
Meir, Golda, 155
Meisar, 77, 80
Meretz (party), 41
Messerschmid, Clemens, 184
Metzer kibbutz, 75–80
Mevasseret Zion, 125

Mitchell, George, 210
Mitzna, Amram, 46
Modi'in, 180
Modi'in Illit, 61, 207
Mofaz, Shaul, 39, 42–43, 45, 110, 162
Mohammad, Abu, 19–20
Mordechai, Yitzhak, 32–33
Mount Gilboa, 62
Mount Moriah, 117
Mount Scopus, 11, 141
Mouqata (Arafat's compound), 45
Moussa, Nasser, 92
Mrabe, Rafik, *86*, 92–94

Nabi Samuel, 134
Nablus, 31, 45, 146, 163, 164, 167, 168, 169, 177, 180, 181
Nachman, Ron, 30, 61, 153–62
Nahmias, Sami, 125
Nasser, Ghiath, 124–25
National Religious Party, 41, 62
National Security Council, 64
Naveh, Dani, 62–63
Nazareth Illit, 197
Nazlat Issa, 68, 72, 80, 81
Negev Desert, 206
Nes Ziona, 154
Netanya attack, 39, 43, 51
Netanyahu, Binyamin, 32, 63, 95, 142, 145, 210–11
Neve Ya'akov settlement, 137
Nof Hasharon, 94
Nofim, 164
Nof Kana, 164
North America, immigrants from, 171

Obama, Barack, 210–11
Occupied Territories
  refusal of Reservists to serve in, 108
  the term, 2

travel restrictions within, 10
  See also West Bank
Ofarim, 161, 203
Ofer military base, 134
Ofra settlement, 169
Ohayon, Revital, murder of, with children Matan and Noam, 79
olive trees, *34, 60,* 71–73, 84, 103
Olmert, Ehud, 43, 59, 101, 145–46, 162, 177, 187, 190, 192–93, 202
Operation Rampart, 45
Orient House, 130
Oslo Accords I (1993), 3, 44, 56, 186, 209
Oslo Accords II (1995), 141, 171–72
Oxford Public Interest Lawyers (OXPIL), 197

Palestine Liberation Organization, 129, 170
Palestinian Authority, 45, 79, 139, 172, 190
  corruption and ineffectiveness of, 105, 182
  errors in the peace process negotiations, 54
  negotiations with, 208–9
  powerlessness of, 84
Palestinian Legislative Council, 106
Palestinians
  accused of Islamic jihad, 58
  economy of, ravaged by the wall, 18, 102–5, 139, 180
  in Israel, suppression of, 130–33
  number of, 239n.5 (ch.5)
  patience of, 82
  the term, 153
  vocabulary of, 2
Palestinian State, future, 133, 182
  border of, 207–11
  Sharon's proposal for, 36
Pardes Hanna-Karkur, 196

passage points, 12, 81, 138
  designed like airport security
    gates, 149–50
  unofficial, 205–6
Paz, General Ilan, 70
Peace Now, 187, 207
peace process (1990s), 24, 56, 85,
  170
Peduel, 161
Peres, Shimon, 37, 57, 168, 194
Peretz, Amir, 190, 192, 195, 204
permits
  for entering Jerusalem, 124
  for permanent residency in
    Jerusalem (for Palestinians), 10,
    13, 70–72, 88, 121
  for residency outside Jerusalem
    (for Palestinians), 185, 186
  for travel, 88
  for vehicles, 88–89, 178–79
  for work on own farm, 83, 93
Petah Tikva, 96
Poraz, Avraham, 64
Powell, Colin, 58
Project 115/8, 94
Public Council for a Security Fence
  for Israel, 52–53, 63

Qadum, 168
Qadumim settlement, 169
Qaffin, 67, 74, 75, 77–85
Qalandiya, 137
  refugee camp, 136
Qalqiliya, 66, 68, 70, 72, 73, 88, 89,
  92, 96, 97, 101–6, 113, 181, 182,
  202, 203, 204
Qalqiliya Hospital, 89, 93
Qalqiliya Road, 87
Qarne Shomron, 164
Qawas, Wajih, 105
Qurei, Ahmed (Abu Ala), 54

Rabin, Yitzhak, 3–4, 31–32, 41, 56,
  130, 141, 167, 171
  assassination, 32, 43, 141, 208
Rafah, 106
Rainbow Project, 24
Ramadan, 139
Ramallah, 14, 17, 31, 36, 45, 134,
  135, 144, 146, 147, 169, 180,
  181, 182, 183, 197
Ramallah Hospital, 21, 135
Ramat HaSharon, 87
Ramon, Haim, 42, 97, 98, 201–2
Ramot Allon, 134
Ras al-Amud, 7–8, 10–13
Ras al-Amuda, 142
Ras a-Tira, 86, 87–89, 91–93, 110,
  112, 115
Ras Atiya, 88, 89, 93, 97
refugee camps, 25, 79, 136, 138
Reihan, 67
religious Right, 168
requisition notices, 7, 69
Resolution ES-10/7, 199
Resolution ES-10/15, 198–99
resolutions, UN Security Council,
  209–10
Rice, Condoleezza, 58–59, 63–64,
  144–45
Right, the, 41
Roadmap for Peace, 59, 194, 209
roads
  forbidden to Palestinians, *176*
  linking Palestinian enclaves,
    182–83
  linking settlements but
    inaccessible to Palestinians,
    170, 177–83
rocket attacks, 190, 191, 192
Route. *See* Highway
Russia, 209
  immigrants from, 171

Salem, 46, 62, 67

Salfit, 72, 153, 154, 163, 169, 181, 182

Sal'it settlement, 67

Sand, Shiomo, 56

Sarta, 163

Sasson, Talia, 208

Sawahira a-Sharqiya, 122, 145, 203

Sbitany, Mohsen, 20

Seam Line Administration, 147

Second Intifada, 4, 10, 24, 25, 30, 33, 36, 53, 82, 102, 124, 136, 172, 179, 180, 185

security
    airport, 149
    as all-purpose justification, 179
    imperiled by Israel's actions, 199
    Israeli preoccupation with, 25–26, 53

security zones, 160–61

separation, idea of, 52, 159

separation line. *See* wall, the

September 11, 2001, terrorist attacks, 57–58

settlements
    annexation to Israel, 47, 61, 141–47, 153
    evacuated ones, 167
    in Greater Jerusalem, 23
    history of, 167–74
    isolation of, in Palestinian territory, 35, 41
    new building in, without permits, 173–74
    number built, 167, 169, 170, 172
    number of settlers, 167, 170, 171, 173–74, 177, 207, 241n.1 (ch.1)
    as an obstacle to peace, 172
    protection of, 33, 37, 184
    public support for, 108, 153, 155–58, 167

purpose, to contain the growth of Palestinian population, 131–32, 169–70

the term, 2

"wild" (outposts), 172, 185, 208, 242n.7

Sfard, Michael, 69, 107–15, 202

Shachal, Moshe, 32

Shaked, 67

Shalit, Gilad, 189–90

Sharansky, Natan, 57, 142

Sharon, Ariel, 24, 29–30, 35–39, 40, 41–48, 80, 95, 97, 101, 110, 132, 145–46, 153, 155–56, 169–70, 184, 194, 208, 209–10
    concerns about the wall, 51, 53
    endorsement of the wall, 61–64, 159–60, 172–73
    settlement policy, 29–30, 56–59, 172–73
    stroke, 146
    visit to Temple Mount, 25, 33

Shas Party, 57

Sheikh Sa'ad, *116*, 117–27, 196

Shilo settlement, 169

Shin Bet (General Security Service), 31

Shinui Party, 62

Shuahani, Muhammad Jamil Mas'ud, 110

Shufat, 138

Sinai, evacuation of, 157

Sirhan, Sirhan Burhan Hassin, 80

Sivirski, Amikam, 98

Six-Day War, 23, 77, 122, 167

smuggling, 236n.13

snipers, 24–25, 66, 96, 113

Socialist Zionist movement, 75

Sofer, Arnon, 35–36

Solana, Javier, 144

Spain, 144

Spiegel, Baruch, report of, 173–74
stone throwing, *74*
suicide attacks, 4, 25, 31–32, 53, 137, 191
suicide bombers, mindset of, 41
Supreme Court (Israel), 69, 109–15, 125, 137, 187, 202–4
Swisher, Clayton E., 54

Taba Summit (2001), 4, 36, 53, 131, 209
Tafnit movement ("Turnaround"), 38, 47, 187
Tal Hill, 94, 115
Talpiot, 117, 125
Tapuah, 158, 160, 161
Tayasir, 186
Tel Aviv, 37, *96*, 107, 133, 180
    District Court of, 125–27
Temple Mount, Sharon's visit to, 25, 33
terminals, 122, 138, *188*
terrorist attacks
    against civilians, 80, 237n.1
    deaths, Israeli and Palestinian, since 2000, 26, 37, *196*
    Israel traumatized by, 56
    on soldiers, 31–32
terrorists, infiltration by, 31, 237n.1, 245n.9
Tiberiade, 42
Tirat Zvi (kibbutz), 62
Tirza, Dany (Abu Karita), 23–25, 32, 42, 61, 64, 66, 69, 95, 97, 101, 112–13, 117–18, 126, 143, 149, 160, 184, 195–96
Toufakji, Khalil, 129–31, 133, 143
Trans-Israel Highway, 66, *96*, 102
travel
    circuitous routes for Palestinians, 80–81, 89, 134, 146–50, 163–64
    permits for, 88

restrictions on, 1–2, 10, 146–50, 163–64, *176*, 178–86
Tubas, 181
Tulkarem, 38, *45*, 66, 67, 68, 70, 72, 73, *75*, 84, 181, 182
    refugee camp, 79
tunnel roads, 147
tunnels, attacks through, 189–91
two-state solution, 51–52, 161, 211
Tzufin settlement, 202

Udah, Abd el Rahim Ismail Daud, 110
Udah, Adnan Abd el Rahman Daud, 110
Udah, Bessam Salah Abd el Rahman, 110
Um el-Fahm, 38
unemployment, 139
United Nations
    food assistance, 139
    General Assembly, 197–99
    observers, 118–19
    reports on settlements, 161, 177, 180
United Nations Office for the Coordination of Humanitarian Affairs in the Occupied Palestinian Territory (OCHA/OPT), 71, 81, 136, 199, 206
United Nations Relief and Works Agency for Palestine Refugees in the Near East (UNRWA), 191
United Nations Security Council, 119, 133, 194
    resolutions 194, 242, and 338, 209–10
United States
    errors in the peace process negotiations, 54
    lack of opposition to the wall, 63–64

pro-Israel lobby, 57–58
support for Israel, 57–59
Uruguay, immigrants from, 75

Vargas Llosa, Mario, 191
Vilan, Avshalom, 63
Vilnai, Matan, 44, 63

Wadi al-Joz, 129
Wadi a-Rasha, 87, 110, 112, 115
wall, the (comprising a concrete wall,
    fence or separation barrier
    between Israel and West Bank),
    1, 50
  buffer zones around, 66
  building of, 11, 22, 65–67, 100,
    136, 142, 204
  circuitous route of, intended to
    expropriate land, 93–99, 101–2,
    134, 160–65
  components of (ditches, patrol
    routes, sensors, etc.), 65–67
  concerns about, from Israelis, 35–
    49, 51, 62, 78–80, 159
  cost of, 65–67, 201–2, 204
  delays in building, 63–64, 69, 201–
    2, 203–6
  difficulty in following it, even with
    a map, 136–38
  difficulty in living with it up close,
    69–73
  difficulty presented to a terrorist in
    crossing, 65
  effectiveness of, 196–97
  as future border, 207–9
  gaps in, with no immediate plans
    to fill, 205–6
  "good" and "bad" side of, 173
  illegality of, in international law,
    61, 111–12, 197–99
  "invention" of, 23–33
  length of, completed, 201

  lobbying in favor of, 52
  maps of, 136, 160
  moving of, at behest of settlers, 101
  moving of, by legal action, 106–15
  names given to, 3
  notices of building of, 7–8
  opposition to building of, 35–49
  passage points through, 12, 81,
    138
  path of, lawsuits and petitions
    against, 125–27, 134, 196,
    202–5
  path of, only partly following the
    Green Line, 37, 41, 62, 67–68,
    75, 83, 96, 98
  Phase I, 46–47
  security as objective, 64–65, 112,
    195–96, 206
  supporters of, 52, 167
  temporary nature of, claimed, 49
  terrorists successfully crossing,
    237n.1, 245n.9
  timetable for building, 63
  true purpose of, to annex territory,
    109, 112, 173, 183–84, 195–96
  unofficial crossing points, 6,
    205–6
Wallerstein, Pinhas, 173
walls, security (generally)
  doubts about effectiveness of,
    190–91, 196
  in other lands and times, 15, 17,
    26–27
Wanchope, Sir Arthur, 118
war on terror, 58
water
  access to, 184
  polluted by Israeli sewage and
    chemicals, 164–65
Weisglass, Dov, 45, 59, 194
Weizman, Ezer, 157
Weizmann, Chaim, 133

West Bank
  boundary of, 23. *See also* Green
    Line
  plan to annex part of, 39, 168–69
  plan to cut into three "sausages,"
    36, 181
  plan to return some to Jordan, 168
  plan to withdraw from, 43
  splitting of, by East-1, 143–47
  the term, 2, 153
  See also Occupied Territories
World Zionist Organization, 169

Yacoub, Elie, 15–16
Yaqir, 164
Yaron, Amos, 97, 98
Yedioth Ahronoth (newspaper), 53,
  73

Yesh Din (There Is Justice), 87,
  90–93, 106, 109, 165
Yishuv, 28
Yisrael Ba'Aliyah Party, 57
Yitav, 186
Younes, Yassin, 86, 92–93

Zahran, Ma'arouf, 103–4, 106
Zayem, 147
Zbuba, 46
Ze'ev, 134
Ze'evi, Rehavam, 57
Zionism, 27, 91, 154, 239n.5
  (ch.7)
Zissman, Arie, 95–98, 203
zone of separation proposal, 38
Zufin settlement, 67, 204
Zvili, Nissim, 207